Social Pyschology

Published by
Saurabh Publishing House

Social Psychology

Dr. Dev Prakash

Saurabh
Publishing House
4735/22, Prakash Deep Building,
Ansari Road, Daryaganj,
New Delhi - 110002

Published by
SAURABH PUBLISHING HOUSE

Distributed by:
Lotus Press Publishers & Distributors
Unit No. 220, Second Floor, 4735/22, Prakash Deep Building,
Ansari Road, Darya Ganj, New Delhi-110002
Ph: 23280047, 32903912, 098118-38000
www.lotuspress.co.in

Saurabh Publishing House is an imprint of
Lotus Press Publishers & Distributors

Social Psychology

ISBN 978-81-89005-59-7

Printed at: **Afcon Enterprises, New Delhi**

Preface

Psychology has been defined as the science of human and animal behaviour. In other words, psychologists are interested in finding out the causes underlying various types of behaviour. The term behaviour as it is used in psychology is very broad. It does not mean only the things a person does in every day life, such as walking, crying, frowning etc. For the psychologists, however, the term behaviour includes not only how we act or what we do, but also how we think and how we feel. In short, it includes mental processes, such as thinking, feeling, willing, imagining etc. as well as the physical processes.

Social Psychology is interested in the ways in which interactions with other people influence attitudes and behaviour. Individuals belong to several types of groups such as family, club, community, school, friendship and so on. These groups affect our behaviour and shape our attitudes towards life, social psychology is mainly concerned with the behaviour of an individual as a member of a group. It uses its own methods of investigating the influences that a group exerts on an individual's behaviour. It is mainly concerned with such group phenomena as leadership, group behaviour, group dynamics, social perception, social attitudes, customs, traditions, social prejudice and social tensions like strikes, riots and wars. Social psychology also investigates such topics as propaganda and persuasion, conformity and inter-group conflicts. Social psychologists are perhaps best known for their work on public opinion and attitude surveys.

This book deals with the topics of—Basic Facts; Senses Process; Psychology of Social Behaviour; Psychology of Social Motivation; Social Effects and Problems; Psychology of Social Attitude; Social Life and Environmental Change; Social Distance in Society; Rural and Urban Community in Society; Group Structure Psychology; Psychology of Social Control; Family of Social System; Psychology of Social Change; Socio-Cultural Influence; etc.

I hope that students and those in the administration field will find it useful for academic and competitive examinations. I owe a deep sense of gratitude to my publisher for materialising my present endeavour.

Dev Prakash

Contents

1

Basic Facts

Psychology is relatively a young science and yet within a brief span it has made tremendous progress. Psychology touches almost every facet of our lives. There is hardly any single aspect of human life where psychology has not made its contribution. In all the important spheres of life, such as industry, technology, arts, education, law, management, politics, social life, medicine etc., psychology has made its unique contribution by examining the basic psychological processes underlying all these spheres; viewed from this angle, it can be said that the scope of psychology is as vast as our life itself.

Psychology has been defined as the science of human and animal behaviour. In other words, psychologists are interested in finding out the causes underlying various types of behaviour. The term behaviour as it is used in psychology is very broad. It does not mean only the things a person does in every day life, such as walking, crying, frowning etc. For the psychologists, however, the term behaviour includes not only how we act or what we do, but also how we think and how we feel. In short, it includes mental processes, such as thinking, feeling, willing, imagining etc. as well as the physical processes.

Since every organism including man lives in an environment with ever changing energies, objects and other organisms, psychologists believe that behaviour is a means of adjusting to the environment. All our behaviour, therefore, is directed towards achieving an adjustment between the forces within us and those in our environment. Adjustment to inner and outer demands of the body is a continuous process and hence, psychologists aim at the study of organism's attempt to adjust itself to the varying conditions both within itself and in its environment.

Fields of Psychology

Psychology is relatively young compared to other sciences and yet within a very short time it has pervaded practically all fields of human behaviour. Psychology is no longer a subject of academic interest taught in colleges and universities, but its impact has been felt in business, industry, clinics, guidance centres and education. Psychologists do many things depending on their field of specialization. In this chapter we shall attempt to indicate some of the fields of specialization in which psychologists are engaged.

Experimental Psychology. In this category we find psychologists who use experimental methods to study the behaviour of the individual. They study how individuals react to sensory stimuli, perceive the world around them, learn and remember things and events, respond emotionally either in a positive or negative way, and are motivated to action whether because of the organic need of hunger, or because of their desire for some status in society. In short, experimental psychologist by using laboratory techniques, study sensation, perception, learning, remembering and forgetting, emotion and motivation. Usually since these phenomena cannot be investigated with human beings as their subjects due to the ethical consideration, psychologists work with animals. They attempt to relate their animal findings to human behaviour, sometimes they also study animals in order to compare the behaviour of different species and they are known as comparative psychologists. Whatever the interest, experimental psychologists are concerned with developing precise, objective and scientific methods of measurement and control.

The term experimental psychology is really a misnomer because psychologists in several other areas make use of experimental methods. For example, social and personality psychologists also use experimental techniques although, strictly speaking, they are not experimentalists. Experimental psychology, therefore, is distinguished as such by its methods. Experimental psychologists are not primarily engaged in work which has a direct application to practical problems; instead, they are interested understand the fundamental causes of behaviour. In short, they are theoreticians.

Physiological Psychology. Closely related to experimental psychology is physiological psychology. The physiological psychologist tries to discover the relationships between bodily processes and behaviour, it is interested in showing some type of correlation between a given psychological activity and some set of physiological activities within the organism. How do sex hormones influence behaviour? What are the areas of the brain that control speech? How do drugs like marijuana and LSD affect co-ordination and memory? These and several other questions form the subject-matter of physiological psychology. The physiological psychologist, really speaking, is concerned with the whole organism. His interest lies in the reintegration of the total activity of the organism and to accomplish this he must go into the physiology of the living organism as a functional unit.

Developmental Psychology. The main purpose of developmental psychology is to study the human growth and the factors that shape human behaviour from birth to old age. It is much more comprehensive than the child psychology or the psychology of adolescence. Developmental psychology studies the qualitative changes that take place with the changes in age. These changes are directional, that is, they lead forward rather than backward. At every stage of the development, some changes just begin, others are at their peak, and some others are in the process of decline. Different types of changes influence the development in different ways.

Developmental psychology has both research and applied aspects. For example, much of the research in developmental psychology is concerned with the intellectual, emotional, social and moral development. On the applied side, the developmental psychologist works with maladjusted and disturbed children.

Clinical Psychology. Clinical psychology appears to be the largest area in which psychologists work. A clinical psychologist is engaged in the application of psychological principles to the diagnosis and treatment of emotional and behavioural problems such as mental illness, criminal behaviour, drug addiction, juvenile delinquency, mental retardation and other problems of adjustment. Clinical psychologists work in a clinic, in a mental hospital, a mental-health clinic, in a prison, or are in private practice. In most cases, individuals with major personal problems come to them for help.

It is necessary to distinguish between two types of specialists, namely, clinical psychologists and psychiatrists. The psychiatrists are usually medical men with a degree in medicine and special training in the diagnosis and treatment of behavioural disorders. The psychiatrists usually use drugs, surgery and shock treatment in treating their patients.

The clinical psychologists, on the other hand, are trained extensively. In all aspects of psychology and special psychodynamics rather than medicine. They are highly specialized in the work of diagnosis and Psychotherapy. They are also well versed in research techniques used in understanding and treating mental disorders, such as the use of psychological tests, interviews and various psychotherapies. In short, clinical Psychologists are primarily concerned with the diagnosis and treatment of mentally ill persons.

Counselling Psychology. It is rather difficult to draw a sharp dividing line between clinical psychologists and counselling psychologists. The major point of difference is that the counselling psychologists treat those individuals who have relatively minor problems of adjustment. They mainly deal with persons having emotional or personal problems that require some expert advice and guidance. Typically, they work with students in high schools, or universities, giving advice on problems of social adjustment and vocational as well as educational goals.

There are various types of counselling psychologists. Some of them are specialized in helping the people who have problems of marital adjustment; others are specialized in problems related to school, or college, or vocational selection; there are still others who are specialised in helping children's problem or mal-adjusted industrial workers. In short, the main task of a counselling psychologist is to understand the causes of individual's mal-adjustment and help or guide him in reaching normal adjustment. In a way, counselling psychologists are the guardians of the mental health of the people.

Educational and School Psychology. Although educational and school psychologists are concerned with education, their activities differ considerably. The psychologists who are involved in testing and guidance of individual students are called school or college psychologists. Their main task is to help students develop better adjustment to school and college situations. The school psychologists are well verse in psychological testing and also in helping that to overcome their several difficulties or problems such as slow speed in reading, emotional problems, lack of concentration in studying, and several other problems, which are commonly encountered in school life. School psychologists are also train vocational counselling and hence there is no clear dividing line between the work of a school counsellor and a school psychologist.

Educational psychology is closely related to school psychology, but the educational psychologists are not much concerned with the problems of individual students. Instead, they are more concerned with general psychological principles underlying the entire process of education. Their main problems are when to teach, what to teach and how to teach. They use various important psychological processes involved in education such as learning, effective methods of teaching, training and motivating the students. In general then, we may say that the emphasis of educational psychology is to discover the principles upon which a sound and effective educational system can be based.

Social Psychology. Social psychology is interested in the ways in which interactions with other people influence attitudes and behaviour. Individuals belong to several types of groups such as family, club, community, school, friendship and so on. These groups affect our behaviour and shape our attitudes towards life, social psychology is mainly concerned with the behaviour of an individual as a member of a group. It uses its own methods of investigating the influences that a group exerts on an individual's behaviour. It is mainly concerned with such group phenomena as leadership, group behaviour, group dynamics, social perception, social attitudes, customs, traditions, social prejudice and social tensions like strikes, riots and wars. Social psychology also investigates such topics as propaganda and persuasion, conformity and inter-group conflicts. Social psychologists are perhaps best known for their work on public opinion and attitude surveys.

Industrial and Engineering Psychology. Many industrial firms have a trained and specialised psychologist on their staff who is known an industrial psychologist. The main work of an industrial psychologist consists of section of a worker for a job after a very careful consideration of his intelligence, aptitudes, and personality characteristics. Besides, industrial Psychologists are also entrusted with such tasks as training programmes for workers, training of supervisors and related personnel in leadership, improving the organizational efficiency, improvement of conditions which lead to decreased efficiency and productivity, and several other functions.

One specialization of industrial psychology is known as engineering psychology. This branch of industrial psychology is chiefly concerned with the design of the equipment and other related problems used in industry for achieving maximum efficiency and ease for the worker, who operates it. Industrial and engineering psychologists at one level serve the technological process, that is, they are concerned with human factors in industry such as personnel selection, employee morale, and the design of complex machines. At another level, they are concerned with the larger problems of industrial civilization like environmental polution, over-crowding and other influences, which disturb the quality of human life. A new term for this area of investigation is environmental psychology.

Psychology of Personality. This branch of psychology is primarily concerned with normal human personality. The personality psychologists Use various methods and techniques to find out the basic traits of human personality. They use devices like psychological tests, interview, naturalistic observation and so on, for understanding the behaviour of normal people. Sometimes, when needed, even experiments are conducted under carefully controlled conditions.

Psychology of personality primarily aims at constructing theories about human behaviour that will give adequate explanation about human personality as it is revealed through an individual's normal behaviour.

Psychometric Psychology. As in all sciences, in psychology also, great emphasis is laid on measurement and quantification. Measurement and quantification help in describing the events or behaviour under study, in a most precise and objective manner. Since psychology borrows several statistical and mathematical concepts and applies them for objective understanding of behaviour, a new branch of psychology, known as psychometric psychology, has gradually emerged. The psychometricians are mostly concerned with the development of statistical techniques for research purposes as well as construction, development, administration and scoring of psychological tests. Psychometricians supply us with tools to be used by psychologists in the applied fields such as schools, counselling, clinical and industrial psychology.

Methods of Psychology

The aim of science is to use scientific method to collect information in the form of verifiable data. Different sciences use different methods that are suitable for the investigation of their subject-matter. However, all of them have one thing in common, in the sense that, they aim at a very high objectivity in the collection of facts and precise description of the phenomena under investigation.

When discussing the methods used by psychology, we must be sure that they fulfil scientific requirements. The complexity of the subject-matter with which psychology deals is quite obvious. The behaviour of the individual is something that varies not only from person to person but also from time to time. Such variations in behaviour, obviously, are less subject to accurate and objective observation and description than the subject-matter of many sciences like physics, chemistry, biology etc. In spite of these difficulties, psychologists, have tried to confine themselves to the requirements of objectivity, which characterize the methods of science. Like other sciences, psychology also uses several methods to study its problems. The methods which psychology uses can be broadly classified into three categories: (1) Experimental methods; (2) Descriptive methods; and (3) Statistical methods.

Experimental Methods. The experimental method is regarded as one of the most preferred and most full-proof methods because it meets the requirements of objectives. It can be used outside the laboratory as well as inside but most experimentation takes place in special laboratories chiefly because the control of conditions commonly requires special equipment. The distinguishing feature of the experimental methods is that the experimenter can carefully control the conditions and make measurements in order to discover relationships among variables. A variables something which varies; it is a condition which can be measured. For example, in an experiment seeking to discover the relationship between learning ability and age, both learning ability and age are variables which can have different values, learning being either slow or fast and the learner being either young or old. To the extent that learning ability changes systematically with increasing age, we can discover an orderly relationship between them.

The ability to exercise control over variables distinguishes the experimental method from other methods of observation. For example, if the experimenter seeks to discover whether learning ability depends on the amount of sleep, he can control, the amount of sleep by arranging to have several groups of subjects spend the night in the laboratory. First group might be allowed to go to sleep at 11.00 P.M., second at 1.00 A.M. and the third at 4.00 A.M. By waking all the subjects at the same time and giving each one of them the same learning task, the experimenter can find out whether the subjects with more sleep learn the task more quickly than those with less sleep. In this experiment, the different amounts of sleep are the antecedent conditions and the learning performance are the results of these conditions. We call the antecedent condition the independent variable because it is independent of what the subject does. The variable affected by the changes in the antecedent conditions is called the independent variable. In psychological research the dependent variable is usually some measure of the subject's behaviour.

In performing an experiment, the experimenter manipulates the independent variable and tries to find out different effects of the manipulati6n. Another important characteristic of the experimental method is control. Since there may be several factors other than the independent variable which might influence the dependent variable, the experimenter tries to have two groups, that is, the experimental group and the control group. Supposing a scientist has discovered a chemical X, which when taken regularly for a week, in prescribed quantities, results in increase of IQ, the experimenter will employ the control group. To begin with, he will select two groups of subjects with similar IQs. He will treat both the groups exactly in similar manner by keeping all the conditions that are like to affect the IQ, exactly identical for all the subjects in both the groups. However, he will give the drug X to one group and some harmless resembling the drug X to the other group. Now, if at the end of the experimental period, he finds significant differences in the IQ's of the two groups, he can safely conclude that the drug X is effective in increasing the IQ's of the people. He can come to this safe conclusion because he very well knows that the two groups were exactly alike in all conditions except one, that is, the independent variable (the drug X) was administered to one group, whereas a harmless drug was administered to another.

In experimental terminology the group in which independent variable is introduced is called the experimental group whereas, the group in which the independent variable is absent is called the control group. This technique of not letting the subjects know to which group they belong is called the single-blind technique. However, it is possible that the experimenter himself may be unconsciously and in subtle ways influenced regarding the outcome of the experiment. The obvious way to control this effect is to keep the experimenter in the dark about which subjects are in which group. A person who never has any contact with the subjects may assist the experimenter by assigning code numbers to the subjects. The experimenter who does not know the code can conduct the experiment without knowing which subjects are in the experimental or control groups. This technique of disguising group membership from both the subjects and the experimenter is known as the double-blind technique.

Thus then, when an experiment is to be performed the scientist must be able to distinguish between which is the independent variable and which is the dependent variable and what are the relevant variables, which he must control. The experimenter's skill lies in identifying all these variables and also in adequately controlling the relevant variables. The control is the unique feature of an experiment; the better the control of an experiment, the better and more reliable are its results.

Descriptive Methods. Descriptive methods are used both by scientists as well as non-scientists. As the name implies, this technique consists in making direct observation of various events in nature as they occur in their natural surroundings and record them as faithfully as possible. There are three major variations of this method: *(i)* Naturalistic observation; *(ii)* Systematic observation; and *(iii)* Case history methods.

Naturalistic Observation. Ancient Greeks first used this method and thereby laid down the ground work for various sciences. Although many new and refined methods have been developed in recent years, naturalistic observation is still used occasionally to study some events in various sciences. For example, some years ago, a group of child psychologists made a special use of this method to study the behaviour of a seven year old boy. A team of eight child psychologists carefully watched the behaviour of the boy almost round the clock, right from the time he got up till he went to sleep at night. The behaviour was observed so carefully that it filled a volume of 435 pages. Such detailed observations are often useful in supplying us with clues for further systematic research. Similarly, observation of chimpanzees in their natural environment can give us important information about their social observation, which will help us to conduct precise laboratory investigations.

Systematic Observations. The method of naturalistic observation discussed above is unsystematic because the observer simply and faithfully records the things as he observes them happening. However, there is a possibility that the observer may record consciously only those events which he thinks are important from the point of view of understanding the event under observation. By doing so, he may very often ignore many things that take place and keep on looking for only some that he thinks are important. Under such conditions the observation becomes systematic and precise. In such an observation the observer may even have some rough idea about his independent, dependent and even relevant variables. Such systematic observations may come very close to experimentation, but the observer may not have the same control over the event observed, as the experimenter has because he is observing the things as they occur in their natural course; secondly, the naturalistic observer has to wait for the event to take place, or observe it only when it takes place. He cannot like the experimenter, produce an event as and when he wants its. In spite of these disadvantages, this method can be used where the experimental method cannot be used. The most important contribution of this method is that it provides new problems for experimentation and thus serves as an aid to experimentation.

Case History Methods. Scientific biographies, known as case histories, are important sources of data for psychologists studying individuals. Most case histories are prepared by reconstructing the biography of a person according to remembered events and records. Reconstruction is necessary because often the person's earlier history does not become a matter of interest until he develops some sort of problem. In such cases understanding of the past is considered to be important to understand the present behaviour. These methods are usually used by clinical psychologists when patients come to them with some serious psychological problems. Although not all clinical problems need a thorough probe, in many cases the psychologists have to undertake a peep into the personal history of the patient to explore the possible causes of his mental disorder.

Clinical methods come very close to naturalistic observation discussed earlier. The only difference is that these methods are used in tracing out the possible causes of a patient's abnormal behaviour. Clinical methods are not highly reliable because the observations are not made under controlled conditions. They lack the objectivity of the experimental method and yet they are the best available tools that can be used in the study of abnormal behaviour. Case histories may also be based on a longitudinal study. This type of study follows an individual or a group of individuals over an extended period of time, with measurements made at periodic intervals. The case history is constructed from the actual observations made by the investigator according to our plan. The advantage of a longitudinal study is that it does not depend on the memories of those interviewed at a later date.

Survey Method. Some problems, which are difficult to study by direct observation may be studied through the use of questionnaires or interviews. Surveys are usually undertaken to ascertain group trends in behaviour of various types. Thus, a survey may be aimed at finding out opinions of a group of people on various topics such as political opinions, food preferences, health care needs and the like. A survey to be reliable must use carefully selected questions as well as a representative sample of the group about which the findings are made.

Statistical Method. Psychology aims not only at the mere description of behaviour but also at its precise measurement wherever possible. This emphasis on psychology on quantification of its data has given rise to a number of statistical techniques for the analysis of behaviour. The use of statistical analysis has helped psychological research specially in the field of psychological testing and experimental psychology.

Historical Focus

Even since man has been able to think, he has had a desire to understand the psychological processes by which he lives. The history of psychology has been characterized by an increasing use of the empirical method. Psychologists preferred to rely upon reliable observations rather than on verbal reports from their subjects. However, gradually when new methods of investigation developed, many schools of psychology emerged. The most influential psychologists who revolutionized psychology are: Wilhelm Wundt, William

James, Ivan Pavlov, John B. Watson, Max Wertheimer and Sigmund Freud.

Structuralism. Wundt, E. B. Titchener and their followers concerned themselves primarily with the structure of consciousness and with the way that structure interacted with changes in the outside world. They started searching for mental elements into which they believed, all mental contents could be analyzed. The elements they thought must be sensation such as red, cold, sweet, or putrid. In their search for these mental element, they used the method of introspection. Although many valuable observations were collected by the method of introspection, this approach proved too narrow because it was limited to reports of what a person experienced. Further, it also became apparent that the mind cannot be thought of as a structure made up of elementary sensations. This disenchantment led some psychologists to give up structuralism and seek some other avenues to explain psychological events.

Functionalism. Psychologists like William James, John Dewey and others being influenced by the Darwinian theory of evolution turned towards functionalism which lays emphasis on the total organism adjusting to its environment. Thus they sought to study the adaptive functions of behaviour and mental processes and not merely their structure. The methods used by the functionalists were introspection and the observation of behaviour. They did not limit themselves to the description and analysis of sensory experience and of mental content like the structuralists but emphasized the total activity of the individual how he learns, how he is motivated, how he solves problems etc. Functionalism then, was characterized by two important aspects: (1) the study of the total behaviour and experience of an individual, and (2) the nature of the adaptive functions.

Behaviourism. With John B. Watson, its first and most influential advocate, discarded introspection as a method of studying-mental processes used by the structuralists and insisted that psychological experiments be restricted to the study of behaviour. In a way it can be said that Watson tried to remove psychology from inside the skull and apply it only to objectively observable behaviour. He emphasized conditioned reflexes as the elements or building 'blocks of behaviour. Another characteristic of behaviourism was its emphasis on learned rather than unlearned behaviour like instincts. To Watson, almost all that a man becomes is a matter of the conditioning of reflexes. One of his famous statements is that he could take almost any infant and through proper training make him into a beggar, a lawyer, or any other kind of person he desired. Finally, behaviourism emphasized animal behaviour and held that there is no important difference between man and animals; that we can learn much about man by the study of animals particularly since animals are easier to experiment with. These characteristics of behaviourism have left their impact on modern psychology and many psychologists like B. F. Skinner came out with stimulus-response psychology. The S.R. Psychology studies the stimuli that elicit behavioural responses, the rewards and punishments that maintain these responses, and the modifications in behaviour obtained by changing the patterns of rewards and punishments. This type of psychology is not concerned with what goes on inside the Organism. Instead, it maintains that although the brain and the nervous system may carryon complex activities, which we cannot see, a science of psychology can be based strictly on what goes inside and what comes out, without worrying much about what goes on inside. Thus then, a theory of learning can be developed by observing how learned behaviour varies with environmental conditions. For example, what stimulus conditions and patterns of reward and punishment lead to the fastest learning with the fewest errors are sufficient variables and we need not bother to specify the changes that learning produces in the nervous system. A strict S.R. approach does not consider the individual's conscious experiences.

Gestalt Psychology. In nineties, when behaviourism in the United States was displacing introspectionism, another school of thought was gaining ground in Germany. This was Gestalt psychology founded by Max Wertheimer, and his colleagues, K. Koffka and W. Kohler. Gestalt psychology was a protest against the structuralists and also against the elementarism of the behaviourists. Gestalt psychologists held that our experiences and our behaviour are not made up by compounding simple elements. Rather, they are patterns, or organizations similar to a magnetic field in which events in one part of the field are influenced by another part of the field. For example, a gray piece of paper is gray only in relation to its, background because on a black background it appears light and, against a white background it appears dark. Similarly, a series of dots in any orderly arrangements is perceived as a pattern and not as isolated dots. The dots are somehow organized in perception so that they are seen as a configuration. According to them, "the whole is more than some of its parts". Today many psychologists, in studying perception, learning, thought, and problem solving apply the principles of Gestalt psychology and seek for patterns and organisation rather than seek for additive discreteness.

Psychoanalysis. Psychoanalysis is not a school of psychology because it originated outside the laboratory in medical practice and vet it had a considerable impact on psychology. Psychoanalysis was founded and developed in the beginning 20th century by Sigmund Freud. Unlike the ideas discussed so far, psychoanalytic concepts are not based on experimental studies and yet have a profound interest on psychological thinking. The basic assumption of Freud's theory is that much of man's behaviour is determined by innate instincts that are largely unconscious. By unconscious processes Freud meant thoughts, fears and wishes of which the person is unaware but which influence his behaviour. According to him, many forbidden or punished impulses of childhood period are repressed into the unconscious from where they influence behaviour. These unconscious impulses, Freud believed, find expression, in dreams, slips of tongue, mannerisms and symptoms of neurotic illness, as well as through such socially approved behaviour as artistic, literary, or scientific activity.

Freud contributed two important things. In the first place, he developed a method of treatment and the word psychoanalysis primarily refers to that method. At first he used hypnosis with his patients and was not impressed by its efficacy. Consequently, when he heard that a new method had been devised by a Viennese physician, Joseph Breuer, a method by which the patient was cured of his symptoms by talking about them, he tried it out and found it to be effective This method is called the method of free associations. The patient freely associates on his thoughts and experiences with the help of the psychiatrist who analyses the causes of his difficulty. Secondly, he constructed a theory of personality known as the Freudian or psychoanalytic theory. This theory is rather elaborate and stresses the role of motives, often hidden and repressed from the individual and society. The structure of personality is made up of three major systems; the id, the ego, and the superego. Although each of these has its own functions, properties, components, operating principles and mechanisms, they interact so closely with one another that it is difficult to weigh their relative contribution to man's behaviour. Behaviour is almost always the product of an interaction among these three systems.

Freud's theory of personality, rather than his method of treatment has evoked great interest among psychologists. The theory contains many unverified assumptions but it has none the less been very valuable, because it has stimulated further systematic research.

Humanistic Psychology. This school of thought developed from the ideas of existential philosophers (Kierkegaard, Nietzsche and Sartre) emphasizes those human qualities, which distinguish man from the animals primarily his free will and his drive towards self-actualization. The humanistic psychology rejects the concepts of man as a mechanism controlled by external forces or by unconscious instincts. They prefer to see man as an actor capable of controlling his own destiny and changing the world around him. According to humanistic psychology an individual is free to choose and to determine his actions. Each person, therefore, is responsible for his actions and cannot blame the environment, his parents, or even circumstances for what he does. Further, an individual's main motivational force is a tendency towards growth and self-actualization. Every person has a basic need to develop his potential to the fullest, to progress beyond what he is now. He may not know what path to follow or he may be blocked by all sorts and environmental and cultural obstacles, nonetheless, his natural tendency is towards actualization of his potential.

The main thesis of the humanistic psychology is the individual's subjective experience. An individual's perceptions of himself and of the world are considered as more important for study than his actions. Humanistic psychology emerged partly as a reaction against those aspects of technological society that tend to determine man.

Neurobiological Approach. If we wish, we can view the psychological process in neurological and physiological terms. Every time the organisms sense the world, interprets it, responds to it and feels a sense of satisfaction or dissatisfaction with the results of its response, its body and its nervous system are involved. His motives may be construed in terms of physiological imbalances. This approach tries to reduce an observable behaviour and mental events, such as thoughts and emotions to neurobiological processes.

Recent discoveries have clearly demonstrated that there is an intimate relationship between the brain activity and behaviour, or experience. Emotional reactions such as fear and rage, have been produced in animals and humans by mild electrical stimulations of specific areas in the brain. Electrical stimulation of specific areas in the human brain can produce sensations of pleasure and pain, and even vivid memories of the past events. However, because of the complexity of the brain and because live human brains are seldom available for study, there are many gaps in our knowledge regarding the neural functioning.

Since psychology is a new science, which emerged from Philosophy, and since every country in the world had it own philosophy, psychology can be said to have existed in every country. However, psychology as an objective science is of recent origin. The beginnings of scientific psychology were laid down in Europe by such stalwarts as Sir Francis Galton in England and Wilhelm Wundt in Germany. Subsequent development of objective psychology is the reflection of the work undertaken by these two foundling fathers.

The growth of psychology in the form of research both from theoretical and practical angles was interrupted during the World War II. Psychological research in Germany and Austria suffered as a result of great losses of eminent psychologists who were exiled. If American psychology today stands foremost, it is because of the German immigrant psychologists who smuggled themselves into America to escape the horrors of the Nazi regime.

At that time, the German psychologists were involved in research particularly on verbal and personality areas. Some of the great German psychologists who influenced other European and American psychologists are Spranger whose Types of Men led to The Study of Values, by Allport and Vernon. Jung's Psychological Types, gave our language extrovert and introvert Kretschmer's Physique and Character is the early formulation of a classification which has influenced, among others Eysenck to formulate his hierarchy of personality traits such as introversion-extraversion and stability-instability. Finally, Rorschach's psychodiagnostics, are some of the important contributions showing the psychological trends in Germany.

Another area in which German psychology has had a unique position is perception. The Gestalt psychologist like Wertheimer, Kohler, Koffka and Lewin who went into exile exercised a far-reaching influence from 1920 till 1934. However, some of the younger generation like Metzger stayed on and produced a lot of experimental work on perception. Similarly, Von Frisch, whose work on bees had long been famous, made some observations during World War II that roused a good deal of controversy. He claimed that the bee workers returning to the hive after discovering a new source of honey can indicate both the direction and the distance to their fellow beings by performing two types of dances—the "round" dance and the "waggle" dance. Lorenz perhaps is the most important animal psychologist whose contribution is the concept of "imprinting," the process by which the young of a species become attached normally to their mothers. Lorenz, and his disciples Timbergen and Thorpe who made a special study of animal behaviour have contributed considerably to the science of psychology. Lorenz and his disciples fled to England during World War II.

In Great Britain psychology flourished under the stewardship of Bartlett whose books—*Remembering and Thinking* exercised great influence in the university of Cambridge. The most important figure in the development of British psychology was Craik, who died quite young as a result of road accident in 1945. It is said that Craik was a "philosopher by training, and experimentalist by inclination, and a genius at inventing apparatus." Some of his ideas have influenced the psychological thought both in Europe and in America. Some of the basic ideas of the science cybernetics owe their origin to him.

A second line of thought in British psychology can be traced back to Galton through Spearman, Thomson, and Sir Cyril Burt. These psychologists engaged themselves with the problem of intelligence. Spearman stated his theory of intelligence in *The Nature of Intelligence* and *Principles of Cognition,* followed by *The Abilities of Man.* Thomson's The Factorial Analysis of Human Ability and Burt's *The Factors of the Mind* in 1940 are some of the noteworthy contributions to the theory of intelligence.

In the past 40 years, psychologists like Eysenck, Broadbent and Broadhurst have contributed immensely by their original work. Eysenck's output is much greater than that of any other British psychologist and ranges all the way from highly technical to popular writing. His book *The Scientific Study of Personality* shows his theoretical position. Much of his work has been done in a clinical setting in Maudsley Hospital in London.

In France, Pieron has been the influential figure on French psychology. He is both an empiricist and an experimentalism. Pieron has not been well understood by the English speaking world and hence his ideas on physiological and sensory areas, so also on psychophysics are also not adequately understood and hence he is poorly represented to the English speaking psychologists.

In Belgium Michotte and in Switzerland Piaget have been very influential figures. The former is a phenomenalist interested in the characteristics of immediate experience and yet he is a good experimentalist. Piaget's work on the intellectual development of a child needs no mention since it is the best available work now. His *"The growth of logical thinking from childhood to adolescence"* is the landmark in the developmental psychology. Though he wrote in French his works have been translated in English and have influenced the English speaking world. John Flavell's book "*The Developmental Psychology of Jean Piaget*" summarizes Piaget's work. Another important psychologist in Belgium is Joseph Nuttin. His own experimentally based attack upon the Thorndikian view of the law of effect has been largely neglected in the United States. His work on the spread of effect demonstrates this attack.

Italian psychology specially at the Catholic University at Milan is more centered on experimental work. Gemelli has produced a tremendous amount of experimental work in diverse fields. Much of the psychological research in Italy is concerned with applied orientation like accident prevention and occupational activities. Applied work in Italy at the National Institute of Psychology at Rome has been much influenced by Gemelli's contributions and to a lesser extent by Ponzo's contributions to aptitude testing and selection in education, industry, and vocational guidance. Some of the psychologists in Italy have been engaging in the areas of intelligence, risk-taking behaviour and perception.

In Canada, like in the United States, there is a great volume of psychological research specially in the fields of verbal learning and memory by Earhard and Earhard, Mandler, Marshall, Murdock and Murray. The second field is motivation in which research is done by Appley, Bindra and Malmo. Berlyne's work on learning and attention is an attempt to understand the intellectual processes in terms of the behaviourist principles. Hebb seems to have greater influence on Canadian psychology specially from physiological point of view like sensory isolation and neural organization.

In Soviet Russia psychology has been influenced by Pavlovian concepts of conditioning. Soviet psychology is greatly interested in physiological basis of behaviour and attempts to account for psychological phenomena in terms of physiological principles. Luria's work on brain and behaviour, Norkina's work on the "type of highest nervous activity" Miminoshvili's work on experimental neurosis in monkeys by overstraining the cortical excitatory processes, Vygotskii's work on thought and language and Krushinskii's animal behaviour are some of the important strides made in Soviet psychology.

Oriental Psychology. In the orient psychology has been the handmaid of philosophy and as such it is difficult to separate psychological concepts from philosophical ones. In the ancient Hindu and Buddhist literature, there are various systematic approaches to human; nature and experience. A lot of psychological information is to be found in the Rig Vedas and specially in *Upanishads*. According to one of the *Upanishads* as *Akhilananda*, states there are four states of the mental processes like sleeping, dreaming, the waking state, and the superconscious. The first two states which belong to the subconscious; are considered by Hindu philosophers to be important aspects of human experience. It is interesting to note that the Hindu philosophers differentiated between sleeping and dreaming. Recent neurophysiological research by Thompson, seems to support the Hindu thinker's distinction of the dual theory of sleep classical "slow" sleep and, "paradoxical" sleep with dreaming. The Hindu psychologists, like the psychoanalysts, place special importance on the sub-conscious but unlike psychoanalysis, Hindu psychology does not assume sex and death urges as the basic human instincts. According to them, the basic urge is to attain eternal happiness or complete freedom from bondage.

In India, the crowning achievement of the Indian thinkers was metaphysical speculation. However, the philosophical literature of India is not only rich in metaphysics, but also in Psychology, Logic, Ethics, Aesthetics, and Epistemology. Every school of philosophy has made worthy contributions to

Psychology, Logic, Ethics, and other mental sciences, but these have never been treated as a separate branch of study. Perhaps the reason is that the Indian mind is primarily synthetic and it always analyses a problem into its various aspects without destroying its organic unity. Although in the development of Indian though we come across separate monographs on different sciences, we find them mixed up with Metaphysics. In India, there is not a single work that is exclusively devoted to the psychological analysis of mental processes. The Indian philosophers did not believe that psychology, as understood in modern terms, could be treated as a separate discipline. Mrs. Rhys David's book on Buddhist Psychology is indeed a monumental work but only on the psychology of the Buddhists. Indian psychology is not Empirical because it is based on metaphysics. In the words of Jadunath Sinha, "The psychological account of some problems of perception, *e.g.* perception of the self, perception of the universal, etc. is unintelligible without consideration of their metaphysical foundations. So I found it extremely difficult to avoid metaphysical considerations altogether in my treatment of these topics." Indian psychology is based on introspection and observation unlike the psychology in the West, which is based on experiments and this is obvious because introspection is the method of philosophical enquiry.

Comparing psychology in India from Western point of view, though psychology has made great strides in the West because it is treated as an empirical science and the methods used are of experimental nature, in India psychology is in its infancy merely because it is still regarded as part of philosophy. However, modern Indian psychologists trained in psychology as an empirical science are trying to experiment upon some of the problems encountered in Indian psychology. The greatest contribution of modern Indian psychologists, has been in the fields of social psychology and psychological testing. Several studies on communal stereotypes, social distance, regional tensions, caste tensions and attitudes have been reported in Psychological Journals in India and abroad. A study by Desouza on regional and communal stereotypes of Bombay University students, has shown that Maharashtrians have a negative image of South Indians, Muslims and business communities.

In the field of testing, several' psychologists have devised personality inventories and intelligence and vocational tests. Bhatia's Test of Intelligence, Kamath's Test of Intelligence in Marathi and Shukla's Test of Intelligence in Gujarati are some of the widely used tests. Kundu's Neurotic Inventory, Bhagwat's Pre-Medicine and Pre-Engineering Aptitude Test, Bengalee's Multiphasic Personality Scale arid many other such tests devised by research students have come into existence. Besides, several foreign tests and projective techniques have been standardized in India. Desouza standardized the Hand Test on Indian population consisting of 3,000 subjects drawn from seven religious communities such as Hindus, Muslims, Christians, Neo-Buddhists, Jains, Parsees and Sikhs and five occupations such as manufacture, construction, trade and commerce, transport and other unlisted occupations. The norms have been copyrighted by the Western Psychological Association, Los Angeles.

A recent book, *Personality Development: A Critic of Indian Studies* by Kundu is based on Indian researches conducted by Indian psychologists. The book reflects contemporary trends in Psychology and Education with special reference to the area of Personality development. The book is a collection of the material consisting of 180 unpublished Ph.D. thesis and Master's Dissertations.

Psychology in Japan. Zen Buddhism is well known to the Western World because it was early introduced by Dr. Y. Motora of Tokyo University. According to him the essential nature of mind is a dynamic psychic potentiality into which the subject-object division melts away. Apart from the psychological aspects of Zen Buddhism, psychology in Japan has made tremendous strides in research and there are several Japanese Journals of Psychology.

Among the experimental fields, perception has attracted the attention and some of the most intensely studied areas are optical illusions, figural after effects, constancy phenomena, colour vision and binocular vision. Unfortunately, because most of the journals are published in Japanese language, their original work on perception is unknown to foreign workers.

Another area of popular research in experimental psychology is learning and memory. One of the original works on memory is concerned with the function of stimulus and response words in paired-associate learning. Some of the psychologists engaged in learning and memory follow the Gestalt theory. In the field of animal behaviour several psychologists have followed the Pavlovian line of thought and have experimented upon such phenomena as reinforcement, resistance to extinction, discrimination learning and conditioned - avoidance response.

Now, interest in experimental psychology is marked by the interest in physiological psychology. Several psychologists are working on psychophysiological studies of sleep and wakefulness. Interest also has been shown in clinical psychology specially with children who are emotionally disturbed. On the applied side, the psychologists are engaged in investigating such problems as school curricula, traffic safety, industrialization, physical education etc. In short, psychology in Japan has touched practically all facets of human and animal behaviour both from theoretical and applied aspects.

●●●

2

Senses Process

The importance of sense organs in the behaviour of a living organism can hardly be exaggerated. Sense organs are like the doors through which the organism becomes aware of his environment. As we go up the evolutionary stage, sensory mechanisms become more varied and more sensitive. The human organism seems to be well equipped to register his world. The senses provide us with the knowledge of things with which we deal. In fact, it is impossible to think of behaviour without sense organs as it is impossible to think of it without the brain and the nervous system. At every moment of our life, right from the time we are born till we are dead, we are responding to the physical world around us and to various conditions within our body through the action of our senses. Our sense organs then, make us aware of our external world as well as the internal processes in our body. The famous British Philosopher John Locke said many years ago that, "there is nothing in our mind that was not first in our senses."

Our senses are the seat of highly specialized receptors, each capable of reacting to only certain type of changes in the environment or within the organism. These receptors are the nerve endings, which are set in action when a specific energy stimulates them. When they are stimulated, the nerve impulses generated by the stimulation of the receptors begin to travel through the nerves towards the brain. When these impulses reach certain specific areas of the brain, the brain activity caused by their presence results into conscious experience. Each class of sensory activity has its own specialized centers in the brain, which decode the impulses coming from the receptors of a particular sense organ.

Senses of Man

It was a traditional belief that the senses a man possesses are five in number. However, research in human physiology has shown that the senses are closer to ten or eleven. They are the sense of vision, hearing, taste, and smell. The skin itself has four senses namely, the sense of cold, warmth, pain and touch. These are known as the external senses but there is also a kinesthetic sense through which we become aware of the position of our limbs and tensions in our muscles. The vestibular sense located in our ears supplies lots with the information about the movement of our head and helps us to maintain the balance of our body. Besides these, there are other senses located within the body, which give us information about pressure, pain and temperature within the body and hence they are called organic senses. These three are known as internal senses. A minimum list of man's senses includes: vision, hearing, cold, warmth, pain, touch, organic sensibility, smell, taste, kinesthesis and the vestibular sense.

Each sensory receptor responds to a particular type of stimulation. For example, the visual receptors respond to changes in electromagnetic energy or light. The hearing receptors are stimulated by the sound energy; the taste and smell receptors respond to chemical stimulation; the warmth and cold receptor in the skin are stimulated by thermal energy or temperature changes. The sense of touch, pain, kinesthesis and vestibular senses are stimulated by some kind of mechanical movement. These different sense modalities show that our sense organs are highly specialized to respond to only some kind of stimulation. The kind of stimulation, which usually stimulates a sensory receptor is called the adequate stimulus.

Another important feature of sensory stimulation is that the stimulus, which excites the receptors in a particular sense organ must be of certain minimum strength if it is to excite them. We are aware that some lights are too weak to be visible or sounds too feeble to be audible. The minimum strength of the stimulus that is necessary to excite any particular sense organ is known as the lower threshold or limen, sometimes also called the lower absolute threshold. This threshold can be determined by presenting the subject with a stimulus of a given intensity and asking him whether he detects it or not; on the next trail a different stimulus intensity is used and such a procedure is followed through a wide range of intensities. On the basis of certain theoretical considerations, psychologists have agreed to define the absolute threshold as that value at which the stimulus is perceived 50 per cent of the time. Table 2.1 gives the data of absolute threshold for different sense modalities.

Table 2.1

Some Approximate Values for Absolute Thresholds

Sense Modality	Threshold
Vision	A candle flame seen at 30 miles on a dark clear night.
Hearing	The tick of a watch under quiet conditions at 20 feet.
Taste	One teaspoon of sugar in two gallons of water.
Smell	One drop of perfume diffused into the entire volume of a six-room apartment.
Touch	Wing of a fly falling on your cheek from a distance of 1 centimetre.

Besides the least amount of stimulus energy required to detect a sensation, there is also a certain difference between two stimuli before we can distinguish a difference between them. The minimum amount of stimulation necessary to distinguish between the two stimuli is known as the differential threshold or the just noticeable difference (JND). For example, two tones must differ in intensity in some measurable amount of stimulation before one can be heard as louder than the other. Like the absolute threshold, the differential threshold is the amount of change in physical energy necessary for a subject to detect a difference between two stimuli 50 per cent of the time.

One of the remarkable features about the differential threshold is that it is not constant. To illustrate this point, if you are in a room, which is illuminated by one 25-watt bulb and if another 25-watt bulb is added, the addition of this amount of extra light will be at once detected because it is well above the differential threshold. However, if you are in a room, which is illuminated by a thousand 25-watt bulbs, the additional light from one more 25-watt bulb will not be noticed because it is below the differential threshold although the amount of energy added is the same.

From the above illustration it follows that the value of the differential threshold depends upon the intensity of the stimulus to which more energy is added. It has been found that for relatively moderate intensities there is a constant ratio between the amount of energy which must be added, called Δ^I to reach the differential threshold, and the intensity, called I of the stimulation. In other words, Δ^I/I is constant for the middle range of intensities. This has been called Weber's law.

Stimulus Adaptation. An important characteristic in the working of our senses is that they get gradually adapted to continual stimulation. In general, it is true that all senses gradually become less sensitive as they are continually stimulated and more sensitive in the absence of any stimulation. For example, when wearing clothes, our skin senses feel their pressure but soon we become unaware of it because our skin senses: have adapted to the pressure of the clothes. By the same token, in extreme darkness we are able to detect even a faint glimmer of light because there is complete absence of visual stimulation. These changes brought about in our receptor organs either due to their continual stimulation or absence of stimulation are referred to as the phenomenon of adaptation. There are varying degrees of adaptation in different sense modalities. For example, the sense of smell shows a high degree of adaptation to continual stimulation. Everyone has the experience how quickly we become habituated even to strong smells, so much so, we may not perceive them at all. Excepting the sense of hearing all the senses show adaptation to a smaller or greater extent.

Transduction. The process of converting physical energy into activity in the nervous system is known in sensory psychology as transduction. Transduction takes place at the receptors and involves several steps. In general, the specialized cells of the receptor organs act to convert physical energy into a slowly changing electrical potential known as the generator potential. The generator potential, in turn, acts upon the nerve cells and fibres to produce the nerve impulses as already noted, which travel through the central portions of the brain and eventually result in an experience.

Sensation and Perception. The simple experiences, which arise from the stimulation of sense organs have been called sensations. All our experiences of red, white, sound or pain are said to be sensations whereas, more complex experiences, such as house, warning etc. have been called perception. In simple language, the distinction between sensation and perception is that simple ingredients of experience are regarded as sensations, and the experiences that involve several sensations and their interpretation are regarded as perceptions. A perception, therefore, is the interpretation or the meaning given to the sensation and individual experiences.

Vision. Vision has been described as the most important sense in human beings as well as in animals because their survival is closely linked with its normal functioning. In man, this wonderful sense adds colour and movement to life. The experience of the world around us in terms of shapes, sizes and forms in two and three dimensions is made possible because of the functioning of our eye. The electromagnetic energy, which we call visible light, stimulates the specialized receptor cells, the rods and cones of the retina and initiates a series of chemical changes in the light-sensitive substances of these cells. The result of this series of reactions is an electrical event called the generation potential which causes a barrage of nerve impulses to be triggered and it is this barrage, which becomes the input into the central nervous system, which is responsible for seeing. What we see depends upon the objects transmitting light to the retina.

The Human Eye. Anyone who is acquainted with the working of a camera will very well see the similarities between the camera and the human eye. Both are dark chambers, which admit light through an opening in front. Both have a lens behind the opening for focussing the images of outside objects on the rear surface. Both have surfaces behind the lens (film in the case of a camera and retina in the case of the eye) on which the image of an object is projected. Both have images, which fall on their surfaces, which are inverted and turned from right to left. Both can be adjusted to control the amount of light falling on their surfaces, but in the case of the eye, it has its own automatic mechanism for its adjustment. The iris of the eye serves like a diaphragm of the camera. The iris controls the size of the opening known as the pupil, which enlarges its size when light is dim in order to allow more light on the surface, or contracts when the light is bright in order to allow only sufficient light in the eye.

In spite of these several similarities between the camera and the eye, there are some fundamental differences, which must be carefully noted. Firstly, the eye sees because of the activity in the brain and not because we see the image of the external object falling on the retina. Secondly, the eye has a lens like a camera but it is used only for small adjustments in focussing and the main job of bending the light is done by the cornea. Finally, the eye is far more sensitive to light than a film in a camera.

The eye is roughly spherical in shape and its walls are made up of three different layers. The outer layer known as the sclera is made up of tough fibres that protects it and serves to maintain its shape. The sclera layer bulges out and becomes transparent in front of the eye and this bulge is called the cornea. Beneath the sclera layer there is another opaque layer known as the choroid coat, which does not allow any light to enter in the eye except through the cornea and the lens. The innermost layer is known as the retina. It is the most sensitive part of the eye, which enables us to see.

Retina, when examined under a microscope, shows that it is made up of several cells on its surface. Two types of cells—rods and cones—are the light sensitive elements. The rods are cylindrical in shape and the cones are conical. According to a modest estimate there are between 110,000,000 and 125,000,000 rods and between 6,300,000 and 6,800,000 cones. Cones are packed most closely in the central part of the retina known as the fovea. Fovea is the region of the most distinct vision and the part, which we use most when getting clear images of the objects. There are no rods in the fovea. The cones and the nerves leading from them function only in the light and are responsible for colour vision as well as the sharpness of vision. In darkness, the cones are not stimulated and hence only the rods can function. Through the process of dark adaptation, the rods become highly sensitive and responsive to the smallest quantity of light. Thus then, cones are a day vision system whereas, rods are a night vision system. The rods do not respond to the colour of objects but can see only white, grey and black. Further, the rods do not record the fine details and shapes of the objects as the cones do.

Another interesting feature about the cones in the region of fovea is that they have separate connections with the optic nerve. This nerve leaves the retina at the posterior side and goes to the brain. The region in the retina where the optic nerve leaves for the brain is insensitive to light and is known as the blind spot. It is a blind spot because it lacks both rods and cones. As we leave the central part of vision, the fovea on the retina and go towards the periphery, the cones become less and less and the rods become more and more in number.

Focusing Mechanisms. In most cameras, one has to adjust the focus of the lens for objects at different distances by adjusting the lens back and forth. The lens of the human eye, however, becomes thicker or thinner to focus at different distances. It becomes thinner or flat when focusing on far objects and thicker and curved when focusing on nearer objects. These changes are called accommodation. The shape of the lens is controlled by the ciliary muscle, which is attached to the lens. The defects in accommodation lead to visual defects known as short-sightedness and long-sightedness. Inability to see objects, which are far at a distance is called short-sightedness and inability to see near objects is called long-sightedness. Such visual defects are usually corrected by using glasses. The accommodation of the lens occurs for far and near objects.

Nature of Visual Stimulus. The eye is stimulated by electromagnetic energy, commonly called light. However, it is capable of reacting only to a small band of electromagnetic spectrum. As a physical stimulus, the light has three different dimensions. The first one is intensity, the second is wave-length, and the third is the wave-length composition. The intensity of the physical stimulus leads to the experience of brightness. The greater the intensity of the physical stimulus, the greater is the experience of brightness. The characteristic of the wave-length makes us aware of hue or colour and when a mixed light falls on the retina, the experience is of white or grey depending upon the intensity of the wave-length.

Brightness. The sensation of brightness, which is dependent upon the intensity of light, varies from black to white through various shades of grey. Although we usually talk of brightness as extending from black to white, our experience is that colours can be bright or dark. A weak and strong blue light may have the same wave-length but different brightness. Brightness then, depends upon the intensity of light and the intensity of light in turn depends upon the amplitude of the light wave. Thus, one and the same wave-length may have different amplitudes; the smaller amplitude usually is intense whereas the larger amplitude is more intense.

Hue. Hue is the perceived dimension of colour, which we refer to when we use common colour names like red, green, yellow, blue or combinations of them. When we say that some object is red, we mean that it has a red hue. Our sensation of hue or colour depends upon the wavelength of light. Different wave-lengths produce different sensations of hue. For example, when a light of 760 nanometres in wave-length strikes our retina, we experience the sensation of red hue. The entire visual spectrum of light extends from red at one end through oranges, yellows, greens, blues and violets at the other end. The relation between wave-length and hue is not completely stable and the eye also is not equally sensitive to all wave-lengths. The relative sensitivity of the eye changes with the intensity of the light stimulation. Hue also depends upon contrast effects. For example, when two coloured areas are adjacent to each other, they may induce what appears as mutual changes in hue in each other near the border between the two areas. This phenomenon is called simultaneous contrast.

Saturation. When hues are mixed, the reiulting colour is different not only in hue but also in saturation. By saturation we mean the purity of colour. Purity or saturation refers to the degree to which a particular colour is diluted or not diluted by greyness or whiteness. Saturation then, refers to the degree of concentration or dilution of the hue or colour. Saturation or purity of colour can be reduced by mixing it with white. When a hue has no mixture of white, we call it a highly saturated colour. In fact, the most highly saturated colours are made by using only the colour pigments and avoiding any white in the mixture The deep or strong colours are those which are highly saturated whereas, the weak colours are those which are relatively unsaturated.

Functioning of the Eye. When the electromagnetic energy or light from the external objects strikes the eye through its opening and the lens and casts its image on the retina, the rods and cones are stimulated. The rods and cones have in them the light-sensitive substances known as rhodopsin and iodopsin respectively. The former is the major pigment found in the rods whereas the latter is found in the cones. These substances start splitting when light falls on them.

When the electromagnetic energy strikes in the visible range, rhodopsin is broken into orange intermediates and then into two substances called retinene and opsin. Retinene gives the yellowish colour, which was originally called visual yellow. Retinene and opsin spontaneously change back into rhodopsin and a cycle of chemical changes called the visual cycle takes place. In this way, the equilibrium is established between the splitting of rhodopsin and its synthesis from retinene and opsin.

Regarding the cone pigments, three human cone pigments have been identified and these are called blue, green and yellow cones. These changes create generator potential, which triggers the nerve impulses which collectively travel to the brain via the optic nerve. When they reach the visual cortex in the brain and stimulate its activity, we become aware of the things we see.

Colour Vision

Our ability to perceive colours depends upon the capacity of the retina to react differently to various wave lengths in the spectrum of light. The cones on the retina are supposed to be specialized structures, which react differently to different wave lengths. Research on colour vision has shown that there are four different primary wave-lengths which correspond to red, yellow, green and blue which are sufficient to prove all types of colour sensations. These elementary colours are called psychological primaries. Between these elementary colours are the secondary colours in which the primary components can be identified such as, orange between red and yellow; yellow-greens between yellow and green; bluegreen between green and blue and purples and violets between blue and red. Another set of primaries is called the colour-mixture primaries. The three colours usually chosen are red, green and blue, which can be used to produce all the other colours by additive mixture. For example, colours between red and green on the colour circle can be produced by additively mixing a pure red and pure green. Similarly, colours between green and blue on the colour circle can be obtained by their additive mixtures, and the same holds good for blue and red. In fact, with additive mixing the entire colour circle can be produced with just three colours.

It is assumed that the cones have different types of photosensitive chemicals, each capable of reacting to different sets of wave lengths. There are red cones, blue cones and yellowish green cones, which react to the red light. blue light and green light respectively to produce various colour sensations.

Theories of Colour Vision

Psychologists have evolved different theories of colour vision to explain the facts about colour perception, but they do not explain all the facts of colour vision adequately. In Eighteenth Century a theory of colour vision proposed by Thomas Young, an English physicist and later modified by the German physiologist Hermann Von Helmholtz and hence the theory has been called the Young-Helmholtz's theory. This theory proposes that there are three kinds of cones: red cones, green cones and blue cones, each of them is highly sensitive to a different wave-length. All other colours are somehow produced by a combined stimulation of these three cones. For example, yellow is produced when red and green cones are stimulated simultaneously. Similarly, white is produced when all three cones are simultaneously stimulated.

Although there is strong support for this theory from the point of view of colour mixture, yet this theory has not been able to explain many other facts of colour vision. For instance, many red-green colour-blind people can see yellow. The theory as originally stated assumes that yellow is due to the mixture of activity in the red and green cones. If this be so, how can red-green colour-blind persons who presumably lack the red and green cones see yellow?

Another colour theory was formulated by Ewald Hering after the above theory. Hering felt that the Young-Helmholtz's theory did not adequately explain the visual experience. He based his theory on the psychological primaries rather than the colour mixing primaries and argued that yellow is as basic a colour as red, blue or green. He proposed that there were three types of cones (1) one that responded to degrees of brightness, the black-white continuam; (2) two colour cones, one provided the basis for red-green perception and (3) the other for blue-yellow. He also assumed that each cone functioned in two ways. One colour of the pair was produced when the receptor was in a building-up phase (anabolic), and the other appeared when the cone was in a tearing down phase (catabolic). The two phases cannot occur at the same time in a given cone. For example, when a yellow-blue cone is stimulated it responds with either yellow or blue. It cannot react both ways simultaneously. Hering's theory has often been called the opponent-process theory. In its modern form this theory assumes that the opponent processes take place not in the cones but in the coding mechanisms closer to the brain in the optic system.

Recent research suggests that both theories may be partially correct. MacNichol, using her procedure called microspectrophotometry, was able to identify three kinds of light-sensitive pigments in the cones. One type was primarily sensitive to wave-lengths in the blue band, the second sensitive to green, and a third sensitive to yellow. DeValois and Jacobs, took recordings with microelectrods which gave evidence of an "on" and "off" type of process in the bipolar cells and in cells of the portion of the thalamus where visual impulses are relayed to the usual cortex. They found that some cells respond when stimulated by short wave-lengths but do not respond during illumination with long wavelengths, whereas other cells respond when stimulated by long wavelengths and do not respond when stimulated by short wave-lengths. These findings support the opponent-process theory.

Afterimages. Both the Young-Helmholtz and Hering theories explain another phenomenon of colour vision called successive contrast. For instance, if you look steadily at a bright-coloured spot for a while, and then look at a grey sheet of paper, you may see two kinds of successive afteriamages. The first is called the positive afterimage because it is the same colour as the original stimulation. The second, is the negative afterimage which is the complimentary colour of the original colour. Suppose that the original circle is blue green, the positive afterimage will also be blue green whereas, the negative afterimage will be orange. It must be noted, however, that not all afterimages are of the complimentary colour. In fact, after staring at a very bright light you are likely to see a whole succession of colours, but seeing the complimentary colour is very common.

Positive afterimages are supposed to be caused by the continuation of the activity after the removal of the physical energy. Regarding the negative afterimages, the Young-Helmholtz theory makes the assumption that the original stimulation fatigues the special colour cones, which are excited. For example, a blue-green stimulus will fatigue the blue and green elements but not the red elements.

Dark Adaptation or Scotopic Vision. When we enter a dimly lighted room after having come from bright sunlight, we are unable to see anything in the room, but gradually things become visible. You must have experienced that when you have entered a cinema theatre, you could not see the rows of chairs before you. Similarly, when we come out of a dark room into bright sunlight, our eyes are at first blinded by the light, but in a few seconds we are able to adapt ourselves to the bright light. When we remain in a dark room for a long time, our eyes become highly sensitive to light, so much so, we are even able to see a flicker of match from the distance of fifty miles if there is perfect darkness. Experimental evidence demonstrates that after an hour of dark adaptation the sensitivity of the eye can increase from 1000 to 1,00,000 times. Light adaptation of photovision on the other hand, diminishes considerably the sensitivity of our eyes.

Visual Acuity. Colour and brightness are not the only characteristics of objects in our environment. They also have a form. The capacity of our eyes to discriminate between various forms in our environment is called the visual acuity. In other words visual acuity is the ability of the individual to perceive differences in details of the visual environment. There are several ways to determine and measure the visual acuity but the basic procedure is to present the subject with figures with finer details at a specified distance and the subject is asked whether he can perceive them or not. The charts of letters, which the opticians use to determine the extent of the eye defects are based on this principle. For instance, if a person can see at a distance of 20 feet what a normal person can see at a distance of 100 feet, he has 20/100 vision which certainly is defective. Similarly, if a person can see at a distance of 20 feet what a normal person can see at a distance of 10 feet, he has 20/10 vision which is excellent. The standard vision is defined as 20/20, which actually means that a person has a normal or average vision.

Colour Blindness

It is estimated that about four percent of the people in the general population are colour blind and their inability to see certain colours is likely to affect their behaviour in various ways. Colour blindness is not our inability to identify colour by a particular name or even our inability to see colours. Really speaking colour-blindness means mistaking certain colours for some other colours. Colour-blind people usually see a great many colours but they confuse certain critical ones. Colour-blindness is a defect, which makes a person unable to tell the difference between two or more colours which most other people can easily distinguish. The explanation for colour blindness is that the cones on the retina of the colour blind people are in some way different from those who can see all the colours without any difficulty.

There are various types of colour blindness. Firstly, there are people who are totally colour-blind, who cannot see any colour but perceive the world as a sort of black and white photograph. It is assumed that this defect arises from complete absence of the cones on the retina. Such people seem to rely only on rod vision and are very rare. Secondly, there are people who are called partially colour-blind. In other words, such people are capable of seeing certain colours but confuse them with certain other colours. Among the partially colour-blinds, there are two common varieties: (1) those who are known as dicromats whose colour vision is limited to only two colours or hues, namely, the yellows and the blues. These people are also known as Red Green colour-blinds because they usually see these two colours and their shades as some other colours rather than red or green. (2) there are others who confuse very light pinks, greens, tans and browns. Such people are known as suffering from colour weakness called anomalous colour defect.

There are several colour vision theories, which account for colour blindness. According to Ladd-Frankiln theory of colour vision, our capacity to see colours has gradually developed in the course of evolutionary process. In the first phase of development of vision, we are capable of seeing things only in black and white. In the second phase, we develop yellow blue colour vision and at the last phase we develop red green vision. Perhaps because of this phased development we are more likely to lose our red green vision than the colour vision at the two earlier phases. This explains why there are many more red green blind people than blue yellow; colour blinds.

The most interesting feature about colour blindness is that the colour blind persons or even those around them are unable to detect this defect unless it is highly pronounced. There are several good tests to find out whether a person is colour-blind or not. One such very widely used test to detect the defect of colour blindness is known as the Ishihara's Colour Blindness Test.

Most types of colour blindness are supposed to be inherited and the defect has been identified as a sex-linked recessive characteristic. It is also assumed that due to the genetic relations involved, colour blindness is more prevalent among men than among women.

Audition

The sense of hearing, technically known as audition, is in no way inferior to the sense of vision. Its importance as a means of acquiring knowledge of the external world, can be hardly exaggerated both in the case of animals and human beings. In the case of animals, hearing is very closely concerned with their survival and, in certain highly developed species of animals, hearing becomes a sort of underdeveloped means of vocal communication. In the case of man hearing acquires a great importance as a vehicle of communication of language through which we are able to accumulate knowledge. Further, it is through hearing that a man is able to make his visual and other experiences much more meaningful and effective.

The Human Ear. Broadly, the human ear can be divided into three distinct parts: The external ear, the middle ear and the inner ear. The sound waves are collected at the external ear, which consists of the decorative ear called the pinna and a canal through which the sound waves are transmitted to the ear drum. The ear drum is a small thin membrane stretched tightly across the inner end of the canal. Inside the ear drum there is a small cavity filled with air and three small bones called ossicles. This is the middle ear.

The boundary of the middle ear extends from the ear-drum to another membrane separating the inner ear from the middle ear. It is known as the oval window. One of the three ossicles known as malleus (hammer) is attached to the ear drum. The middle bone, known as incus (anvil) is connected with the stapes (stirrup). The arrangement of the three bones and the two membranes is such that the vibrations caused by the ear-drum are conducted through the bones to the oval window.

The inner ear is more complex in structure. It is a seat of two organs the sense of equilibrium and the sense of hearing. The sense organ of hearing is located in a bony snail like spiral called the cochlea. The cochlea has three different canals which are filled with fluids and are separated from each other by membranes. On one such membrane known as the basilar membrane there is a tiny structure called the organ of Corti, which is the real organ for hearing. The receptors of hearing known as the hair cells, are located in the organ of Corti. These hair cells are the real receptors of sound energy. When these hair cells are stimulated the generator potential resulting from such stimulations triggers off nerve impulses which are transmitted through the auditory nerve to the auditory area of the brain. It is only when this process takes place that we experience hearing.

Sound Stimulus. The air is a collection of molecules, which are always moving about, colliding with one another and exerting pressure on one another. If these molecules are closely packed, the air pressure will be greater and if they are few, then the air pressure will be less. Such changes in pressure constitute the physical basis of sound perception. Sound waves are generated by the vibration of a physical object in the air. When an object vibrates in both directions, it results in the condensation and ratification of the air molecules, which create areas of high pressures in the air. This is what we call the sound wave. When the object vibrates, condensation of molecules takes place and this is known as positive pressure. whereas, when ratification of air molecules takes place, a little vacuum is created and this is known as the negative pressure.

A sound wave moves through the air in much the same way as a ripple moves on the water. Sound waves generated in this fashion vary from each other is three important respects: (1) frequency, (2) amplitude, and (3) complexity. These three properties of sound are important because they are the basis of our psychological experiences called: (1) pitch, (2) loudness, and (3) timbre.

Frequency and Pitch. The vibrations in the air molecules vary in frequency depending upon the speed of the vibrating object. Experiments have shown that the vibrations may be as slow as one per second and as fast as one million per second. The frequency of a sound wave is measured in terms of cycles per second (CPS) also known as Hertz (Hz).

The human ear is capable of responding only to a small range of frequencies usually from 16 Hz to about 21,000 Hz. The sounds above and below these frequencies are inaudible to the human ear. It is possible that individuals vary in their sensitivity to the frequency of sound wave but the differences are not very large. Similarly, some animals like dogs, for instance, are capable of hearing sound frequencies beyond human capacity; they can respond to the sound of 40,000 Hz. It is important to note that our experience of pitch (the highness or lowness of a sound) is primarily dependent upon the frequency of sound waves. For example, the higher the frequency of sound, the higher is its pitch.

Amplitude and Loudness. The second factor in which the sound waves differ from each other is known as the amplitude. Amplitude, is determined by the amount of pressure difference between compression and rarification of the wave. Thus then, while the frequency of a sound wave tells us how often the sound wave changes from positive to negative pressure, the amplitude tells us how great the pressure changes are. In other words, the amplitude of a sound wave tells us how intense the sound is. Our psychological experience of the loudness of the sound is primarily dependent upon the intensity of the sound wave.

Scientists have developed special methods of measuring the sound energy. The range of intensity to which the human ear can respond is very great. For instance, the loudest sound that one can hear without discomfort has a pressure of about one million times as great as the weakest sound that is just audible. The intensity of the sound wave is usually measured in terms of decibels. A decibel is equal to the lowest sound pressure that can be recorded by a normal ear.

Complexity and Timbre. The sound waves produced in the world around us are rarely simple (of uniform frequency or intensity). They are usually made up of several complex waves of all considerable types. However, they may be broadly classified into two categories: periodic and aperiodic. The periodic waves are of various heights and widths. The sound waves produced by various musical instruments are also complex but repeat themselves in regular patterns. They are usually periodic. On the other hand, there are many objects, which produce sound waves of irregular and unrelated frequencies which produce auditory sensations called noises. This is due to the aperiodic waves.

We are able to tell the sounds produced by one musical instrument from another, only because each musical instrument is capable of producing certain complex and yet characteristic patterns of sound waves. This characteristic quality of a musical tone is called timbre. It is the timbre (tonal quality) of a tone that tells us whether it is being produced by a piano or a clarinet.

What happens when two tones are sounded together is a problem raised. It has been found that they do not lose their identity as colours do when mixed, but they may lead to a fusion that is heard as consonant (pleasant) or as dissonant (unpleasant). The two tones create a third tone based on the difference in their frequencies. This difference tone may or may not harmonize with the fundamental tones sounded and it is for this reason that some combinations of tones are preferred to others. Musical harmony, for example, depends partly on the interaction between fundamental tones, overtones, and different tones, which combine to make up the complex tonal stimulus.

A noise is sound composed of many frequencies not in harmonious relation to one another. Sound experts sometimes speak of white noise when a noise is composed of all frequencies in the sound spectrum at roughly the same energy level. White noise is like the white light which is composed of all frequencies in the light spectrum. A bathroom shower, for instance, approximates the sound of white noise. Speech sounds make simultaneous use of both, tonal qualities and noise qualities. When we speek, the speech consists of vowels which have a tonal quality and consonants which have a noise quality.

Functioning of the Ear. When the ear drum begins to vibrate in response to the pressures exerted on it by the sound waves, the vibrations are first transmitted to the ossicles and from them to the oval window. The oval window conducts the sounds to the cochlea, which is the auditory portion of the inner ear. Pressure at the oval window sets into motion the fluid inside the cochlea which stimulates the fine hair cells of the basilar membrane in the cochlea on which is located the organ of corti. The pressure changes in the fluids of the canals cause a shearing movement of the hair cells to produce nerve impulses which are carried over to the auditory areas of the brain through the auditory nerve. It is only when the nerve impulses reach the brain that we get the experience of sound. The pathways of the auditory nerves are made up of nerve fibers from each ear, which travel to both the cerebral hemispheres and terminate in the temporal lobes.

How the nerve impulses convey the physical characteristics of a sound stimulus like frequency, amplitude and complexity, and how our corresponding experience of pitch, loudness and timbre result, is yet to be fully understood. However, scientists have tried to offer several theories for these questions. The two most accepted theories are known as the Place Theory suggested by Helmholtz and the Telephone Theory suggested by Rutherford.

The place theory assumes that the frequency of a tone is indicated by the region of the basilar membrane that is maximally displayed by the sound wave. The telephone theory, on the other hand, assumes that the cochlea acts like a microphone and the auditory nerve like a telephone wire. According to this theory, pitch is determined by the frequency of impulses travelling up the auditory nerve. The greater the frequency, the higher is the pitch. Just as when discussing the theories of colour vision, Young-Helmholtz and Hering's theories were said to be partially correct although they did not offer a satisfactory explanation, in hearing also, pitch discrimination may be partly explained by both the theories. Both the place of excitation on the basilar membrane and the frequency of nerve response seem to be involved in transmitting the information about the frequency of a tone. Perhaps, it could be said that precise coding of the auditory information takes place in the auditory pathways closer to the brain and in the auditory cortex itself.

Deafness. It is commonly believed that deafness is simply our inability to hear sounds. However, this is not the complete truth because actually there are many kinds of deafness. In the first instance, there are people who cannot recognize even the faint sounds and such people are regarded as hard of hearing. Technically this phenomenon is known as intensity deafness. Usually people who have to work in deafening noises such as pilots, gunners or factory workers, may develop such intensity deafness. Really speaking, our ears have protective mechanism which shield the delicate organs in the ear by reducing the intensity of sounds that are allowed to reach the inner ear, but obviously, when these mechanisms are over used, the ability to detect lower intensities of sound decreases. Sometimes the age factor also seems to be a possible cause of deafness. Research on the relationship between age and hearing has clearly demonstrated that persons below the age of 20 definitely have better hearing than the persons above that age. There is also some truth in the common belief that hearing is very much impaired in persons above 50 years of age.

The second factor which is often responsible for deafness in young people is the stiffening of the ossicles, particularly when the small bone known as the stirrup gets tightly sealed in the oval widow. This may happen due to different causes like the infection in the middle ear or even the rupture of the ear drum. Such deafness is called conduction deafness. The term conduction deafness is used because the origin of the deafness is to be found in the deficiencies of conduction in the ear.

The third type of deafness is called the nerve deafness. This deafness is caused when something is wrong with the auditory nervous system. Sometimes the nerves themselves are damaged or the damage is done to the cochlea or the basilar membrane. In this type of deafness, the hearing loss is much greater at high frequencies. Such persons are unable to hear high pitched sounds, but can hear low pitched sounds reasonably well. This type of deafness is very common among old people. With advancing age almost everyone shows signs of nerve deafness, but only in a few persons it becomes serious. There is some evidence also to show that nerve deafness is hereditary because it runs through certain families.

Localization of Sound. Every individual with normal hearing capacity can locate the source of sound by carefully listening to it. Psychological research has shown that this capacity to locate sound depends upon several factors. For example, it has been demonstrated that the sounds which are made directly above our heads are difficult to be localized, but those which are made anywhere on the right or left side can be very easily localized. Similarly, the sounds, which are made directly in front or behind are also difficult to be localized. Finally, sounds, which have very high frequencies are also difficult to be correctly located.

In localizing the source of a sound we make use of several physical clues but the time taken by the sound to reach the ears seems to be an important factor. For example, when a sound originates on our right side, it first reaches the right ear and then the left ear. This small difference is sufficient for us to locate the source of sound. Similarly, the sound that reaches one of the ears first is slightly louder than when it reaches the second ear. Such a clue also helps us in locating the sound. Finally, the localization of sound is further helped by the movement of our head and the use of our eyes. Psychologists have devised an apparatus called the sound cage to study the localization of sound. The findings mentioned above are based on such experiments conducted in the laboratory.

The senses of smell (olfactory sense) and taste (gustatory sense) are regarded as chemical senses because the receptors of these senses are stimulated by chemical substances. Both the olfactory sense and the gustatory sense work in close co-ordination with each other to produce a wide variety of experiences both pleasant and unpleasant. For some animals, the experiences of taste and smell are as interesting as those produced by the eyes and ears. In the case of dogs the sense of smell appears to be very highly developed. In most wild animals the sense of smell is connected with their survival because it is through this sense that many wild animals are able to detect the dangers in their environment. In the case of man, both smell and taste have a unique place because they add spice to our lives and make the act of eating either pleasant or unpleasant.

Smell

The receptors of the sense of smell are located in the nasal passage leading from the nostrils to the throat. Ii you look at, you will find that the smell receptors: lie in two small patches, one on the left and one on the right, in the roofs of the passages, and they are known as olfactory bulbs. They are stimulated when chemical substances in vapour form come in contact with them. When the smell receptors are stimulated nerve impulses are generated which are carried to the brain by olfactory nerves. We do not have adequate information regarding the brain mechanisms involved in smelling due to several difficulties, yet physiologists as well as psychologists have done a lot of research and yet the information is inadequate.

Attempts have been made to discover the basic or primary smells and a German researcher Henning has listed six primary smells as follows: (1) flowery (smells of flowers), (2) fruity (smells of fruits), (3) spicy (smells of spices like cloves and cardmom), (4) resinous (smells of pine), (5) burnt (smells of tar or burning substances), and (6) putrid (smells of rotting or decomposing substances). The industrial chemists, on the other hand, who are concerned with the manufacture of perfumes, prefer a four-fold classification of smells. According to this classification, the four basic smells are: (1) fragrant (musk), (2) acid (vigegar), (3) burnt (roasted coffee) and (4) caprylic (goaty or sweaty).

Whatever may be the number of basic smells, it is interesting to note that the nose is an extremely sensitive sense organ. Only a few molecules of odorous substance are enough to give rise to the sensation of smell. For example, the artificial musk, which is supposed to be the most ordorous substance can be smelt when it is mixed with a litre of air in such a small quantity as 0.00004 miligram. It is believed that smell sensitivity far surpasses the sensitivity, which we find in human beings. The extreme sensitivity of the sense of smell would have been a great nuisance to us had it not been for the phenomenon of adaptation. Adaptation is a process by which a sense organ gradually ceases to respond to constant stimulation. It is everybody's experience that smells of soaps, powders or perfumes, which we use constantly are no longer sensed by us. In the same manner we can get ourselves used to very strong foul smells rather quickly. This is only because of very quick adaptation of the sense of smell.

Theories of Smell. Although there is a disagreement regarding the basic ordours, many scientists have advanced theories to account for the transduction and the psycho-physical characteristics of smell. However, none of these theories has gained widespread acceptance. The basic idea is that certain smells are produced by molecules with particular shapes. This theory is called the lock-and-key theory because these molecules are supposed to fit into the "sockets" in the olfactory receptors. For example, the molecules of camphor, and substances, which have a camphor like smell, are supposed to have a spherical shape and fit into a bowl-shaped depression in the olfactory receptor. This theory considers five of the smells—camphoraceous, musky, floral, pepperminty, and ethereal—to be basic because they are supposed to have distinctive shapes. The other two basic smells—pungent and putrid—are supposed to arise from molecules having special patterns of electrical charge which allow them to fit in the sockets in the olfactory receptor. The evidence for this theory is highly suggestive specially regarding the molecular shapes and the electrical charges but the evidence has not been conclusively proved.

Taste

The receptors for taste are usually to be found in little clusters known as the taste buds. Normally there are 245 of these buds located on the top and sides of the tongue, and more sparsly on the back of the mouth and in the throat. Receptor for the sour taste are located mainly on the side of the tongue. Sweetness is best experienced by the tip of the tongue. Salt receptors are at the top and sides of the tongue and the bitter sensitive areas are at its base. All taste receptors, it has been found, operate with reduced sensitivity after smoking. Smokers who give up smoking often find that foods now taste so good that the habit of over-eating easily replaces the habit of smoking. Old people do not taste as well as do the younger people, and children, with all taste buds functioning fully, seem to have very active tastes.

The stimulation of the receptors in the taste buds can occur only when the substance to be tasted is soluable in saliva. When the taste cells are stimulated by such solution they generate nerve impulses, which are transmitted to the brain. The areas of the brain, which are involved in interpretting the impulses from taste cells are not yet precisely known. In dealing with smell we had said that there was no agreement among scientists regarding the basic odours. However, we have a better knowledge about the basic taste qualities. The research evidence in general is that there are four basic or primary taste qualities: salty, sour, sweet, and bitter. The evidence for these qualities comes from the fact that the tongue is not uniformly sensitive to all stimuli. It is true that we taste a lot of other flavours besides the four mentioned above but, this is due to the sense of smell. This in fact is the reason why we find the foods flavourless and tasteless when we are suffering from a heavy cold or when our nose is blocked.

Like all other senses, taste also shows adaptation. In other words, it becomes less and less sensitive during the course of constant stimulation. Research points out that the stronger the stimulation, the greater is the adaptation. Further, as compared with the senses of vision and hearing, the senses of smell and taste show a very rapid adaptation. Although we believe that we taste with our tongues and smell with our noses, most of us do not realize that we commonly confuse taste and smell. In fact, we often think that we are identifying a flavour by taste when smell is more important.

●●●

3

Psychology of Social Behaviour

We can survey the social behaviour among animals in a broad way by distinguishing the patterns of social behaviour among the invertebrates and the patterns among the vertebrates. The adjustments of organisms to the environment as well as to each other among the in ertebrates is more or less automatic, determined by the physico-chemical forces. Hence the terms tropism, reflex and instinct are used to denote the relatively inflexible patterns of behaviour. On the other hand the vertebrates reveal an increasing degree of flexibility. ·While the invertebrates show certain more or less fixed patterns of adaptation, the vertebrates show a good deal of individual variability and a capacity to profit by experience. Nature, as it were, has conducted two experiments: one at the invertebrate level where the relationship between the organism and environment is rather inflexible, with little scope for learning, and consequently, with little scope for the development of individuality, whereas at the vertebrate level the relation is more flexible and consequently with greater possibilities for learning and the development of individuality. In other words we can look upon the rigidity in behaviour at the invertebrate level as a stage in transition from the fixed relations at the inorganic level to the high degree of individuality possible among the higher animals and among the human beings.

Invertebrate Social Behaviour

Jennings studied the reasons for a collection of bacteria. He found that behaviour is fundamentally adaptive: the responses tend to promote life activities. He placed water containing bacteria on a slide. At first they scatter uniformly, swimming in all directions. Gradually they all collect around the air bubble. They come to the oxygen-saturated zone. Thus it, is the protoplasmic constitution that is responsible for the collection. There is nothing 'social' in their behaviour.

Similarly there is collective, but non-social, behaviour in the protozoa. Euglenae, for example, collect around a lighted spot. This is because each individual is whipped around by its flagellum when it enters into the shaded border zone. Alverdes distinguishes between 'associations (mere collections) and societies (organic wholes)'. "By associations I understand those chance gatherings produced solely by external factors (*e.g.*, insects round a source of light). Societies, on the other hand, are genuine communities. (*e.g.*, the ant-state, a horde of monkeys). In the formation of an association the individual is guided by environmental factors, and not by other members of its own species; a society, on the other hand, is formed when the individual is guided in the first place by the presence of others of its own species and only in the second place by environment factors". According to Alverdes not only the aggregations of protozoa, but also the collection of beetles around the corpses of mice or birds and the gathering of birds and other animals round the dead body of an animal are all instances of association and not of a society. Elsewhere Alverdes distinguishes between asocietary and societary animals. The lower animals, beginning from protozoa are societary. Each individual lives for itself whether it is alone or in the neighbourhood of others of its species. At the most they may attack each other or defend themselves against others. But they are incapable of entering into any kind ot relationship with the others. On the other hand the societary animals form relationship with one another when they are thrown together. "What differentiates a social group of any complexity from the above situation—(simple association or in sub-social aggregations) is that in social aggregations the unity rests upon an interdependence of individuals, a condition deriving from the effects exerted by group members as individuals with given qualities".

Swarms of dance flies form as a result of similar individual responses to local conditions such as light, humidity and temperature. These incidental aggregations may have possible adaptive benefits. The swarms assure the meeting of sexual forms and the survival of species. Thus we find that at the lowest levels organisms collect together because of *(a)* common environmental conditions and *(b)* for purposes of procreation.

It is at the level of the insects like the ants, bees and termites that we find true social organization. As Maier and Schneirla put it "The true social organization may be defined as an aggregation of individuals into a fairly well integrated and self-consistent group in which the unity is based upon the interdependence of the separate organisms and upon their responses one to another". The typical insect colony is based upon the grouping of parents and offspring. A second feature is the communication within the whole. The insect community is aroused through the propagation of excitement from individual to individual. An ant excites her nest mates through antennal vibrations. Finally we find a division of labour, a caste system among the ants. There are the fertile individuals and the infertile workers. In the insect colonies there is the soldier caste besides the worker caste. The fertile female or the queen loses her wings and becomes an egg-laying machine. She shuns the light and makes a small burrow. As the first eggs are laid she licks them. When the larvae develop she feeds them upon a salivary gland secretion. The offspring become the workers. They are very active, they look after the queen, gather food, excavate or build the nest. They pick up the further eggs, lick them and gather them in packets as the queen did to start with. The adult workers constantly feed one another, lick one another's bodies and stroke one another with antennae. They attack ants from other colonies even though they belong to the same. species. The ant learns to respond positively to the specific chemical of her own colony. One investigator took eggs from the nests of different species and hatched them artificially. Raised in a common nest they lived in peace. But the adult ants taken from the original nests and put together attacked one another. When an ant finds food and meets another individual in the nest, there is an excited and rapid exchange of antennal taps.

We thus find sex and reproduction constitute a very important element in social formation. Even the incidental aggregations of dance flies assure the meeting of the two sexes and thus of the survival of the species. With respect to the social insects, as we have seen, the whole colony gets started with the fertilized queen laying her eggs and hatching them. The colony consists of the mother and offspring. Allport wrote, "Society originates in the sex instinct. It leads to the institution of the family, which is the essential unit of survival within the family the principle of sympathy takes over; a child survives not because he is strong and fit but because his defencelessness arouses some grade of sympathy in others". We need not agree with Allport that there is 'sympathy' when the queen ant licks the first laid eggs and feeds them upon its salivary gland secretion. But here is the biological basis of what later manifests itself as psychological process—sympathy.

The divisions of labour among the social insects is very exact and rigid based on the needs of reproduction, nutrition and protection. Each insect caste is dedicated to one function. The queens have the task of reproduction, the workers that of nutrition and protection in some insects; while in others the soldiers are in charge of only protection. Each caste has the special structure to perform its function. As far as the reproductive castes are concerned, the males and the queens, the determination appears to be genetic. In bees and wasps the determination of the queen and worker castes depends largely on nutritional factors. As Wheeler puts it the workers are "nutritionally castrated" by being fed only on the "bee nectar" whereas the queens are fed entirely on "royal jelly". "In general, caste determination appears to be fairly flexible in the first stages of growth in the social insects but, once determined, an individual's caste seems to remain rigidly fixed".

Social Life among the Lower Vertebrates

Sexual differentiation itself as we have seen makes for social interaction. When we come to the warm-blooded forms, especially the birds and mammals, there is increasing care of offspring by the parents. The young depend on the mother for survival, involving feeding and protection. There is also communal living with a view to feeding protection and play. As we have seen above this development in social behaviour depends on the gradual decrease in the more or less fixed patterns of stimulus and response and the increase in the importance of maturation and learning. These, in their turn, depend on the growing domination of the higher brain centres. As Scott puts it, "The major roots of social organization appear to be con tactual behaviour, which leads eventually to advanced types of cooperation, and sexual behaviour, which, when related to more elaborate types of reproduction and protection of the young, may result in what may be termed altruistic behaviour".

Thus there appear to be the following four basic roots for social organization: *(a)* contactual behaviour, all the way from bacteria and protozoa, which lead to measurable physiological benefits like protection against temperature and other environmental factors, *(b)* reproduction, *(c)* protection of the young and *(d)* group living among the higher vertebrates for feeding, protection and play. Secondly the actual kind of social relationships developed depend upon the capacity of the animal for various kinds of learning. Thus there appear to be two biological roots to social behaviour: *(a)* organic needs and *(b)* the neuro-muscular structure enabling learning processes. The two together determine the level of social behaviour among the prehuman animal species.

We can now turn to a study of the social factors among the lower vertebrate species. There is not much in the literature regarding the extent of social stimulation and response among them. There are seasonal aggregations among the fishes related to feeding and reproduction. There may also be the influence of con tactual behaviour. We, however, do not know whether there is any domination or subordination among the fishes. As regards the amphibians, particularly among the frogs, there is not only contactual interplay but also some vocal interstimulation. But it is not clear whether there is any cooperation in feeding and care of the young among the fishes and the amphibians. Among the rcptiles, however, there is evidence of nesting, some care and defence of the young and even some attempts to control some areas of movement. The lizards acquire and hold certain territory. The resident male wills according to Evans "in 91 per cent of the combats". He fights harder to defend the territory.

Among the birds we find a good deal of social life. There is flocking for purposes of feeding, migration and nesting. Secondly mating is mostly monogamous and the pairing persists through a period of nest-building, hatching and caring for the young. Thirdly, in many species there is some form of dominance and suboradination. Finally there is development of vocal communication.

Most birds have a social background. It has had nestling with parents and fellow fledglings in the nest. Most of the characteristic activities of the birds are associated with the reproductive cycle—migration, courting, mating, nest-building, brooding, care of the young. Breeding cycle is accompanied by some kind of migration. The birds more in flocks to a shorter or longer distance. Decrease in available food, decrease in temperature, decrease in available light are some of the conditions associated with bird migration. The mating and breeding activities start when the birds reach the breeding ground. In most species the male arrives first. He establishes a "territory" and drives out the other males. He fights other males and sings with great vigour to attract the female. She is not particularly responsive at first. Her presence, however, excites him and there is surplus energy which takes the form of "strutting" and "display", particularly in the peacock. After mating the nest-building activity starts. The nest is completed by the time the egg-laying starts. Then there is the brooding. When the young are hatched, the female and the male as well supply the nestlings with food at regular intervals. Birds may come together on the basis of family groups or as a reaction to some common external condition. As the group forms they become adjusted to one another. They respond to the sounds made by others when frightened or when food is discovered. It is not possible to call this communication because the sounds are made not to get the attention of the others but are incidental to their own condition. Studies have also shown that there is dominance submission among the birds. There are reports of observation of "despotism" of one bird over the other. The ascendancy is shown by pecking another. There is also evidence of hierarchy. A may peck Band B subbmits to A but it may peck C. The subordinate bird demonstrates fear, submissiveness, avoidance or flight. Age, strength and sex differences determine the dominance submission relations. The most aggressive and active birds become 'leaders' since other individuals learn not to push ahead of them.

Social Life among the Primate

Studies of the social life of monkeys and apes have been very extensive and rewarding. There are four basic biological factors: *(a)* the erect posture *(b)* the freeing of the hands from locomotion and their use in manipulation, *(c)* elaborate vocalisation and *(d)* further advancement in the cerebral cortex, which differentiates the monkeys and apes from the other higher mammals.

Both among the monkeys and apes the societies are loose associations of adults and young, generally a male, some females and their children. Sometimes several of these groups may combine and form a bigger group. Thus group life is connected with reproduction, care of the young, securing of food, protection. They also derive a good deal of pleasure in mutual grooming. We find this even among rats and lower mammals. There is the avoidance of individual isolation. In most of the groups studied for one adult male there will be two to three females, indicating polygyny. The new-born is quite helpless and is entirely dependent on the mother, The young monkey takes about one month to become independent and the chimpanzee takes about three months. The mother not only feeds the infant but grooms it and instruct it in numerous responses. There is the dependency relation not only to the mother but also to the other adults as well as to the human care-taker in captivity.

In all species there is some hierarchy of power, particularly with respect to sexuality and feeding. Zuckerman reports that in captivity there is continual fighting among the males to control the females. On some occasions the struggles were so fierce that the weaker male as well as the intervening female have been killed. There is domination resulting in rudimentary leadership when a pack of monkeys arrive at a feeding ground or when the group fights another group. Maslow reports that the stronger and more ascendant monkey reserves to itself all the available food, shows aggression towards all the other members of the group and is dominant in sex. The subordinate monkey gets little or no food, responds to aggression by passivity, by flight.

According to Yerkes "The young chimpanzee is a lively, extrovert, active, energetic, impulsive, enthusiastic, sangunine, very sociable, ordinarily good-natured and fairly good-tempered, somewhat mercurial, timid before the unfamiliar, extremely expressive of its continuous flow of feelings and rapidly changing moods". It is eager to play and is mischievous. In adolescence and maturity playfulness and purposeless activity become less and it becomes serious, reserved and relatively quiet. "That social stimuli are powerful determiners of chimpanzee behaviour is readily demonstrated. An individual who refuses to eat a new food, to go into a strange place, or, perform some simple act which involves the novel use of objects in its environment may intently watch a companion of the experimenter act in the appropriate way and thereupon, as of stirred and emboldened by example, make a trial for itself. Having been pleasantly rewarded or discovered that nothing disagreeable happens, it may carry on without further social aid or encouragement". This is what Kohler identified as insightful behaviour.

Yerkes traces the development of the mother-child relationship. The dependence on the mother is complete, just as in the human infant. Further the infant needs something to cling to. McCulloch used a paper towel and Harlow has studied the need of the infant for some towel or blanket to cling to. At first the mother encourages the infant to be dependent; she prevents the infant from taking risks. But after two or three months she changes her attitude and encourages the child to move about and explore. She even' teaches' the young one to stand up, climb, walk etc. Finally she becomes antagonistic to the clinging reaction of the child. She pushes him aside and even drives him away. Thus the physiological status of the mother and the stage of the development of the infant determine the time for weaning and promotion of self-dependence. We find active socialization in the mother-child relationship. Further the initial specific clinging dependence on the mother is replaced by a generalized dependence on the other adults. It now seeks the companionship of other members. We can now understand why the chimpanzee is scared of loneliness. Isolation causes in it varied symptoms of deprivation. When forcibly deprived of companionship or when it is left alone, the ape cries, screams and struggles desperately to return to its companions.

There are also elementary forms of cooperation among the apes as well as monkeys. When there is an appropriate cry of distress, when an individual is threatened or injured and cries, the whole group rushes to its rescue. We shall refer to Crawford's experimental work on cooperativeness among the chimpanzees in a later chapter. We may now consider the 'grooming' behaviour. We have seen in the zoo the monkeys as well as apes picking lice. But the behaviour is much more than 'lice-picking'. It is an expression of mutuality and the ability to cooperate. Grooming takes the place of human washing and bathing; the animal makes a thorough search of its skin and hair and removes all bits etc. There is both self-grooming and mutual grooming. The animal may solicit grooming or initiate the activity. The animals express great satisfaction in this social relation. Neither the monkeys nor the apes possess true speech.

Thus we find development in social behaviour among animals from the most primitive congregations and contacts due to environmental conditions to the formation of families, and groups with dominance hierarchy. The biological and the social elements lead to the complex social interactions among the monkeys and the apes. Learnings and socialization play a very important part. Is there an ape culture? The basic element of culture is the transmission of tradition. This is associated with language. Both these are linked with the existence of more or less persistent thought patterns which are at the basis of tools, skills, codes and values. The ape groups do not give evidence of any of these. It is only in the human society that the cultural element is added to the biological and social elements.

Social Development among Children

In the last few decades objective studies have been made regarding the development of social behaviour among children. In the following section we will rely mainly on the observations of Gesell, Shirley, Charlotte Buhler and other pioneers in the study of child development.

The First Six Months of Life

In the first month of life there are hardly any signs of the infant's awareness of the social aspects of the environment. By the end of the fourth week the infant stares at the faces of human beings who are close by. If he is crying, he becomes quiet when picked up. Here is the beginning of response to social stimulation. However, this may yet be a response to warmth.

By the end of the eighth week he responds to the adult smile for smile. His interest in people is evident by the way he follows the movement of persons in the room. He enjoys seeing people move about the room. At the end of 16 weeks he shows more definite signs of social awareness. He likes people to speak to him. He likes when the mother or nurse sings to him. By 20 weeks he may cry when people leave him.

At 28 weeks he participates more in social interaction. He likes to be handed back and forth from one person to another. He responds to more than one person at a time. There is now the beginning of discrimination. He differentiates between people. He can recognize the mother who feeds him and looks after him. With discrimination arises a certain awareness of the strangers. He is lively with those whom he knows and reacts with shyness to others, particularly when he meets strangers in new places. He shows signs of fear when he is accosted by strangers.

Thus we find a gradual increase in the infant's social awareness from the fourth month to sixth month. In the fourth month the infant ceases crying when a person comes, pays attention to the face and the voice, whimpers or cries when a person leaves the room. He smiles in response to another's gaze. By the fifth month he becomes more active, responds by vocalization and attempts to grasp and to touch.

The Second Half-Year

The child enjoys the company of other people in the second half of the first year. He may easily become overexcited. The instability of his emotional life is evidenced by quick changes from crying to laughter and from laughter to crying. By 40 weeks he becomes more shy of the strangers. He demands more of his mother or nurse. He enjoys, 'peek-a-boo', 'rock-a-bye' and other, activities of social interplay. He learns to say 'bye-bye'.

He also loves the game of being chased while he is creeping. He enjoys hiding behind chairs to play the game of 'where's the baby?'. At the age of one year he likes to walk when his hands are held. Another game that he delights in is to throw the toys on the floor with the expectation that they will be restored to him. He cries when the adult gets tired and does not restore. He whimpers or cries when things are taken from him. He thus gives evidence of some sense of possession.

Another development is the awareness of other children by the age of six months. His interest in other children increases as he grows older. He pays heed to the crying of other children. There may be babbling to gain the attention of other children.

Though before six months the infant is unable to discriminate between the facial expressions and tones of friendliness or anger by 8 months he shows astonishing capacity for interpreting and understanding the gestures of others.

The Second Year of Life

By 15 months he overcomes the shyness towards strangers. He is now eager to go out. He enjoys imitating others. He may cough, blow the nose, sneeze in imitation. He may demand anything he sees and puts his parents in an embarrassing situation. By 18 months we find him greatly interested in household activities. He enjoys sweeping and dusting. He also takes delight in fetching things. At this time he refuses to be held. He wants to be free. He resents even being touched. In these situations he may develop temper tantrums.

At the age of 21 months his awareness of the people is very great compared to what it was when he was one year old. Further he knows what articles belong to whom in the house. He can identify things which belong to his mother, his father and himself. Thus the sense of property right becomes stronger. His interest in household activities also becomes stronger and he helps his mother in the kitchen. He can now bring things which are in the drawer and put them back again after use. But there is also the beginning of 'negativism'. He responds less quickly to requests than before. He may do the opposite of what is asked of him.

When he is two years old his property rights become, stronger. He tries to possess as many things as he can. He insists on his rights by asserting 'it is mine'.

Maudry and Nekula studied the social relations of the children of same age by placing them in standard situations and by observing their reaction to one another. They found that up to the age of nine months there was very little social response to one another. From 9 to 14 months though they paid attention to each other they were more engrossed in their play things than in one another. There were negative responses such as pushing the other child aside. From 14 to 18 months there was a gradual transition. There was the positive response to one another. Responses became friendly and cooperative. Positive responses predominated over the negative responses by the time the children were two years of age. The cooperative give-and-take between the children at this age was not likely to be of long duration. The authors observed that when many children were together they tended to take notice of one another and make contacts. But their play tended to be more parallel, each child playing the same game like the other children, with only occasional interchanges.

Thus we find a big difference between the social and emotional life of the child in its first year as compared to that in his second year. As we have seen the child does not differentiate much between individuals in the first year except in recognizing the mother and nurse. Otherwise the child smiles, babbles and makes physical contacts with everyone. Similarly negative responses like fight and defence occur when there is some interference with the freedom of movement of the child or when it encounters strange people or familiar people in strange clothes. But in the second year of life both the positive and the negative social reactions become much more strong. The child manifests its affection by caresses, fond words, by offering assistance and even by giving presents. Further he change to his mother or other favourite person when there is the prospect of separation. He also shows jealousy when some one else approaches the mother. All these are definite signs of love. Similarly the negative reactions become signs of hatred. The child may show violent negative behaviour by hitting, pushing away, shouting and so on.

The Two-and-Half Year Old

According to Gesell ritualism is very characteristic of the 30-month child. He knows the position of the various things of the household and insists that they should be kept in their proper places. He resents any rearrangement or alteration. Parents can recall the way in which the child of this age insists upon his father removing his shoes and socks in a particular manner in the particular place. He will insist upon being put on the cycle or the car when father goes to work or returns home after work. "His imperial domineering ways are sometimes hard for others to accept. He may command one to sit here, another to do something else, and still another to go away. If the parent realizes that the child is only passing through a temporary regal, dictatorial stage he may respond to the child's orders more graciously, more whimsically".

At this age the child will do a number of simple household tasks in a systematic manner. He likes to be with other people, adults as well as children. He likes to play with one other child out of doors. Gesell has found that the child who likes to play with the other child in the house will be rather poor in making adjustments to new places. So it is in the interest of healthy development to take the child out to others' houses or to parks and play centres to play with other's at this age.

Three Years

By three years. the child likes to play outdoors with another child. He will not only play, he will also quarrel. He may attack the other child and scratch, or bite or push or kick him. So the play must be supervised. He is of greater help to his mother in doing household work and in running errands.

He has a new emotional awareness of himself. He enjoys speaking of himself and his mother as 'we'. He wants to know more about himself and so the mother has to tell him about his earlier experiences and actions. Thus we find around this age, with the growth of language and with the increase in interactional processes a growing awareness of oneself. Some children cling to their past but others will look forward and are planning to go to school or go out for a holiday. At this age the child is able to make a choice of his food, his clothes, play, toys etc. The child may even learn to play one parent against another. When he wants to go out and knows that the mother will not allow, he gets the consent of the father and later tells the mother that he was asked to go out by the father. When there is disagreement between the parents, the child makes use of this technique. The best thing is for the parents to give up the appearance of divided authority. The mother must make decisions about food, clothes etc., and the father about other things.

The imaginative life of the child increases. The child of three or three and half-years may speak to and play with imaginary companions. Even when the child is two years old the imaginative play starts. The child of two and a half-year may give tea out of its toy tea-pot and cups with or without water. The child may also imagine that he is an animal and make the appropriate movements and cries as he perceives them. All these various activities are coincident with the self-discovery of his own identity. The child may also impersonate the postman or the policeman or the doctor or the hawker or the mother at play with other children or with the adults.

Four Years and After

The four year old child is a social being. He desires to play with other children. His preference for children may be so much that he may even refuse to go to houses where there are no children. He is now so busy with his own play and friends that he loses interest in helping his mother in the household work.

At the same time he will also develop strong family and home ties. He often quotes his father and mother as authorities. He is given to a good deal of boasting about his home and his parents. He makes comparisons and magnifies the things in his house and the attributes of his parents.

His imaginary playmates do not figure much at this age. His imaginative play is more closely related to the social life. Impersonation of animals gives place to impersonation of father, mother, doctor, grocer ete. He likes to go out for a walk with the father or mother and asks no end of questions.

The social development of the individual is a continuous one. There will be always something we learn about ourselves and something about the others right through the years of life. We may now give brief reviews about certain specific social relationships.

Some Specific Social Relationships

We find that the infant starts his life with no awareness of others nor of his utter dependence on others. With time he not only becomes aware of others, but also of himself. He gradually becomes more and more independent of others. He becomes self-assertive. He may even become defiant. "But whatever front he may assume, he is never completely weaned from his dependence on others; he never becomes so self-sufficient that he is immune to the approval or disapproval of his fellows or free from a desire for affection and security in his relation with his fellow men". As we have seen above, according to Charlotte Buhler, there are three phases in the growth of the child with respect to love or positive reactions as she puts it: in the first four to six months the child's perceptions are not clear and specific. He reacts in a positive way to all human beings. In the second half-year he can distinguish between the familiar persons and the strangers. He reacts positively to the familiar persons and negatively to the strangers. At the third stage from the second to the fourth year the child shows extreme dependence on specific individuals like the mother, father and others in the household. Charlotte Buhler refers to the study of Amy Daniels who made a study of the far-reaching importance of sympathetic individual care. "Two groups of two-years-old children living in the same institution were segregated from each other and subjected to two divergent types of treatment. One group was given very little tenderness. although adequately cared for in every other respect. In the other group, a nurse was assigned to each child and there was no lack of tenderness and affection. At the end of half a year the first group was mentally and physically retarded, in comparison with the second. In order to effect normal psychic and physical maturity, individual care and devotion are indispensable in the upbringing of small children". Thus we find that particularly in the first five years of life the child needs the mother's affection very greatly. Psychoanalysts, psychiatrists and psychologists are now convinced that it is essential for mental health that the infant and young child should experience an intimate, warm and continuous relationship with his mother or mother-substitute, in which both the child and the mother find satisfaction and enjoyment. The ill-effects of 'maternal deprivation' are very great. "Partial deprivation brings in its train anxiety, excessive need for love, powerful feelings, of revenge, and, arising from these last, guilt and depression. The young child, still immature in mind and body, cannot cope with all these emotions and drives". Bowlby shows that complete deprivation of mother love, particularly from two to five years of age, is disastrous to the individual and renders him incapable of making love relationships with others.

●●●

4

Psychology of Social Motivation

It must be realised that motivation is a concept in order to explain behaviour that can be observed and described. It is an inference based on our observations of the behaviour of animals and human beings under conditions of every day life as well as under experimental conditions. The rat which is hungry will learn to go through a maze and obtain its food; a rat which has been fed may go through the maze but its learning will be very slow. Consequently, we infer that there is some tension in the organism which arises out of the deprival of food. The energetic action of the organism, its goal-directed activities, its variability and its persistence and the way in which its activities cease when it consumes the food, all these lead us to infer that the behaviour of the rat is motivated by hunger. Behaviour is looked upon as an activity which arises when there is a state of tension in the organism and the activity itself is looked upon as 'tension-reducing'. If the organism is not allowed to move about, it becomes more and more restless, more and more active wherever it is. When the activity leads to the reaching of the particular goal, then the organism becomes quiet. This kind of motivated behaviour, as we have seen, is not only based upon the physiological drives but it is also based upon drives which are of social origin. A man struggles to obtain food, clothing and shelter not only for himself but for his family. When these minimum requirements are obtained, he does not stop working. His restlessness does not cease with the provision of minimum requirements. He wants to be like his neighbours with better food to eat, bettter clothes to wear and better house to live in. And so he works harder, earns more and profits more. What is the limit for this? It depends upon the group in which he is living. If he is living in a village, he is quite satisfied with a little more than his neighbours. On the other hand, because in the city the neighbours have a good deal of amenities he will have to struggle for much more. Irrespective of how much food or clothing or shelter a man obtains the basic consideration is to have the same standards as his neighbours or better standards than his neighbours whether it is in the village or in the city. Consequently, the physiological motives do not operate purely at the somatic level.

Interpersonal Relationship Based on Motives

Before proceeding further we can pause for a moment to understand the place or motives in social relationships. We enter into interpersonal relationships in order to achieve certain ends, probably to secure livelihood or to find a mate or to achieve status or recognition. Thus motives constitute the basis for entering into social relationships. In other words, we cannot understand social interaction if we do not take into account the motivations underlying the interpersonal relationships or group interactions.

Physiological Drives

Whatever the cultural pattern may be, whether it is western or oriental, highly industrialized and technological or very primitive, among rich as well as among the poor, there are certain universal activities which are biogenic. Man eats, drinks, sleeps and tries to keep warm. In other words, he tries to sustain life as a biological organism. How he satisfies these basic physiological needs depends upon the cultural group in which he has been brought up. We find that such behaviour is reaction to an organic demand. It is a reaction to a chemical deficit or to some organic state. The organism under such conditions is roused to action and this action continues till the equilibrium is restored by the taking of oxygen or food or water etc. Apart from such reactions being universal in the species, a second distinguishing mark of the biogenic motives is that they are unlearned or innate. It is true that human behaviour aroused by any motive is modified by learning. Even the simplest activity like breathing is regulated by learning; for example, among the singers and athletes. As we know the Yogic exercises have developed systematic ways of training how to breathe and the, control of breathing. Consequently, these activities are looked upon as 'unlearned' not because they are not affected by learning but because we are thinking of the conditions under which they first appear in the organism. The biogenic motives are present either at birth or through maturation.

Among the biogenic motives we can include. hunger, thirst, activity-sleep cycle, temperature regulation, sex, evacuation, urination and defecation and avoidance of organic injuries. These activities are found not only among all human beings but also among all the animals. Most of these physiological motives recur periodically. They are cyclic. We take our food and go to sleep at regular intervals. Of course, even this periodicity may be affected by social influences. For instance, people in the cities take four meals a day while those in the villages take two meals a day.

The Social Drives

Just as we find that physiological drives are universal, similarly we find that human beings strive to belong to a group and to acquire a position or a status in every society. Motives like these are to be found universally among all the human groups. Undoubtedly such activities are affected by the social setting to a much greater extent than the physiological drives.

(a) The Need for Affection

The most fundamental social drive arises out of the need for affection. This need has two expressions. We have the need to receive affection from others, we have also the need to give affection to others. This need is not something peculiarly human. We find it among birds as well as the animals. The domesticated animal gives affection and longs for affection. Often times we find people expressing that a dog is much more reliable than the human beings. The dog runs to the master the moment he goes home and the master feels that here at least is one being which needs him. To be needed is something basic. When a man feels that he is not needed by anybody, when nobody wants him, nobody loves him, he feels that life is not worth living. This is where we find that family is a very important unit in social life. The parent-child relationship, the husband-wife relationship, the love of siblings, these have a very important position in the family situation. How important this fundamental need for affection is to the personality of man. Due to wrong upbringing man becomes selfish and finds that nobody needs him, nobody loves him. He forgets that he has not developed the art of giving affection to others. We receive affection to the extent that we are able to give affection. The domesticated animal as well as the child who do not receive affection will become 'wild'.

(b) Self-Assertion

Self-assertion is another very important social drive. This may manifest itself in the form of self-display. An individual may undertake difficult tasks to prove his abilities and to demonstrate his powers. He may try to differentiate himself from other people through dress, professional status, club-membership and such other activities, or he may fight for economic, political or intellectual freedom. It may even take the form of physical fighting or verbal argument.

Self-assertion also takes the form of domination. Each tends to dominate over the small primary group or even over the whole secondary group. As we have seen before even lizards show patterns of domination and subordination. The heaviest males are at the top of the hierarchy of power. Further the lizards fight hard to defend the territory and control some area of movement. Similarly birds also try to establish a 'territory'; the male drives out the other males. There is also the dominance-submission pattern among the birds. Cases of 'despotism' of one bird over the other have also been observed and reported. The most aggressive bird becomes the 'leader'. The studies of Zukerman and Maslow have shown that there is the struggle for dominance among the monkeys and the apes. The dominant monkey reserves all the available food for itself and shows aggression towards the other members of the group who show subordination by being passive or by flight. There is also social hierarchy of power among the monkeys and the apes. Thus we find that dominance-submission behaviour is not peculiar to the human beings. On the other hand, it is through cultural efforts that an individual or a group renounces domination. These two tendencies of social behaviour are closely correlated when an individual shouts loudly. He may become dominant and the others in the primary group may become submissive. It is quite possible that a person who is dominant in one situation may become quite submissive in another situation.

Another manifestation of self-assertion is the desire to be recognized, to be accepted as an equal, or as a superior, by the other individuals in the group. We find the prototype of this need for recognition even among the animals and children. It is a familiar fact that there is jealousy among the little dogs brought up in the house; if one dog is petted the other becomes restless and starts barking and attacking the favoured dog. There is the jealousy among the little children below 4 or 5 years. When the younger child is fondled the elder child becomes jealous. He may become aggressive or he may become sullen. This desire for preference and resentment of preference being shown to the rivals is a characteristic feature among children. Unfortunately, many adults also are unable to get over this childish way of reacting. It is well known that there are rivalries based on the need for recognition not only among the individuals but also among groups. A small country may feel hurt if a big country shows preference to the neighbouring country by giving it economic aid. It is well known that the Army officers, civilian officers, as well as artists vie with each other to obtain the recognition of the feudal Raja or Maharaja. That is why the palaces of the small as well as the big countries in the East as well as in the West are always full of plots and counterplots to gain preference and recognition from the ruler. We experience a great pleasure when our work is approved and recognized and rewarded. On the other hand, to be ignored is a severe form of punishment. We resent that nobody recognizes our virtues, our skills and our accom-plishments. Society has developed many forms to show its approval and recognition of individuals as well as groups. We find this, not only in the feudal and imperialistic organizations but even in the socialistic and communistic organizations. The British set-up a number of titles and awards as a sign of recognition of 'loyalty' among the Indian citizens. This was greatly resented as a technique adopted by the foreigner to win the loyalty of the colonial. But even in the communist Russia, Stalin prizes and Stalin medals were greatly coveted. In India also, a new system of awards for distinction has been developed. This is an indication of a double attitude towards recognition. Every individual needs recognition but is also shy of it and he resents if another is recognized. This need for recognition is a very powerful motive which makes an individual as well as a group to put forth the highest effort whether it is at home, in the class room, or in the wider society. Whether we are children, adolescents or adults we are all of us eager to obtain recognition and work incessantly and put forth our best efforts to obtain it.

In brief, we may say that the two basic drives are, the need to belong and the need for status and power. These two needs may manifest themselves in diverse forms. Both these have their roots in animal behaviour as well as child behaviour. But both are greatly influenced by the group in which the individual is brought up. An individual may strive to attain status by destroying his whole property or by acquiring untold wealth or learning. Similarly the need to belong may express itself in juvenile delinquency depending upon the situation and circumstances of the individual upbringing.

Physiological and Social Drives

It is very difficult to tell whether the social drives are more powerful or the physiological drives are more powerful. When there is tremendous physiological deprivation then the social needs may be thrown to the winds. Neither consideration of belonging nor consideration of status will prevent an individual forced to starve due to natural reasons like being isolated by devastating floods, or due to social reasons like a concentration camp, none of these reasons will prevent him from begging food or water, from any person. Similarly pursuit of wealth or pursuit of fame may impel an individual to even deny bodily needs. He may work without food, without taking rest in order to obtain status. A woman may mortify her body in order to maintain her slender figure or a Sanyasi may mortify his body in order to attain salvation. So it is difficult to determine whether the social drives or the physiological drives are more potent. It depends upon the individual as well as the circumstances.

Social Drives are affected by Social Norms

The physiological drives as well as the social drives are both greatly modified by the group in which the individual has been brought up. As we have seen above, eating, satisfaction of hunger, is a physiological drive common not only to all human groups but common to animal as well as human beings. How we eat, when we eat, what we eat is determined by the group in which we have been brought up. This is where we can distinguish between the biogenic aspect and the sociogenic aspect of motives. Among human beings, eating rice or eating chapatis is sociogenic while eating itself is biogenic. Similarly wearing clothes depends upon the social drive regarding status and recognition. It is affected by the norms of the group in which we have been brought up. Whether we wear cheap cotton clothes or costly cotton clothes depends upon several conditions under which we have been brought up and in which we are living. To take another illustration, pursuit of wealth is one of the important motives among the civilized groups in the world today. This is not a primary drive, it is only a secondary drive. Wealth is sought because it enables us to satisfy certain physiological needs and certain social needs. But pursuit of wealth may itself become a powerful motive without relevance either to the physiological needs or to the social needs. In this respect, the way of life of the Indian is rather peculiar. Pursuit of wealth is perfectly in order for a grihasta. But when a man has done his social duty by his children, the Indian way of life enjoins renunciation of wealth. Accumulation of wealth according to Indian traditions is good neither to the individual nor to the society. All modern societies are now approaching this standpoint. In the capitalistic countries as well as in the communist countries it is now well recognized that accumulation of wealth beyond a certain limit by an individual should be prevented. Incomes are taxed and inheritance of wealth is taxed. In India, today we have besides these taxes, wealth tax, as well as expenditure tax.

Social Incentives

Motives and Incentives. Motives are based upon biological as well as the social needs of the organism. As we have seen among the human beings the physiological as well as social drives are affected by the cultural patterns. Motives are a set of internal conditions which give rise to action in an organism. Society sets up conditions to support or initiate, decrease or inhibit or to direct activities. These are incentives. Thus we find that incentives are conditions setup in order to alter behaviour of other individuals. Thus incentives may be positive or negative. A positive incentive reinforces action while a negative incentive inhibits action. 'The modification of the individual by the society is based upon the operation of these incentives. This is how social learning takes place.

Incentives Modify Behaviour. Material rewards are positive incentives which release drives and thus influence the speed and accuracy of performance. Similarly punishment or the removal of a reward is a negative incentive which inhibits certain drives. Apart from rewards and punishments, praise and reproof or scolding are also very powerful as incentives affecting behaviour. This is how the puppy learns to respond to its name and to give up urination and defecation within the house. It is rewarded with a biscuit if it does what the owner wants him to do. We use not only rewards and punishments, we also use affection as an incentive to socialize puppies. If the puppy responds correctly we bestow affection on it by patting it, embracing it; if it commits errors we show our displeasure through our facial expression as well as through language, particularly the aspect of intonation. In the socialization of the infant also all these various incentives are used by the parents and later on by the teachers in the school. The leader of the group is one who is an adept in fitting incentives to the personality of his followers. It is the man who is able to make use of the appropriate incentives that can become a leader of a group. These incentives aid the learning process. They do not originate behaviour. They can only modify behaviour. Incentives tap the motives and change the attitudes of the individuals in the group. When appropriate incentives are given the efficiency of performance improves considerably.

Rewards and Punishments. A good deal of experimental work has been done in the last half a century regarding the influence of rewards and punishments on behaviour. We may give an account of some of these studies. In the mirror-drawing experiment, punishments as well as rewards are used as incentives to study their effect upon learning. Punishment informs the individual that his response is not correct. It does not indicate what is the right response. On the other hand, reward, as it is associated with the correct response, is of a greater value in fixing the right response. A combination of rewards for right responses, and punishments for wrong responses will lead to more efficient learning. Long ago Hamilton showed that the same physical stimulus may be used as a reward or as punishment depending upon the situation. For example, the ringing of the bell may be used as a punishment if it is rung whenever there is an error. When this is done the individual develops a negative attitude towards the bell. He does not like the ringing of the bell and his aim is to try to see that the bell does not ring. On the other hand, when the bell is used as a reward the attitude towards the bell changes. He likes the ringing of the bell and he tries hard to make it ring.

Experimental work has also been done to study the effects of monetary reward. Meier reported that mentally retarded children improved their reading skill when money or candy were offered. Money was immediately exchanged to candy by these children. On the other hand, in industrial units the effect of monetary reward on production is different.

Several reasons like the inevitable increase of the output norm, the possible retrenchment of workers, the likelihood of wage-cuts in depression, and the most important of all, the social norms within the primary groups in the factory, all these make money incentives valueless in industry.

Competition and Cooperation

It is not always easy to differentiate between motives and incentives in their concrete operation in a complex society. A student who enters the college may work hard, or may not work hard, because of a number of motives and incentives. A student may join college because he wants to train himself for a profession or because he wants to earn more money by becoming highly qualified. It may be that he wants to earn approval and social recognition by becoming a highly educated man, or his motive may be to meet young people of the same age, or to meet people who are higher in status and more cultured. Consequently, in a complex social activity it is neither possible nor necessary to draw any fine distinctions between motives and incentives. An individual may engage himself in gardening because he wants to attract more people to his garden than the neighbour or it may be due to an incentive he wants to win the first prize in the garden competition.

Competition means striving to equal or surpass the speed and quality of another person's performance, or it may be to improve on one's own past performance. The basic characteristic here is to do better than what one has done or what another has done. This is a very powerful incentive in social life; particularly in the modern Western society competition plays a very important part. The high level of prosperity among the nations of Western Europe and United States is due to this strong incentive to compete and to do better than other people.

Competition and Rivalry

We must distinguish between competition and rivalry. Rivalry is a drive to equal or surpass the skill of another person. Sibling rivalry is a very important and outstanding phenomenon within the home. Constantly brothers and sisters become rivals and try to excel each other. In the same way in the old Indian society, there was a great deal of rivalry among the different wives of a single individual. What is the difference between competition and rivalry?

In ordinary language as well as in social psychology, we do not make any distinction between these two terms. However, it will be better to draw a clear distinction between these two terms. It is here suggested that the term rivalry may be limited to those situations where a person or a group tries to crush the rival. In other words, they try to surpass the rival not by themselves doing better, but by pulling down the rival. Thus in rivalry an attempt is made to become superior to the other not by improving one's performance but by dislodging the other individual or group from the position occupied, so that one is superior to the other. The term competition may be restricted to the attempt by an individual or group to improve the level of performance so that one is superior to the other. Probably, a second distinction between the two may be made on the basis of the area of social relation in which the two individuals or groups are operating. Rivalry is limited to the face-to-face relationship, whereas competition is much more impersonal. Competition does not lead to jealousy and hatred whereas rivalry inevitably leads to both of them. Rivalry may ultimately lead one to violence because the first aim is to bring down the prestige of the other man or of the other group in the eyes of the rest and the ultimate aim is to annihilate the rival.

Development of Competition

Even in small children we find evidence of competitive behaviour. There are the acts of aggression when another child takes away his possessions. The toy becomes a part of the child's self. Its possession yields considerable satisfaction and consequently when a companion tries to take away the toy the child becomes aggressive. There may be conflict and free fight between the two children. In this situation the essence of competition is to acquire or to retrieve the possession of an object rather than to excel the competitor. The aim is the possession of the object rather than depriving. the other of the object. When the child sees a bright object or toy with an elder brother or sister state of disequilibrium is set up and the act of snatching that object is tension-reducing. On the other hand, the snatching away of the object leads to a new state of disequilibrium and frustration in the other individual and consequently there is conflict which is primarily directed towards the possession of the toy. Thus even in the first year the child learns these simple aggressive habits. Competition is also dependent on the behaviour of the elders at home. The parents spur their children to do better than the other children,—"to beat the other fellow". A child who just surrenders his play object is encouraged to be aggressive. Thus the child may be aggressive not only to regain the object taken away by the other child, but also to earn the approval of the elders. It is in this way that the child learns the technique of domination. It learns to find satisfaction in controlling others. Attitudes of rivalry may also be built up. The competition has its biological as well as cultural roots. Differences in size and strength, possibly in temperament and intelligence, all these may foster competition. In modern society aggression and violence do not serve the same purpose as they used to serve in the more primitive societies. This is where we find a big difference between the other biological drives like hunger, thirst and sex and this drive for mastery. In modern society there is plenty of scope for mastery without aggressiveness and violence.

Thus by the time the child enters the school most children will have learnt how to compete with others. Long ago

Allport showed there is social facilitation when an individual is working in a group. Dashiell showed that there is social facilitation even when the individual is by himself but knows that there are other persons in other rooms doing the same task. Under such conditions the individual will do much better than when he is alone, and when nobody else is doing similar work. Thus the sights and sounds of others working reinforces our work. There is this reinforcement also when there are no sights and sounds but we know that other individuals are doing similar tasks. To give a simple illustration when an individual who is cycling sees another cyclist ahead of him he competes with him and surpasses him. This may spur the other individual to compete. We see that cyclists compete with even motorists and feel very happy if they can surpass. It is a familiar sight that the tonga drivers compete with each other, probably to the dismay of the people sitting. But most times the people who have hired a tonga enjoy the fun. Thus the sights and sounds of other people working rouses individuals to work better for self-enhancement. The presence of spectators enhances competition in games and sports. Sometimes, however, the audience may affect adversely and become a source of inhibition.

Experimental work has also been done with children in schools. For example, Hurlock used arithmetic tests and found that the experimental groups surpassed the control groups equal in age and initial ability. It was found that the girls made slightly larger gains than boys under the impact of competition. Similarly the younger children seemed to profit more than the elder children. Finally, it was found that the initially inferior children seem to profit much from competition. It is a well-known fact that most adults do not work to the maximum they are capable of working. Green studied 80 men and 80 women in spool packing and card sorting. Groups of 8 sitting in front of groups of 8, all of them worked: some were instructed to compete with the group in front and some were instructed not to compete. It was found that all groups improved as a result of practice. They began with 196 spools and at the end of the experiment the control group did 210 spools, the non-competitive groups did 219 spools and competitive group did 228 spools. There was significant difference between the control group and the competition group while there was no significant difference between the other groups. This experiment showed that (1) practice improves performance, (2) the mere sights and sounds of others working improves performance—social facilitation—and thirdly that competition, over and above and social facilitation, also leads to improvement in performance.

Co-operation

Our knowledge of the psychological process involved in co-operation is not as much as our knowledge with respect to competition. With respect to competition as well as co-operation the field studies of the anthropologists have given us considerable knowledge. In general it may be stated that co-operation occurs when the ends sought are unlimited, while competition occurs when the ends sought are limited. Experimental studies of the children's play suggest that two factors determine cooperation, namely, the kinds of material available and the age of the development of children. Ross reported that children of 2-3 years exhibited cooperative behaviour more frequently when playing with clay than when playing with blocks. It has also been found that cooperative play was evident most dearly among the children who were 3 years of age and older. Thus we find that both competition and cooperation are displayed clearly approximately at about the same age, namely, after 3 years of age.

Crawford made a very interesting study of cooperative behaviour among the chimpanzees. He gave 3 problems to the chimpanzees. In the first problem, there was a heavy box with two ropes. It required cooperative effort of two chimpanzees to move this heavy box. In the second problem, the door of the food box would open only when two vertically suspended ropes were pulled simultaneously. In the third problem, the box had two handles and it was only when both these were manipulated and that in a coordinated way by two different chimpanzees that the door was opened and food tray obtained. In the preliminary stages, each chimpanzee was trained to pull boxes. Next the animals were put in pairs. It was found that there was evidence of social facilitation. When the animals were in pairs each animal could pull a heavier box than what it could when it was it the alone-situation. But it was found that the chimpanzees could not learn to cooperate. Crawford asserts that probably the animals themselves may have never learn to work cooperatively. After 12 sessions the animals learnt to pull two boxes at the same time. Even then each pulled without regard to the activity of the other chimpanzee. This is similar to the parallel play activity of children under three. In the 35th session Crawford gave the auditory stimulus 'pull' when one of the partners began to pull. It was found that by the 40th session one of the animals learnt to respond to the visual cues, from the partner. After the two chimpanzees had learnt to cooperate in pulling two ropes to move one heavy box, the situation was changed by giving a single rope. It was found that there was no transfer effect. Thus according to this study cooperation requires attention to the visual and auditory cues. Even with a good deal of training the chimpanzees were not able to coordinate their acts with a single rope.

In organized games we have both competition and cooperation operating. There is team work within the group and competition between the teams.

Thus competition as well as cooperation depends on age, experience, social training and attitude. Anthrologists have shown that different cultures stress competitive and cooperative activities. In those societies there position of power or prestige are achieved competitively there is emphasis upon competition. Among the children there is competition and aggressive behaviour when the objects desired are few. Extending this principle it is generally asserted that where many individuals desire to reach the same limited goal there is competition.

●●●

5

Social Effects and Problems

The advances in technology in recent years and particularly in the present century have been of an unprecedented magnitude. Today man has been able to banish fear of famine and epidemics practically completely. Great changes in the agricultural methods due to the application of science and technology have brought about great improvements in the production of food. When there was famine in India, particularly in Bengal State, in 1945, food was rushed from United States, Canada and Australia. The government was accused for its inefficiency. This is a great change in the attitude of people. In the olden days when floods and famines came people accepted them with helplessness and fortitude. But today they are shocked that there should be so much of suffering. They are convinced that the suffering is due not to nature, but to the inaction of man in counteracting these disastrous effects of nature.

Side by side there is also the other problem of resistance to change. Indians, as a nation, are looked upon as conservative people who do not change quickly. Still we find that in the last few years after Independence vast changes have taken place in the country. The Five Year Plans are deliberate attempts to industrialise India so that there is increased production of goods and services. This is a very big change. People are now realising that the existence of poverty in the country is due to either inefficiency or inability to face and solve the problems. It technological improvements are made both in the production of food and of other goods, then poverty can be banished from the land. One of the basic reasons for this change in the attitude of the people as a whole is the concept of sarvodaya introduced by Gandhi and developed by Vinoba Bhave.

Even though, there is a change in the overall position still there are resistances to change in particular spheres of activity. We can take as an illustration the resistance of the Indian farmer to the use of artificial manure. Though India was the most highly developed agricultural country of the ancient times in the last few centuries there has been an utter stagnation in the techniques of production in agriculture. This was attributed to the ignorance and illiteracy of the Indian farmer. But recent events have shown that acceptance of change and resistance to change are due, not to knowledge and ignorance respectively, but to our attitude towards the change. When artificial fertilisers were introduced the farmers were against accepting the change. But when practical demonstrations showed that artificial manure increases very greatly the yield per acre, the Indian farmer readily accepted the change. Five years ago when the Sindri fertilisers went into production the Government was despairing whether the stocks would be cleared from the factory. After some time we are finding that the Sindri plant is unable to meet the demands for the fertilisers. It is proposed to setup a few more plants.

Studies among the people living in isolated areas have shown that modern technology has very great influence upon certain basic concepts and attitudes towards the physical world. In America, Sherman and Henry studied four groups of people who were living in an isolated area about a hundred miles from Washington. In Colvin Hollow, they found a scattered collection of cabins each with about two acres of garden. There were no roads. A trader brought them a few things to satisfy some of their needs. Apart from gardening the only industry that the people were engaged in was basket making. They were all illiterate people who took up unskilled jobs during summer in a summer resort four miles away. They had few and vague concepts regarding distance, length, time and such other aspects. Even adolescents did not know the days of the week, or the names of, the months. They looked upon people from outside as strangers and viewed them with suspicion. Their work-habits were slow and irregular. Consequently the people in the summer resort looked upon them as "unreliable people." In Rigby Hollow conditions were far better because these people had greater contacts with the cities. These studies of 1933 among the Hollow folk showed profound contrasts in concepts and attitudes among the people with differing degrees of contacts with modern technology. It also showed that the routine of life changes when there is contact with modern technology. Finally the study showed that there are differences in level of aspirations of the individuals. It was found that the children in Colvin Hollow could not understand the problem when they were asked, "What do you want to be when you grow up"? Such a question appeared to them to be meaningless.

Studies have also shown that modern technology has brought about certain changes in the family organization and the interrelationship among the members of the family.

Ogburn found a number of changes in the family structure as a result of the advances in technology. He found that there was a decline in the authority of the husband and father. He says that this is due to the increase in status of the women and children. In the joint family, whether it is a farming family or one of craftsmen, the father is the actual and traditional manager of the family. This was so in Europe and this is so in India. With the industrial revolution in Europe two things happened: *(a)* the increased mechanization took the jobs outside the home, *(b)* the jobs required little manual work. These two factors led to a change in woman's economic role. She was able to get employment in a factory. She was also able to get money income. This also led to a decrease in the number of children in the family. Kolb and Brunner found that rural people of America advocated birth control even in the thirties. Mechanization of agriculture made the labour of children less valuable.

With rapid industrialisation it has been found that there are great changes in the attitude of people towards their parents, relatives and others. Dube found that there were several complaints in the Indian village that the members of the castes, particularly the occupational castes, were not rendering their traditional obligations. He found that the boy does not want to work in the village. He wants to go to the city and work. He is not satisfied with the arrangement of payment. Urban contacts and education make the young man refuse to work in the families to which his family was attached through generations. The barber's son and the Harijan landless labourer's son, when they get educated, do not want to go back and pursue the traditional occupations. Similarly Lang reports that in the Chinese society also the father who was once honoured is now treated with less respect and is neglected by the children who work in a modern industrial organization. She also found that the girls who worked in factories found that their status as well as the treatment in the family had changed. They were no more submissive to parental authority according to custom. They became independent, they earned their own money and spent it. Thus, in the various countries of the world, the family organization has shown a change with the disappearance of the feudal social pattern and the introduction of the modern industrial organization. For example, in India the rural youth, particularly the Harijan youth, are now coming in large numbers to the liberal arts colleges, as well as to the professional colleges. The son of an illiterate landless labourer becomes a professional man.

Educational opportunities are altering the attitudes of people towards their caste occupations and this is one of the greatest and most revolutionary changes thin is going on in the country today. Political changes have also contributed to the situation; because the democratic form of government needs a representative from the area, the son of a peasant or the son of a landless labourer gets elected to the State Legislature or to the Central Parliament. He may become a Deputy Minister or a Minister in a State or in the Centre. One of the most important consequences of the modern developments in technology is attitude towards change. The industrialised societies now have a very favourable attitude towards change. People are eager to try new things developed on the basis of research.

Social Factors in Modern Industry

Till recently the management of a factory looked upon itself as being chiefly concerned with the finances, machinery, marketing and such other aspects of industry. Today we find that the management is looking upon the factory as a social organization, as well as an economic organization. This change in outlook can be traced to the famous research work of the Mayo group in the Hawthorne Plant of the Western Electric Co., in U.S. in 1927. These researches showed the importance of the employee's attitudes and of group pressures on productivity. Five employees and the supervisors were put into a situation and made to work by varying several environmental factors like illumination, ventilation etc. Further the working hours and the number of working days were altered and rest pauses were introduced. The aim was to study the influence of these variations upon output. It was found to the astonishment of the research workers that in spite of these changes in working conditions, as well as in working hours, the output went on increasing. They found that these contradictory results were due to the fact that there was a social change in the group. They were no longer isolated individuals. So the direction of alteration of the environmental and other factors did not affect their work adversely. A detailed analysis of the wage incentives also showed that the wage by itself was not adequate to account for the changes in the output. These investigations showed that the management as well as the industrial psychologist have to pay attention to the following two factors:

(a) The operators as individuals with their attitudes and motives, *(b)* the work group as a significant factor with its own influence on the members. According to Haire, "Not only the reality of the group, but the strength of the group became apparent. The group operated quickly and effectively both to protect itself from internal violations of its own patterns and also to protect itself from outside. The group effectively restricted the output of the individual. Acting in fear of real or fancied consequences of a high production rate, the group put social pressures (ridicule, ostracism and the like) on those who exceeded the implicit group rate of production".

This study of a group of five girls showed that the absence of constraint by supervisors, freedom of conversation and interpersonal contacts, group decision and such other aspects of the work appeared to be operating to give satisfaction to the workers and led to increased output. There was a certain team spirit, which gave rise to satisfaction and led to steady, as well as increased, production. It was found that in the beginning there was very low inter-correlation between the output of the different individuals but as the team was built up, the inter-correlations between the individual workers rose up.

In another study of a group of nine wiremen, three welders and three solderers and two inspectors, it was found that the output in the group remained astonishingly constant irrespective of changes in their environment. It was found that there the group as a whole had set a target of output, and reproached the persons who worked too fast or too slow. This informal grouping, which takes place among the workers, prevents the operation of other motives to increase the work. This is one of the big impediments to the operation of wage incentives. The man who works more to earn more, is looked upon as a selfish individual, who is sacrificing the interest of the group as a whole for his own interests. Such a person will be ridiculed and shunned.

Yet another result of this study was the importance of the supervisor as a leader. The personality of the supervisor is a very important factor to persuade people to work and to maintain discipline. In an investigation in Rowntree cocoa works it was found that, next to the wages, the influence of the supervisor was the most important element in maintaining the level of production and in increasing contentment. We have already seen that Lippitt and White have experimentally demonstrated the influence of the democratic attitude of the leader towards the followers on work. These studies have shown that there is a shift in the role of the leader from one who makes others to work, to one who enlists the co-operation of others to fulfil the task. Katz and others have shown that three things stand out in the successful supervisors' role: *(a)* It has been found that the supervisors of high production groups tend to spend more time in leadership functions and less time on actual production by themselves. The supervisor who works hard and produces a good amount himself will not be able to get a good output from his group as a whole; *(b)* It has also been found that the successful supervisor is employee-centred rather than production centred. When the supervisor is considerate to the employees the output of the group as a whole goes up; *(c)* The operators look upon the effective leader as less punitive, while the less successful leader is seen as being punitive. The man who threatens the workers with punishment induces fear. On the other hand, the leader, who succeeds in making the workers realise that any reproof flows out of the nature of the situation itself, rather than from himself, is a more successful supervisor. Consequently there is today a growing realisation of the need for giving special training to the supervisor to develop qualities of leadership.

Human Relations in Industry

The Hawthorne studies and a number of other studies have shown the importance of the attitude of workers towards management and the attitude of the management towards the workers. The attitudes, which the workers have towards the management depend not only on the economic aspect of the situation but also on the social environment. Industrial conflict which is of great significance in modern society and which may paralyse the life of the whole country or even of the whole world, is based upon the attitudes, which the management has towards the workers and the attitudes of the workers towards the management. Industrial revolution particularly in the last century in England, Germany and other Western European countries brought in its train a good deal of exploitation of the workers. The working conditions as well as the wages were the most deplorable. It is this condition, which led to the campaign of Karl Mark against capitalism. Marx asserted that industrialisation by itself does not lead to plenty and prosperity but that prosperity of the workers can come only by a class war, by the workers capturing the political power as well as the means of production from the capitalists. Now the most important problem of the world is the conflict between the ideologies of democracy on the one hand and communism on the other.

As we have seen above, the technological changes, which brought about the industrial revolution resulted in thousands of labourers working in a factory. Their dissatisfaction with the working conditions, wages, and particularly the social treatment, led them to organize labour unions. In the last century there was a good deal of opposition towards the formation of labour unions. But the attitude of the society changed. Labour unions were reorganized. In India laws were passed making labour unions into legal organizations.

The general tendency is for the management to have attitudes of fear towards the labour organizations and the labour organizations to become suspicious and hostile towards the management. It is these attitudes of fear and hostility that are at the root of industrial conflict. The members of each group perceive their relation to the other differently. However, both of them are motivated essentially by the same social needs of security, self-esteem, power and so on. The employer perceives the demands of the workers for higher wages, for the "closed shop" and for the right to strike, as a threat to his own security, status and prestige. On the other hand, the workers look upon the management as a threat to their security and status. While the labour organization threatens the management with strike, the management threatens the workers with lockout, dismissal from employment and resistance to wage increase. While the worker seeks more money and prestige through increased wages, the management seeks more money and prestige from increased profits.

The modern labourer is a joyless worker. He is engaged in monotonous tasks. Particularly in India, the labouers come mostly from the rural areas. They are uprooted from their own social environment and have to live in miserable conditions in a strange city. In the village they have a sense of security because they are living in the midst of people who are their kinsmen and who will come to their rescue whenever they are faced with disease or poverty. But in the city they are in the midst of people who are strangers. Bonds of family and caste make the ties of kinship very strong. The labourer in the city is cut off from his joint family and is cut off from the members of his caste in the village. There is also the threat of unemployment. He has no sense of security that his job is a permanent one. Because he is an uneducated, untrained, unskilled labourer he has nothing to look forward to by way of promotion. He starts his career as an unskilled labourer and he dies as an unskilled labourer. So there is no joy for him, no hope, no aspiration. Disease and accident ever threaten him. If there is an accident, or if he falls ill, his whole family will be reduced to a state of starvation. Labour inquiry committees have reported that the wages of the factory workers are not enough from the point of view of nutrition and elementary needs for housing, fuel, lights, clothing etc. Though the unskilled labourer in the factory as well as the casual labourer, today get a higher wage than about ten years ago, still, the wage is hardly sufficient to make him and his family survive. They can never hope for a decent and comfortable life. Added to this there is the big gulf between the standard of life of the workers in the factory and the standard of life of the members of the management.

Day in and day out the difficulties in the home, the humiliations in the work situation, the lack of joy due to an occupation that has no creative aspect whatever, all these lead the workers to be in a state of unrest. When there is a particular situation in which the management and the workers are unable to see eye to eye, there will be a strike in the factory. From this point of view the strike with all its violence and suffering is not due to some particular problem alone. It is due to a number of situations in the life of each individual worker. The individual hostilities are all channelised into a group hostility and this makes the situation very difficult to handle. Each group exerts its pressure to enforce specific demands. The industrial strike is essentially a situation, which arises out of a breakdown in understanding the mutual purposes and goals among the workers as well as the management. Both the parties start the negotiations at a wrong time in a wrong setting and so both of them become desperate and resort to either lockout or strike. The government have passed several legislations in the recent years regarding the formalities to be observed before lockout or strike is started. Otherwise the government can declare either the lockout or the strike as an illegal action. But the main problem is not one of legality, but one of willingness and a readiness to understand the viewpoint of the other group. Thus industrial conflict today is not merely the matter of either the management or the workers. It is a concern of the society as a whole. A strike in some essential organizations or a general strike may completely paralyse the life of the society as a whole. In India the strike of the Central Government employees in 1960 was declared illegal as it threatened the whole government and society. The society also did not sympathise with the strikers. So it had to be called off.

Industrial conflict is the manifestation of the social changes, which are going on today. It is a reflection of the changed relationships between the workers and the owners or managers of industrial concerns. There are three clear cut elements in modern society, which are responsible for the industrial conflicts: *(a)* The technological character of modern industry which leads to the employment of hundreds and thousands of skilled as well as unskilled labourers in one organization; *(b)* The growth of labour organizations; the poor and powerless workers become very powerful when they organize themselves into a trade union. This organization is perceived as a threat by the management. It is also perceived as a source of power and aggrandizement by the authorities of the labour union. Thus the growth of labour organizations is the result of, and has induced, mutual fear, suspicion and hostility between the workers and the management; *(c)* There is an increasing tendency on the part of the government to control the labour as well as the industry. Particularly in India, by means of legislation, the government have not only defined the procedures but have also laid down the conditions under which it could interfere when there is a breakdown.

Industrial Peace

It is impossible to assert that there will be industrial peace as a permanent condition in any or all of the industrial units. Nevertheless it is true to state that under certain conditions a state of tension and conflict will exist between the workers and the management, whereas under certain other conditions this state of tension will be reduced considerably. It may not be eliminated altogether. As we have seen earlier the industrial worker is motivated in a number of ways to do his work. Wage is not the only motive force. Attitude studies among the workers have shown that they hold status and recognition and sense of security to be as important if not more important than the wage itself. It is a notorious fact that in the feudal organization, human beings were perfectly content to work for a few rupees if certain nominal facilities were provided. Even today we find that in the villages and even in the cities, children as well as adults work very willingly and with loyalty if they are given some food, shelter and clothing. If they are sure that they will continue to get good treatment by the employer they will be perfectly contented. But with technological changes, the modern social conditions have completely altered and the labourer today is not satisfied with the feudal conditions of treatment. He wants to live in a house of his own, he wants to have all the amenities and facilities for his wife and children. He wants to be treated as an equal. He wants to be respected as a citizen. He has the same right to vote as an employer or the managing director. He wants his child to have the educational facilities so that he can compete with the children of the employer or the managing director.

By law, as well as by necessity, modern industrial concerns have started a personnel department where an officer is appointed to look after the recruitment, training and discharge of workers. The managing director himself cannot now interfere in all these aspects of factory organization. The personnel department follows some rules and regulations in the recruitment of people to the factory. This reduces, if it does not altogether eliminate, personal considerations and bias in the recruitment of workers. The personnel department also interviews each recruit and tries to find out his strong points and his weak points so that he is allotted to the job best suited to him. Even when a man is discharged, when a man wants to resign and give up his job, the personnel department conducts an interview to find out the attitude of the worker towards the organization, so that it can help the management to understand the difficulties of the workers. Another very important feature of modern organization within the factory is the appointment of labour welfare officers who study the grievances of the individual workers. Utmost attention is now paid to the prompt settlement of grievances. The worker is also assured that he can take his grievances to the higher levels if he is not satisfied with the way in which his case has been handled. A strong trade union organization is also very helpful. The individual worker has now the faith that the labour organization will support him if his grievances are just.

Modern industrial units are also developing "suggestion schemes". They invite suggestions for the improvement of working conditions, as well as changes in equipment, from the workers. In the recent years several large industrial organizations in India have benefited very greatly from the suggestions from the workers. When a suggestion is adopted the worker is given a big money award. Over and above the money, which the worker gets, he has now the great satisfaction that his ideas are being accepted and put into effect. This gives him a sense of prestige and satisfaction.

Establishing and maintaining contact between management and labour is a fundamental problem in labour management relationships. In the olden days the policies of the management and the work assignments were being transmitted from top to bottom. But there was no communication from the bottom to the top. What actually the workers felt was, not known to the management. It was only when a crisis came that the management started trying to meet the problem and that would be too late. Now several methods are being adopted to study and understand the attitude of the workers so that their genuine grievances are understood and remedied. An analysis of the attitudes of textile workers in some mills of Ahmedabad in India, revealed that the highest degree of dissatisfaction was, felt by the workers regarding the nature of the amenities provided. This shows that the amenities provided by the management for the welfare of the family and the children are very basic to bring about contentment of the worker. No man can work with enthusiasm if his wife and children are suffering because of inadequate housing or inadequate medical facilities, if his children do not have adequate facilities for education. It is a well-known fact that the industrial worker in India lives in utter poverty. His only satisfaction may be that he is better than the landless labourer in the village and the destitute who is begging in the streets in the city. It is necessary for the management to plough in a part of the profits to improve amenities for the workers, as well as to improve the working conditions within the factory itself. A satisfied worker is less likely, than a frustrated and oppressed worker, to agitate for a breakdown in negotiations. It is wrong to assume that the trade union leaders set up the workmen. A satisfied workman will refuse to oblige the demands of the agitator. As we have seen earlier the agitator exploits the existing dissatisfaction among the workers for his own ends.

It has been found that participation and consultation are of very great value to reduce industrial conflict and promote industrial peace. If each worker identifies himself with the industrial unit as a whole he will tend to be more efficient in his work and he will tend to promote social harmony. This depends upon the expectations of the management. If the management expects the cooperation and support of the workers then the workers will have the sense of participation. Allport has shown that if the worker is made to feel that he is a member of the group as a whole, and is given an active role to play in it, he will have a sense of participation. Attempts are now being made to setup profit-sharing schemes as well as management-sharing schemes. Consultative committees are now set up where representatives of workers meet as equal members with the representatives of management to consider problems of policy of the unit as a whole.

By way of illustration we may refer to some of the studies regarding the influence of transfer, from one section to another of the workers, or of the change in technique of production, on the production itself. It has been found that when there is a transfer of workers there is a drop in production. It has also been found that when there is a change in the technique or in the machinery there will be a drop in production. But studies have shown that this change is more due to social and psychological factors rather than to any technical difficulties in learning. It has further been found that before the transfer or the change, if the problem is discussed in the group and if the workers understand the reality considerations then they will help the management to bring about certain changes in the nature of work, type of the work or the kind of tools or machinery and there will not be any drop in production. Workers then have the sense of participation. The decision is not now something, which is forced from above but something which is necessitated by reality considerations.

Another outstanding feature of modern industry is the tripartite agreement. In several industries in India, the representatives of the workers, and the management, and of the government have met together and discussed about certain industrial problems. When all the three sets of representatives are convinced that the social situation demands that the production should not be impeded and that it is necessary that there should be an increased production in the interests of national development and national security, then they enter into a tripartite agreement according to which, for a period of three or five years, each group agrees not to bring about a deadlock so that the production will not be impeded. When they have a tripartite agreement like this, any problem which brings about a difference between the management and the workers is perceived from a different angle altogether and neither the management nor the leaders will allow the problem to assume a magnitude which results in a deadlock. There is a certain readiness to come to an agreement to solve the problem. Often it is egoistic considerations regarding the prestige of the individual, or the prestige of the group, which the individual is representing, which will stand in the way of realistic assessment of the situation. When there is a tripartite agreement, the realistic considerations become more dominant than other considerations. All the various groups in modern industry must endeavour to have these realistic considerations because ultimately, when there is a deadlock arising out of the frustrations, either in the management, or in the workers, the society as a whole, including the management and the workers, will suffer.

In order to promote the proper understanding and the assessment of the situations, vast training programmes are now being undertaken. The trade unions themselves are now coming forward to give training to the trade union leaders so that they understand the problems involved in industrial conflict. Similarly the management authorities are now trying to set up institutes of management where training will be given to the people in managerial positions. Government also is setting up programmes of training for the Labour Department officials. One of the new features is the organization of courses by the universities on trade union movements and labour-management relationships. Courses given in the universities will enable individuals to get the right attitude towards these problems.

We may conclude this chapter by drawing attention to some of the important problems regarding the motives of individuals and the social organization involved in modern industry. The members of an industrial plant are members of several interlocking social systems. Each system has its own pattern of rewards and punishments, which may or may not coincide with the rewards and punishments that are set up by the management to motivate the workers. It is this situation which gives rise to conflict in the minds of the individuals. The same individual, because he belongs to different groups at the same time, will have to follow the appropriate social norms of the groups to which he belongs. But these may bring about a conflict in him.

Problems of Social Psychology

The description of the several problems studied by social psychology should enable us to formulate a tentative definition of the subject. In a broad way it can be realized that this discipline is on the borderland between the two branches of knowledge—Sociology and Psychology. Instead of looking upon it as a branch of psychology some thinkers even go to the extent of looking upon social psychology as a branch of knowledge by itself, as a special science by itself. Some look upon it as a discipline that engages itself in the study of those problems of social life, which are not adequately studied by either sociology or psychology.

Though such extreme position may not give us an accurate picture of the scope and task of social psychology, there is no doubt that with the development of this branch of psychology, there is a considerable change in our views of what was called 'human nature'. The rapid strides made by cultural anthropology have also helped us to question a number of our assumptions about human behaviour. It is now evident that there can be no group life apart from the individual human beings and that no individual human being can exist as such apart from the group in which he lives. It is the task of the social psychologist to study the relationship between the individual human being and his society. We now realize the importance of the concept of interaction. Behaviour is largely determined by the interaction of men with men.

We may, therefore, define social psychology as the branch of knowledge, which studies the relationships arising out of the interaction of individuals with each other in social situations.

Social Situation and Social Behaviour

In order to understand this definition it is now necessary for us to explain the terms social situation and social behaviour. A social situation consists of the various visual, auditory and other stimuli lived through by the individuals. It also involves besides the present perceptions, the attitudes as well as the revival of past experiences. Thus a mere analysis of the separate stimuli will not help us to understand the social situation. An example may clarify the point. A boy of eight or ten may be hit by his friend. There may even be some contusion. The pain may not be felt at all or even if felt, the boy may laugh over it. It is possible that a few hours later the same boy may have been accidentally hit by his brother or sister at home. The immediate response may be a loud cry, tears, abuse of the sibling, complaint to the mother. The stimulus may be more or less the same but the response is absolutely different. The difference in behaviour can be understood only by the realization of the difference in the social situation. You cannot cry or complain when you are hit by a playmate. This is the social code. On the other hand sibling rivalry can be satisfied by loud cries and loud complaints. This is permitted in the home. Thus we find that social behaviour is determined not merely by the physical stimuli but also by the rules and codes. Social behaviour is a reciprocal interplay of personalities. It must, however, be realized that not all reactions of persons to each other are social response. It is possible that we may avoid collision with a person on the footpath just as we avoid a lamp post. It is converted from non-social to social interaction if one or both smile or exclaim 'pardon me' or 'I am sorry'. This depends on the social conditions, which have moulded the individual through his life history. In other words it involves the traditions, customs and standards of value. It is the task of social psychology to trace the situations, which have operated to socialize the individual. Social behaviour implies interaction between or among persons. But it must not be understood that social interaction always involves face-to-face contacts. Social behaviour may also arise indirectly through the medium of symbols. Objects or signs may have social values. The sign 'Halt and Proceed' leads to social behaviour. We react to it in the same way as we would have reacted to a policeman in uniform speaking those words. We know that if we disregard the sign and dash forwards on our cycle we may be caught by a constable a few yards ahead.

Social and Non-social Situations

Before we proceed further it may be desirable to distinguish somewhat more clearly between social and non-social situations on the one hand and social and non-social behaviour on the other hand. It is obvious that social situation involves the presence of other persons. But as we have already seen social behaviour involves not only face-to-face situations, but it also involves symbols, which lead to psychological events connected with people. The traffic sign is a social situation. It involves the social effects of its observance and non-observance. It also implies the extent to which the individual has been socialized. The famous parable associated with Kanakadasa, a medieval Karnatak saint, may be recalled in this connection. The story goes that the Guru gave a plantain to each of the disciples and asked them to eat it in a place where nobody observed them. All excepting Kanakadasa returned after consuming the plantain. Each reported that he went to a place where there was no human being and ate it so that nobody could observe. When Kanakadasa was asked why he was unable to find a suitable place, he replied that wherever he went he found that he was in the presence of God and so he had to return with the plantain. Similarly a properly socialized individual will obey the law regarding the use of a lamp for his cycle after dusk whether the minion of law is in sight or not. Thus social behaviour arises not only when we are in the presence of others it also arises in the absence of people but when the situation involves reference to others. Similarly when we are alone we are often influenced by what other people might think of us or would like us to do or would like us not to do. The young man who chooses a particular tie to match his shirt and hat and the young woman who chooses a particular blouse to match her sari are influenced not merely by considerations of aesthetic taste but also by what other members of their group would comment about their choice when they meet them later. Thus even when one is alone he may be affected by the psychological presence of others. Similarly, though not as frequently, we may be in company of others and yet not be reciprocally reactive to them. This is one of the characteristic features of urbanization. In the rural atmosphere the neighbours react socially to one another. But in the apartment houses in Mumbai or Kolkata and even in some of the other big cities, people may live as neighbours for a long time, they may perceive each other several times and yet be total strangers to each other. We do not react socially to each person who sits in the same bus or travels by the same 'local' train. On the other hand individuals may react socially to animals and even plants and inanimate objects. We are familiar with the affectionate way in which people play with their pets. They may also dominate over them. The child may 'abuse' the table against which he knocks himself or 'swear' at the stone that trips him.

Social Psychology and Other Sciences

Our appreciation of the scope and problems of social psychology will become more clear if we consider its relationship to other sciences.

Every human being is born into two worlds: the physical world and the social world. He has to learn about the world around him so that he can survive and contribute his mite towards the survival of the human race. He starts as a psycho-physical organism with the biological equipment for survival. But he is such a helpless individual that unless he is protected during prolonged infancy there is very little chance of his survival. Thus the social influences have a very important bearing on the growth of the individual. Still General Psychology studies the individual without reference to his social environment. Any deviation caused by the influence of the social environment is merely looked upon as something contributing to variability. These are merely disturbing influences, which have to be pierced through in order to discover the underlying laws of behaviour and experience The aim of General Psychology is to establish laws of oehaviour which are not affected by the differences in upbringing. The fundamental laws of motivation, perception, learning, memory, thinking and so on are universal to all human beings irrespective of the culture in which they are brought up. On the other hand since social psychology deals with the experience and behaviour of the individual in relation to the social stimulus situations, we find that what is irrelevant to general psychology becomes very significant to social psychology. It studies man in his concrete social and cultural setting. As we have seen above there are practically no situations, which are without a social significance. Hunger is a biological need. Studies in racial differences in intelligence show that it is very difficult to determine to what extent these differences are due to biological equipment and to what extent they are due to rich or poor social stimulation. Considered from this angle, it is clear that social psychology is a necessary complement to general psychology. The full significance of the laws of behaviour cannot be understood unless the study of general psychology is supplemented by a study of social psychology. It must not, however, be thought that the laws of social psychology are different from the laws of general psychology. They are identical. 'Social perception' and 'social learning' are not different from the perception or learning in the non-social situations. From this point of view it may be asserted that social psychology applies the general principles to social interactions.

We may now consider briefly the relation of social psychology to sociology. Sociology is the science, which studies the development and principles of social organization and generally group behaviour as distinct from the behaviour of the individuals in the group. It is concerned with the structure and organization of groups. The group is its unit of study. It studies the origin and development of groups, the means by which a group endures, how it imposes its own discipline on the members and demands their compliance. It also studies how groups and social institutions change. For example, it not only studies the family as a group, it also studies how it has changed from time to time. Social Psychology on the other hand is concerned with the individual, how he interacts with other individuals and group of individuals. Its scope is more limited. From another point of view it is basic to sociology. Psychological factors play a very important part in the formation, development and change of social institutions. Suggestibility, imitation, loyalty, fear, norms etc., explain the persistence as well as change in social practices. As Maciver and Page put it, "When we study the nature of the behaving individuals, the structure of the individual consciousness which expresses itself in social relationships, we are taking the psychological point of view. When we study the relationships themselves we take the sociological point of view. Both sciences are concerned with different aspects of an indivisible reality. 1ndividuals cannot be understood apart from their relations with one another; the relations cannot be understood apart from the units (or terms) of the relationship". The social psychologist studies how the individual is socialized, how he utilities and expresses the social patterns, how he builds within himself the attitudes and opinions of the family and the group in which he has been brought up and in which he lives, and how in turn he leaves his impress more or less effectively on the social patterns. To quote Murphy "Social psychology is the study of the way in which the individual becomes a member of, and functions in, a social group".

We can now proceed to study the relationship between social psychology and anthropology. In a broad way anthropology is defined as the science of man. It involves the biological as well as the socio-cultural aspects. Man is not only a social animal living in groups, but he is also a unique animal possessing the ability to speak and the ability to symbolize, abstract and generalize. Because of these two abilities he is able to communicate his skills and knowledge to his fellow-human beings and descendants. He transmits not only his skills and products of skills to his descendants he also transmits his beliefs, customs, values and social institutions. It is this totality we call culture. "Culture stands for the sum total of human behaviour, verbal and non-verbal and its products, material and non-material". According to Majumdar and Madan, Socio-Cultural Anthropology studies four types of human activities: *(i)* activities that provide satisfaction of bio-psychic needs like hunger and sex by wresting from nature food, clothing and shelter—the economic organization of a group; *(ii)* activities which have led to the social organization of a group so that by organizing group effort he is able to exploit nature effectively to satisfy the bio-psychic needs and also to satisfy his affectional needs. "Family, marriage and such other social institutions provide the medium in which and through which social life exists. And political institutions supply the controlling factors which hold social life at the useful level of inter-action; *(iii)* activities and attitudes towards the unseen presence of supennatural powers—the magico-religious organization of a group; *(iv)* activities connected with the expression of beauty, the aesthetic activities of a group. Anthropology studies the patterns of culture in the various part of the world, particularly among the preliterate and pre-urban groups. It uses concepts like' culture' 'custom' and 'mores' to explain the differences between the various groups. Consequently some anthropologists go and live in the group and study the pattern of the culture of the group. On the other hand some anthropologists make a comparative analysis of the specific reports and try to formulate laws regarding the growth, functioning and change of human societies. Although it is recognized that the bio-psychic needs of man are at the basis of group organization, the cultural anthropologists point out that the culture itself is not psychologically conditioned. Social life is not tied down to the biological and psychological level. Social life "emerges out to attain a new level, the social level, which is more or less super-psychic and super-organic... A society is a system of social relations; these social relations are the products of history; they are held together by moral values and not natural forces. Therefore, a society is a social and a moral system" . The culture determinists like Kroeber look upon culture as a super-organic, super-psychic and supersocial force, which determines how an individual behaves and what he values and cherishes. There is no doubt that the individual is fashioned by the group and that the vast majority of the individuals in any given group are of the conforming type. But it is also realized that some individuals do contribute to the change of culture.

While it is the task of social and cultural anthropology to study the patterns of culture, the task of social psychology is to study the way in which the individual in a given group acquires the culture. Thus we find that while anthropology makes use of culture and custom as concepts to understand patterns of social organization, it is the task of social psychology to analyse the processes underlying these concepts. It endeavours to determine how customs are found and transmitted from generation to generation.

●●●

6

Psychology of Social Attitude

An attitude denotes an adjustment of the individual towards some selected' person, group or institution. In forming an attitude towards some aspect of the environment an individual shows a readiness to respond. In reaction-time experiments, it has been found that there are differences in reaction-time depending upon the attitude taken by the individual. It is conceived as a state of preparation for discriminating among stimuli (sensorial attitude) or as a state of preparation for reacting as quickly as possible upon the occurrence of a definite stimulus (motor-attitude). Thus an attitude results in a state of preparation or a state of readiness to respond in a particular manner under particular circumstances. An attitude determines a certain expectation; if the events are in line with these expectations then there is satisfaction. But if the events are contrary to the attitude then there will be dissatisfaction. Attitudes could be formed to social as well as non-social aspects of the environment. We are now concerned only with social attitudes, that is, attitudes formed in relation to social stimulus situations. Thus social attitudes may be formed towards persons or groups of persons towards the products of human interaction.

People in different cultures form definite attitudes towards what is desirable and what is undesirable. In other words social attitudes involve values. There is a readiness to do or not to do certain things. For example, people in different cultures have definite attitudes about what is desirable to eat and at what time food should be taken. Thus the attitude sets a person for or against persons, groups, things, and institutions. Thus attitudes define what is to be preferred, expected and desired and what is desirable and what should be avoided. Thus, in terms of its consequence, an attitude is goal-directed. Attitudes may be referred to as sociogenic motives. Attitudes arise out of the socialization of an individual in a group. It must be emphasised that we cannot observe attitudes. Social attitudes can only be inferred from the speech and behaviour of individuals. Some social psychologists refer to attitudes as "conforming behaviour". Similarly, if we stand near a temple and observe the reaction of the people as they pass the temple on the street, we will find that a very large number of Hindus will stop for a second and offer prayer and a very small number will just pass by. Such conformity to social norms is based on the development of social attitudes.

Distinguish Features of Attitude

An attitude, which determines the characteristic, or a consistent, mode of behaviour in relation to a particular aspect of the environment is an internal factor. What are the criteria, which differentiate attitudes as internal factors from other internal factors? Sherif has given a few criteria, which help not only to differentiate attitudes as internal factors from other internal factors, but also to learn about the characteristics of the attitudes themselves. According to Sherif the following are the distinguishing features of attitudes.

1. ***Attitudes are not innate.*** They are formed or learnt by the individual as he grows up in the group. Consequently, attitudes are not biogenic though they are based on the biogenic motives, for *e.g.*, craving for food is biogenic but strong preference for rice or for wheat, is an attitude that is formed because of the family in which one is brought up: If the children

in the south, and in other predominantly rice-eating parts of India, have to change their attitudes towards wheat, then wheat should be introduced right from childhood. But it will be accepted by the children only if the mother and father also take it as a part of the food. Thus unless the parents change their attitudes towards food, children cannot change their attitudes.

2. ***Attitudes involve individuals as well as groups.*** An individual may deyelop an attitude of hostility towards another individual or he may look upon the whole group to which the other individual belongs as hateful. A gang of boys may develop hatred towards a rival gang. They may consider not only that a particular individual in the rival gang is treacherous, but that all the individuals in that gang are treacherous. Fundamentalists of one religion hate the people of other religion. To a capitalist century not only the communist countries like Russia and China are hateful, but even the non-aligned countries are undesirable. Thus our social attitudes may encompass not only individuals but also groups, small as well as vast. There is a process of generalisation and consequently all the out-groups are looked upon as aggressive, dishonest and so on.

3. ***Attitudes are more or less lasting.*** They are enduring. But since attitudes are formed they are subject to change. They are not immutable. Because we conform to attitudes we can also change the attitudes provided there are the proper conditions. Our previous illustration gives us an insight about the changing of attitudes.

4. ***Attitudes have motivational-affective properties.*** As we have seen already, attitudes are learnt. How can

we then distinguish attitudes from other learnt items? According to Sherif attitudes have the motivational-affective properties. Unlike other learnt items, an attitude is goal-directed in a positive or negative way.

5. ***Attitudes imply a subject-object relationship.*** Attitudes are always formed in relation to certain persons, groups, objects of institutions. So attitudes are not just internal factors without any relationship with the external factors. On the other hand, they can arise only in relation to some aspect of the environment.

6. ***Attitudes are shared by the members of a group.*** All the above criteria apply to attitudes, which are social as well as non-social. The distinguishing features of the social attitudes are *(a)* that they are formed in relation to social situations and *(b)* that they are shared by the members of the group. That social attitudes are more or less common among the members of a group, with the exception of a few members who are deviant, is an essential feature. It is this that leads to conforming behaviour of the large majority of the members of a group and the deviation only by a small minority. The norms and values of a group are internalised through the formation of attitudes.

There is another peculiar feature in the learning of attitudes as compared with the other learnt items from an individual's behaviour. We find that the new members of the group form attitudes through short-cut verbal dicta like proverbs and aphorisms, Verbal formulae like proverbs induce certain attitudes by being accepted. The elder or the senior members of a family present these value judgments with an air of finality and the younger and junior members of a group accept them who are in the process of becoming members. Thus social attitudes are formed, not on the basis of individual and personal experiences, as much as through the acceptance of the verbal formulae. Even when the personal experience contradicts the prevailing social attitude, the chances are that the individual will tend to look upon the personal experience as an exception rather than as the truth.

In a general way, it may be stated that an attitude is a readiness to respond to certain situations, persons, objects or ideas in a consistent manner. This kind of readiness is the result of learning and it becomes a habitual mode of response. Thus an attitude implies on the one hand a well-defined object of reference and on the other a variation in the degree or strength of a person s attitude from extremely positive to extremely negative.

It is now generally accepted that a social attitude determines the characteristic and consistent mode of behaviour. Further, there is a selective mode of response towards the relevant stimuli from the environment on the basis of the attitude. We can give a few experiments, which have been conducted to study these problems. Marks conducted an experiment to study the influence of attitudes on the, judgement of skin colour in America. He obtained the ratings regarding skin-colour and also ratings regarding attractiveness from four groups of Negro students. The sociologist Johnson has observed a preference for light brown skin colour among the Negro youth. Marks found that there was a tendency to displace the ratings of subjects considered attractive in the direction of the preferred skin colour. It was further found that the rating of a person's skin colour served as an anchorage for judgment. The persons who were lighter in skin colour than the rater were judged as light and those darker than the rater were judged as 'dark'. Thus a person's rating of himself influenced how he rated the skin colour of the other people. Further, those who are looked upon as attractive were given lighter rating and those who were looked upon as unattractive were given a darker rating. In another study, Asch obtained ratings for two political figures, Roosevelt and Hitler, with respect to 'intellectual power' and 'physical attractiveness'. It was found that the large majority of American students looked upon Roosevelt as having the highest ranking and Hitler as having the lowest ranking with respect to intellectual power and physical attractiveness. This study confirms the ordinary experience we have with respect to our judgments about the attractiveness of the parents, the teachers, and other leaders in society whom we love and like, and the opposite with respect to those whom we dislike or hate. Our attitudes influence our judgment regarding the behaviour and the desirability of the individual around us. If we like people, we overlook their deficiencies and defects but if we dislike people, we tend exaggerate their defects. 'This is why the *Bhagavadgita* bids us to give up *Raaga* and *Dvesha* when we are dealing with the other people. It is our likes and dislikes that lead us to prejudice. Probably if the same study of Asch referred to above had been conducted among the German students at that time the results would have been quite the reverse. Postman and his associates gave the Allport-Vernon test of values and the presented 36 words representing the six values included in the test in a tachistoscope. The words were exposed for a very short time and they gradually increased the exposure till each word was recognized. It was found that the greater the value of a word for the subject the shorter the time needed to recognize it. Murphy chose two groups of students who had strong and opposite views on a political issue. The members of each group were presented with two communications from opposing points of view through loudspeakers at the same time. It was found that the individuals favouring one view heard the relevant communication as the figure and the other as the background, while the control subjects were almost equally divided in hearing one or the other communication as figure. Reference may also be made to the study of Proshansky who devised a projective method for the study of attitudes. He gave pictures of social conflict situation to two extreme groups who had strong prolabour or anti-labour attitudes. He asked them to describe the pictures. He found that the individuals with pro-labour attitudes stressed that the government was callous and was not providing proper housing conditions for the poor people. On the other hand the individuals with anti-labour attitudes described the pictures as depicting sloppy people who seem to enjoy dwelling in slums. Finally, reference may be made to an interesting study by Kubany.

Measurement of Social Attitudes

An attitude involves belief or disbelief, acceptance or rejection and favouring or not favouring some aspect of the environment. In order to measure attitudes, scales have been constructed consisting of short statements dealing with several aspects of some issue or institution under consideration. The statements involve favourable or unfavourable estimations, acceptance or rejection. Consequently, the central problem of the measurement of attitude is the scaling of test items. It is presumed that a senes of statements can be made which serve as the marks of a yardstick for the measurement of attitudes. Each statement will represent a specified degree of acceptance or rejection of a belief. Further these statements have to be equally spaced throughout the entire range of attitude continuum from complete acceptance of a belief to its complete rejection.

Thurstone's Method

The theory underlying Thurstone's method of equal appearing intervals is that if a person indicates the statements he accepts and rejects he can be located at a definite position on the attitude continuum. Consequently, the problem is to select an appropriate series of statements and to determine what positions on the attitude continuum each statement represents. In order to solve this problem Thurstone collected a list of statements from several sources like newspaper articles, legislature proceedings on issues, pamphlets, opinions of colleagues etc. The important thing is that these statements should represent all the various stand-points from complete acceptance to complete rejection. Generally about 200-300 statements will have to be collected in order to prepare an attitude scale according to this method. The next step is to edit these statements. Several statements, which are not very pertinent to the issue under consideration or which are ambiguous could be eliminated. Similarly statements, which are duplicating could also be eliminated and the statements could be re-worded so that they are more effective. It is important to see that each statement is a reflection of opinion and not a fact. The statements should be simple, short, complete, definite and direct so that they could be accepted or rejected. The investigator must avoid his prejudices when he is collecting and editing these statements. The next step is to arrange these statements from extremely favourable to extremely unfavourable continuum. They should also be arranged in equal appearing intervals so that a scale resembling a foot rule could be constructed. In order to do this Thurstone followed the procedure of getting each statement typed on a slip of paper. He got several people to serve as judges and each was asked to sort the slips of paper in 9 to 11 groups. For example, if we take up statements expressing our attitude towards prohibition or language issue we can collect hundreds of statements involving definite opinions all the way from complete acceptance to complete rejection. The judges could be asked to sort the statements in such a way that all those which express the greatest appreciation of prohibition are put into one pile and at the other end all those statements expressing the strongest disapproval of prohibition could be piled up as the 9th or 11th pile, as the case may be. Then the other statements could be classified in between these two depending on the degree of appreciation or deprecation of prohibition. Each judge is now trying to sort these statements purely on the basis of whether the statement is favourable or unfavourable regarding the issue. The judge is not thinking about his own preference now.

After getting the judges to classify the statements into the various piles, the next step is to find out the median value of each statement. There is the problem whether the personal attitude of the judges will not affect their evaluation. Thurstone assumed that when a man is asked to evaluate the statements he, will not be influenced by his own attitude towards the issue. Studies have been made to find out if Thurstone's assumption is correct. In America, Hinckley asked a group of Negro students, a group of white students from the north and a group of white students from the south to evaluate 114 statements in order to build up a scale of attitude towards Negroes. He constructed 3 scales on the basis of the evaluation of the 3 groups. He found that these 3 scales were identical in content. Only one statement was found not to occupy the same relative position in all the three scales. Thus the Negroes who were involved in the problem as well as the whites who' were un favourable to the Negroes, and the whites who were favourable to the Negroes, all these three different groups gave the same evaluation for the various statements when they were asked to sit in judgement over each statement.

Ferguson tried to find out if the evaluation of the statements by different groups with status differences will affect the evaluation. He tried to construct an Assistant Managerial evaluation form and he obtained judgements from a group of Managers, Assistant Managers and Agents. It is clear that among these three groups, the Assistant Managers are ego-involved as the statements relate to them directly while the Managers are a superior status group and the Agents are an inferior status group. But Ferguson found that all the three groups rated in the same way. Thus, this technique of using judges in preparing the equal appearing interval scales is satisfactory.

Another problem with respect to this procedure of establishing the scale values is the influence of different time periods and changing cultural trends. Farnsworth found a high degree of correlation (.97) between the evaluation of items with respect to Peterson's scale for the measurement of attitude towards war prepared in 1930 with the values obtained in 1940.

After determining the median value for each statement the next problem is to select a small number of statements representing each value position along the attitude continuum. Roughly about 20-25 items will have to be selected. All the statements, which are judged to be ambiguous or irrelevant to the continuum are eliminated. Finally, the 'Scaled attitude test is administered and the respondent is asked to check those statements with which he is in agreement. His score is the median of the scale values of the items that he has checked. Thus the subject is required to indicate his agreement or disagreement with each statement. Before closing this section, we may give some illustrations of the way in which Thurstone's scale to measure the attitude towards Church works. It was found that the mean value for Catholics was 2.90 while that for Protestants was 3.97 and for Jews 5.44. In this scale, the lower the score the more favourable is the attitude towards the Church. It was found that the mean value for those who attend the Church was 3.06 while for those who are not attending the Church was 5.93.

Likert's Method of Summated Rating

This method is much simpler than that of Thurstone. In this method also, a number of statements regarding the issue have to be collected. The subject is asked to indicate the degree or the strength of his attitude towards each statement on a 5-point scale: strongly agree, agree, undecided, disagree, strongly disagree. These answers are assigned numerical values ranging from 5-1 or from 1-5 according; as the response is favourable or unfavourable. Thus high scores indicate a favourable attitude. The individual score on a particular attitude scale is the sum of all his ratings on each of the items in the scale. It is obvious that this scale does not have any absolute system of units such as Thurstone's scale. The scores of this scale have to be interpreted merely on a relative basis, that is, on the basis of whether the score is higher or lower indicating 'whether the attitude of the individual is more favourable or more unfavourable. In this method also elaborate steps are followed in order to eliminate all the weak items by finding out the correlation of each item with the total test. This is how the internal consistency is established.

Studies have been made to compare the results obtained by Likert's technique with the results obtained by the more complicated method of preparing the scale following Thurstone's technique. It has been found that there is a high correlation between the measurements of the two different scales. But it must be realised that Thurstone's scale has an absolute system of units and also shows higher reliability. Thus even though Likert's method does not make use of evaluation by judges we find that it is quite useful. Another advantage of Likert's technique is that it indicates the intensity of opinion as well as the direction of opinion.

Method of Social Distance

This method has been developed by Bogardus. It is a familiar fact that there are various degrees of social intimacy. For example, when strangers come to our house we may speak to them for a few minutes. Further, we may not take them inside our house. On the other hand, if close friends come to meet us we take them into our room and probably we may give them a cup of coffee, or invite them for dinner. There are also degrees of intimacy or social distance when we are dealing with people of different religions or people of different castes or people of different classes; we tend to have various degrees of social intimacy with them. It is the usual practice in several homes not to admit the servants, other than cooks, into the kitchen. Similarly it is the usual practice not to admit people of other castes or groups into the kitchen, or even into the dining room. Even with respect to the offering of seats we find that differences are made on the basis of class, caste and other considerations. A man of lower caste or class may be asked to sit on the floor whereas a mat or a chair may be provided for a person of superior caste or class. Thus in various degrees in our personal relationships with other individuals as well as in our social relationships with members belonging to other groups we tend to maintain a certain social distance. The most obvious illustration of the operation of this principle of social distance is the old practice in ancient India where, in the cities, and even more so in the villages, the members of the Harijan group are made to live in the outskirts of the town or the village. It is only recently, with the changes in the attitude of people towards this problem, that members of the Harijan groups are allwed to live in houses in any area of the city.

Attitude Formation and Change

In the recent years there has been a widespread interest in actively changing the attitudes of people within the country and towards people in other countries. Groups within the country, as well as the government, are engaged in changing the attitudes of people towards the various problems. In the United States, during the 1930s Roosevelt brought about a big change in the attitude of people towards workers as well as farmers because of the measures he took to counteract the disastrous economic consequences of 'depression'. Similarly, the Labour Party of Great Britain brought about vast changes among the people towards the problems of the working classes. In India, Gandhiji undertook the enormous task of changing the attitudes of the millions of people who were either apathetic or actually frightened of the British suzerainty. He adopted several techniques to make the Indians develop an attitude favourable to 'swaraj' and democracy and against the foreign rule. At the same time, he tried to change the attitude of the British so that they became favourable to end colonialism and unfavourable to the use of violence against unarmed Satyagrahis. Further, he tried to change the attitude of the Hindus so that it became favourable towards Muslims, Harijans and other minority groups. Similarly, he tried to change the attitude of Muslims so that it became favourable to Hindus. It is needless to list all the various changes, which Gandhiji brought about in the political, social, economic, religious, educational, and other fields.

The governments in every country of the world are actively engaged in changing attitudes of people. For example, all the highly developed countries like United States, Great Britian, Germany, Japan, Russia and other countries are now feeling it their duty to help the undeveloped countries of Asia, Africa and South-America, so that these countries can become economically prosperous. This is something absolutely new in the history of man. From plunder, conquest and colonialism, there is this change towards helping the weak and undeveloped countries to become self-reliant and economically prosperous. In India, for example, many attempts are being made to change the attitude of the farmers and peasants so that they take up to new methods of agriculture, chemical manures, cattle breeding, cooperative societies etc. Similarly attempts are being made to change the attitude of the industrialists so that they work, not only for their own profit, but also for the well being and economic prosperity of the country as a whole. Similarly attitudes of the businessmen are being changed so that they do not make a profit at the cost of the helpless customers.

This accelerated rate of social change in our times is due to several changes in political, economic and technological fields. Politically it is now realised that colonialism is outmoded and that each country has the right to have a government of its own. In the economic field it is accepted that m every country the poorest and the under-privileged groups must have the means to live in comfort. Consequently, in every country, attempts are being made to raise the standard of life so that no family is without resources for decent living conditions. The great advances made in technology have now brought the whole world very close so that with the radio, we know what is happening at the ends of the world within a few minutes, and in the jet plane we can travel to any part of the world within a few hours. All these developments in thought as well as in technology have forced the pace of change in every part of the world. Consequently, in every country, attempts are being made to change the outlook of the people so that they can have faith in themselves, work hard, and change their living conditions, so that the disparity in standards of life from group to group within a country or between countries is reduced.

Problem of Attitude Change

As we have seen earlier, we can only infer attitudes on the basis of the readiness of the people to respond positively or negatively towards certain situations or areas. Further, attitude formation brings about a consistent and characteristic mode of reaction to particular situation. Consequently, attitude change means a change in the stand of the individual regarding a given issue or problem. It may be asked, how we can find out whether a person's attitude with respect to some issue has changed. We can measure the change of attitude by the same methods as we employed in our study of the existence of attitude. Attitude change implies that the issue towards which we were unfavourable produces now an attitude of being favourable towards it or vice versa.

It must be borne in mind that both the formation of attitude and change of attitude are not self-generating. Formation as-well-as change of attitude involve inter-personal relations. Consequently, there are both internal factors as well as external factors involved in the formation and change of attitudes. The internal factors refer to the motives of the individuals, the ideals of the individuals and so on.

Group Discussion and Group Decision

During World War II, it was used to bring about a change in the food habits of people. Some varieties of food, though very nutritious, were not used by the Americans. Lewin conducted his experiments on six Red Cross groups of volunteers. Each group had from 13 to 17 individuals. "Lecture Method" was used for three groups and the "Discussion Method" was used for the other three groups. In both cases, the time was the same, that is, 45 minutes. In the lecture method the nutritional value of the unused food was dilated upon. The volunteers were told how economical these foods were; they were exhorted to use these foods so that they could save the usual meat-cuts for the war-effort. Cyclostyled copies of the recipes to prepare these unused foods were distributed. In the second set of groups, the discussion groups, the problem was introduced, the participants were allowed to discuss how housewives could be induced to participate in a programme of change of foods to help in war-effort and to improve general health. The discussion turned to the several obstacles in the way of using these new foods and possible objections, which the family may have. After this the nutrition expert provided the recipes. At the end of the period a group decision was requested by show of hands. Sometime later the subjects were checked in order to find out how many of them had included the new food items as part of their meals. It was found that while 3% of the lecture group included new items, 32% of the discussion group had acted in a similar way. Thus this experiment shows two significant facts. One is that the discussion method is far superior to the lecture method in inducing change in attitude and behaviour. Secondly, it shows clearly that it is not possible to change some individuals of a group by either of the techniques.

This experiment served as a model for other studies of attitude and behaviour change. One of the defects of the first experiment was that two different people were leaders in the two different groups. Consequently, in a second experiment, the same person was used as a leader of the lecture group as well as the discussion group. In this experiment, the subjects were housewives. In each session, there were 6 to 9 individuals in the group. Two check-ups were made, one after 2 weeks interval and another after 4 weeks interval. Again, it was found that the discussion group was decisively more responsive. It was also found that the change endured longer for the discussion group. Leville and Butler confirmed these results in a study in an industrial plant. There were 29 supervisors in this factory. They tended to over-rate men in higher grade jobs and under-rate those in lower grade jobs. The problem was to alter their attitudes so that they did not have bias for or against the men whom they represented. The supervisors were divided into three groups, one group was exposed to the lecture technique. They were informed how to correct the errors in rating. The second group was made to discuss the problem and arrive at a group decision. While the third group served as a control group.

It is clear from the above that active participation in a discussion group is much more effective to change attitude and behaviour than passive reception in a lecture group. "Then individuals actively participate they become personally involved in the issue. Further, group decision has a more binding influence on the individuals than any possible individual resolve. This as Sherif points out, "the crucial step in attempting to bring about an effective change in attitude is getting the individual personally involved (ego-involved) in the issue at hand. Getting the individual personally involved means arousing related ego-attitudes. Such personal involvement is enhanced in the give-and-take process of social interaction". Mere information or logical argument alone does not bring about a change in attitude because if the individual changes his attitude he may be breaking away from the security of cherished group ties".

As we have seen above, an individual derives his attitudes from the group norms even when an individual has to change his attitude. This implies that he is breaking away from the group norms in some way. This is not an easy thing to do. It is against socialization. On the other hand, when an individual discusses the problem in a group, then he can safely put forth his views in favour of change. When several individuals in the group point out the advantages in the change, then the group as a whole will change. When the group changes, the group norm is changed. This will influence and reinforce the change in the individual. Further, as we have already seen, the new group norm becomes the individual's autonomous norm. Consequently, as Sherif's experimental work has made it clear, the individual will behave in a new way whether he is with the group or alone. Later on, if the individual member deviates from the norm thus reached, he feels that he is violating his own values, because he is now incorporating these group values into his personality.

Radicalism—Conservatism

We can now give some illustrations of the way in, which attitude scales are prepared and what results have been obtained by using these scales. There is a general attitude towards the direction and rate of change in the social, economic and political institutions. This is indicated by the words 'racial' and 'conservative '. In every society, there are people who are eager for a change in the social institutions. On the other hand, there are also people who do not want such changes to take place and who feel quite satisfied with the things as they are. Kirk asserts that the conservatives have a belief that Providence rules society, they are attached to tradition, have belief in the inevitability of the class system in society, they link up private property and freedom. The 'radicals' are characterised by a belief in the equality of all men, that if the environment is changed, all men could become perfect, that there is no limit to the progress of society. These people have a contempt for tradition and believe in political levelling, as well as economic levelling. The 'reactionary' prefers to restore the social institutions to their past state while the 'conservative' is attached to the things as they are. But the 'liberal' desires to modify the present in accordance with the needs of the times, while the 'radical' desires to bring about drastic changes in the existing social order. In general it may be stated that the' radical' is not only favourable to the sweeping changes in social institutions, but is particularly opposed to class interests.

How the Scale in Constructed

In fifties Miss M. N. Kamala made an attempt to construct an attitude scale to measure conservatism-radicalism among the people. She chose the problems of divorce, widow-marriage, land problem, private property, income distribution, problem of labour and problem of nationalisation. To prepare the scales for the problems of divorce and widow-remarriage she used Thurstone's technique of equal appearing intervals. She collected about 200 statements on each problem. After editing, she reduced them to 98 statements on divorce and 96 statements on widow-remarriage. Care was taken to see that the statements represented the full range of possible opinions on the issue.

The next step was to prepare an attitude continuum with the following 7 points:

(1) Reactionary, (2) Conservative, (3) Comformist, (4) Moderate, (5) Liberal, (6) Progressive, (7) Radical.

Fifty-six judges among whom were 42 men and 14 women consisting of Teachers (18), Lawyers (10), Engineers (5), Doctors (10), Authors (3), Socio-Political Workers (10), were given this attitude continuum. These seven words were printed on separate cards. In order to see that there is a common basis for judgment for all the judges, the following brief description for each item was given:

1. **Reactionary.** One who struggles to reverse the course of social progress by restoring old and out-worn customs and institutions that are actually losing social approval.

2. **Conformist.** One who conforms in his thought and action to the traditions and conventions in the existing order of society.

3. **Conservative.** One who attaches a sacredness to tradition, tries to preserve the existing order of society and opposes all changes and progress.

4. **Liberal.** One who prefers a few modifications and changes in the prevailing social order that are not radical and opposed to the existing order.

5. **Moderate.** One who conforms to conventions usually but does not resist a few necessary changes, in minor matters, in the existing order of society.

6. **Radical.** One who tries to uproot the existing order of society and struggles to supplant it by drastic and sweeping changes.

7. **Progressive.** One who advocates a large number of gradual changes in the existing order of society and opposes a blind faith in conventions.

With respect to the problems of land, private property, income, labour and nationalisation, Likert's method of summated rating was made use of in order to develop the scales. The following are some of the statements used:

1. Abolition of landlordism, personal and religious Inams, is a hasty measure.
2. That government should own all means of production is an extreme measure.
3. The difference in salaries between the labourers and other professional people must be minimised.
4. Labour Unions must not merely be tolerated but activity encouraged.

Some Results

Hunter has included statements regarding the Negroes, labour, social issues, religion, democracy and national defence in his test on social attitudes. Nelson tested 3780 students in various parts of United States and found that the senior students were the most liberal among the college students. He found that education has a liberalising tendency. Remmers and Weltman tested the attitude of 207 pupils in Senior High Schools and also the attitude of their parents and teachers and found a strong positive relationship among the attitudes of the members of the family. They also found greater similarity in the attitudes between parents and children, than between teachers and pupils. Shepero found a relationship between social attitudes and child Tearing practices. He found that the radical parents were lenient and affectionate and gave more liberty to their children while the conservative parents were more disciplinarian and expected the children to be submissive. Adamo constructed a scale of political-economic-conservatism to determine authoritarian personality. He found a high relationship between conservatism and ethno-centrism. Centers found a relationship between social classes and social attitude. He found that the people of higher social status were more conservative while the people of lower social status were more liberal. Eysenck prepared a 40 item scale to study social attitudes. He postulates that there are two dimensions *(a)* radicalism-conservatism, *(b)* tough mind (authoritarian)—tender mind (democratic) at right angles to each other. He found that the middle class group, were more tender minded and working-class group were more tough-minded irrespective of whether they belong to the conservative, the socialist or the communist party. He further found that the working-class people were more conservative than the middle class people.

●●●

7

Social Life and Environmental Change

There are two fundamental forces which influence the social life and behaviour of the individuals and these are 'heredity' and 'environment'. While heredity is purely a biological factor, the environment seems to be a partially social element. As to the question what environment means, a definite answer can be given here. In general use the term environment indicates all those things which environ or surround the people. It is made of all those things which though distinct or close to the people influence their life and activities in certain ways. It consists of all surroundings and influences whatsoever, that are present at the time of the occurrence of different events.

It is an external force influencing the life and behaviour of the people. In this way environment is not a simple but a complex phenomenon which has several forms. The chief among these being physical environment, social environment, and economic environment. The physical environment is the most fundamental and first in importance of all these forms and may therefore be considered here in detail.

Physical Environment

Physical environment consists of all those things which nature creates for the individuals. They are the product of nature and not the artificial creations of the human beings.

Physical environment is also called natural and geographical environment. To explain it in the words of Maciver and Page, "The geographical environment consists of those conditions that Nature provides for man. It includes the earth's surface with all its physical features and natural resources—the distribution of land and water mountains and plains, minerals, plants and animals, the climate and all the cosmic forces, gravitational, electric, radiational that play upon the earth and affect the life of man." Similarly Sorokin also writes, "By geographical environment we mean all cosmic conditions and phenomena which exist independent of man's existence and activity, which are created by man and which change and vary through their own spontaneity independent of man's existence and activity."

Physical environment is further subdivided into uncontrolled or natural environment and the controlled or artificial environment. The former is composed of those external material objects or phenomena which though in some points may be modified by man, are, in general out of his control. That is to say, most of these man can change only slightly but mostly the change depends on forces beyond his power. Among this aspect of the physical environment we may place the objects which are more commonly known as Nature. It includes the sun and stars, the winds and rains,the mountains and the seas, the seasons, the tides and the ocean currents. However, it may be said that man may not be able to establish his full control on the so called uncontrollable aspects of physical environment, but he can certainly put them to use to serve his needs. On the other hand, the controllable environment consists of those elements which are amenable to the direct control of man and which he can modify in a large measure. Some of the instances of this type are the vast stretches of land which he brings under cultivation, the rivers and streams which he tames with dams and embankments and such other natural resources. There can be drawn a more subtle distinction between these two categories of natural environment and it is that the first category mostly contains the abstract and the hidden objects of Nature while the second category largely consists of the concrete and visible objects of the physical world.

Role of Physical Environment on Social Life

It is an unimpeachable truth that physical environment plays a predominant role in determining the behaviour of individuals and groups. So great is the influence of physical environment on human life that special studies hwe been made about this relationship since the time of Montesquieu. The close relationship between physical environment and social phenomena has led to the rise of Geographical School of Sociology in the modern time. Referring to the work of this school Maciver and Page, observe, "The writers of this school have added tremendously to our knowledge of the role of geography in man's development. They have made us aware of the interplay between climate and topography and the various aspects of the physical environment, on the one side, and political and economic, technological and cultural phenomena on the other. But their interpretations have sometimes misled us also." But this fact need not tempt any body to belittle the impact of physical elements on society. There are several ways through which the various aspects of physical environment have affected the human society and the more important of these facts may be stated here in the following order.

1. ***Influence of Rivers.*** It cannot be denied that the movement and the growth of population largely depend upon favourable physical conditions. In this respect the rivers have ween seen playing a vital role. It is a matter of history that the earliest dense population appeared in certain fertile plains and valleys of the east where great rivers assured ample food supply and easy means of communication. For

instance the Indus, the Ganges, the Nile, and the Yangtze-kiany nurtured the earlier civilizations as certainly as they fertilised the soil. Besides this the river is the first great highway which made possible the movement of the people from place to place. There followed in its train the contacts of commerce and migration and invasion according to their kind stimulating or curshing social development. The civilization of Europe would have been very different, had there been no Danube or Rhine. Most of the great cities of the world are situated on streams and particularly on their tidal reaches. Even the course of the rise of Indian civilization would have been quite different if there had been no Indus and Ganges. Thus it is obvious that rivers have proved to be the creator and the nurse of the earliest human civilizations.

2. ***Role of Oceans.*** The oceans are another element of physical environment to have its bearing on human civilization. The seacoasts are often seen playing a vital role in determining its course. To quote Maciver, "Barrier and threshold" these are the roles which the seacoasts have played in history." The open seas have often placed limits on the aggressive instincts of the people, but at the same time they have helped in developing the spirit of adventure in them. Oceans offer many opportunities of advance to the adventurous people and the countries close to the sea easily become great powers of the world. For instance, the power of Spain, Holland and England had arisen not only by historical circumstances but also by improvements in the techniques of navigation. Britain could establish a vast empire in the world solely by virtue of being the mistress of the sea. Now the vast development of international trade has thrown into bold relief the vital importance of the sea for all the people and nations. No country can think of its all round development without having access to the sea.

3. ***Influence of Climate.*** Now this fact has been throughly established that the climatic conditions also exercise a powerful

influence on the health, habits and activities of men. For instance, it is observed that extremes of heat or of cold have a deterrent effect on social development. On the other hand, a certain moderate temperature is best calculated to evoke all kinds of human activities. No matter if they are physical, mental or intellectual, but their performance under moderate climatic conditions is definitely much better than is the case under the extremes of climate. People develop inertia and laziness while living in extremely hot places, but on the other hand, too much cold cripples human activities and slackens their energy. The variance of human activities and social life under different climatic conditions is best examplified by the difference in the life pattern of the people living in the hills and in the plains.

4. ***Effect of Seasons.*** Some western writers have tried to exhibit the existence of co-relation between seasonal changes and the frequency of crimes. It is held that crime against the persons and suicides occur more frequently in summer and crime against property in winter. However, it should be kept in view that it is not climate or season alone which produce these phenomena. The environment of man is many sided of which climates, seasons and other geographical features are only a part. There are so many other forces at work which together with physical environments dffect the human life and activities.

5. ***Impact of Natural Resources on Social Life.*** The geographical environment influences the life of the people in one more way also. Every piece of territory which is inhabited by a group of people has its own natural resources. These varying kinds of natural resources of the different places influence the social life of the people living there and also determine their occupations. For instance, if on a particular place the land is fertile and irrigation facilities are sufficiently available the people of that region will mostly do agriculture or will adopt such other occupations as are connected with

agriculture. On the other hand, if a particular region is full of mineral resources there industry will predominate and the people, in general, will adopt industrial and commercial occupations. These people living in different regions and doing dissimilar occupations are sure to differ from one another in their social ways, customs, manners, ideas and mode of life.

Limits on the Role of Physical Environment

It has been noted above that physical environments play a vital role in the determination and direction of the social life of the people. Changes which occur from time to time in the different social phenomena are taken to be the direct or indirect results of the interaction and influence of the objects of natural environment. But it cannot be viewed as an exclusive factor in the shaping of social life. There are certainly operating a large number of limits on the role assigned to physical environment, which proves that it is a partial factor in changing the social life and human civilization.

To begin with the critics assert that it is not the exclusive physical environment which determines the social phenomena. There is no consistent relation between the two. In many instances, similar cultural practices are found among people living under very different physical circumstances. For instance, monogamous marriage is practised all over the world and similarly Christian religion has been followed by the people living under extremely different physical conditions. If the effect of physical environment on soical situations had been absolute and exclusive, we could have nowhere found social and religious institutions monogamy and Christianity as all pervasive in character.

Secondly, it is customary to regard climatic conditions as an influential factor in the matter of changes in population. For example, birth-rate and death-rate are, in general, higher in tropical regions than in temperate zones. There may be some reality in this assumption, but even then it would be improper to place the whole responsibility for it on climate alone. There are differences in racial character, economic development, cultural heritage and religious beliefs which have large bearing on this issue. It would be quite a drastic view to hold that climate is the only explanation for the social phenomena of high birth and high death rates in certain regions. The correct view on this question is that climate is not the sole, but one of the factors which influence population.

Thirdly, it has been so happening that different social institutions develop under similar climatic conditions. It is usually found that different groups of people living under similar climates exhibit a wide contrast in their customs, manners and temperaments. Westermarck in his study of the origin and development of the moral ideas has amply illustrated this fact. Moreover, none of the changes that have occurred in a certain culture can be directly related geographic changes.

Fourthly, it is contended that growth of civilization has minimised the influence of physical environment. There have occured a large number of changes in the mutual relations of geographical conditions and social progress. Now the distribution of agricultural resources is less determinative as civilization progresses regarding the distribution of population. For instance, in the pre-industrial age the most populous part of England was that of the greatest fertility of soil and rich in agricultural produce, whereas now the density of population is found in the regions rich in mineral resources and industrial prospects. Similarly natural routes of migration and trade matter less than of old, as men have learnt to build railways through mountains and over swamps and to use the unbounded highways.

Fifthly, it has been conclusively proved now that the geographical environment alone never explains the rise and fall of civilizations. Similar geographical conditions have produced short-lived and long-lived civilizations. The age-old and the popular assumption has been that civilizations emerge when environment offers unusually easy conditions of life.

Sixthly, the march of civilization has lessened the influence of climatic conditions on human affairs. It is now possible to overcome the natural disadvantages of certain climates. By the use of the developed techniques of science and technology. The Panama Canal Zone has, for instance, been delivered from malaria through the application of science. Even the extremes of heat and of cold grow less deterrent as the arts of warming and cooling dwelling places improve. In this way it is clear that an individual's energy and health are not determined by climate alone as they are the result of many factors of diet, hygienic conditions, living standards, attitudes and values. Bowman is of the opinion that as the social heritage grows immediate geographical factors assume a less determinant role in the interpretation of society.

Seventhly, it is noteworthy that there is hardly any connection between the climate factor and the commission of crime particularly of suicide. The actual temperature level has little to do with the correlation between the two phenomena.

Thus as Maciver puts it, "These facts suggest an explanation of a social character that suicide occurs characteristically where conditions encourage social isolation, where people lack the sense of solidarity created by strong social responsibilities, where they are most apt to be thrown back on their own resources for comfort, companionship and consolation."

It may be said on the basis of these facts that geography by and in itself, never absolutely determines the course of human events. Every advance in the scientific technology increases man's ability to modify his environments. The net result of all this is that in the present day world the impact of physical environments on social phenomena is not as much conclusive and marked as was thought of it in the past times, It may be therefore, said that physical environment without playing a determinant role provides an external set of condition under which the life of man in society proceeds. These conditions can hardly be ignored in the study of social behaviour, the attitudes and interests of men. The physical environment is more of a limiting than of a determining nature.

Different Aspects of Environment

It has been stated above that the term environment is a wide and all pervasive phenomenon. It consists of all surroundings and influences whatsoever, that are present whenever an event occurs. It is any external force which influences us. Environment is thus not a simple but a complex phenomenon and consists of various forms. The chief among these may be discussed in the following order:

(1) *Natural Environment.* The natural environment is composed of those external material objects or phenomena which are out of man's control. Such are, for instance, the winds and rains, the sun and stars, the mountains and the seas. These objects are, in general, out of man's power and can be subjected to no drastic modification at the instance of human energy and skill. Thus with the help of science and technology man has harnessed and modified some of the forces of Nature. but by and large they are still beyond human domination.

(2) *Artificial Environment.* Artificial environment refers to every material thing that is considerably modified by the action of man. Such are the vast stretches of land which he brings under cultivation, the dams and embankments with which he directs rivers and streams to useful purposes, the vast system of industry and machinery created by his ingenuity.

The natural and artificial environments may be taken as two parts of the same physical environment. They are also called the uncontrolable and controllable environments respectively.

(3) ***Psychological Environment.*** The psychological environment consists of those attitudes and dispositions built and organized by previous experiences which affect condition or otherwise influence the individual s behaviour without always determining it. When we reflect upon our own psychological acts we often realize that in making a decision we are inclined towards a certain type of action by our own previous experiences and training. It is finally by an act of self-determination that we make our own choices and decisions and accept full responsibilty for them. These free acts,difficult to understand in a mechanistic theory of the universe are the most genuine manifestation of man's personality. They always work as a centre of man's psychological activity and creativeness capable of self-direction and master in a way-limited but real of his own acts and destiny. The internal forces which influence and condition the self cannot be identical with the self. They are in general opinion its internal or psychological environment intimately connected with, though distinct from the social environment. The reality of this power of self-determination in man, acting upon previous experiences and actual tendencies has acquired such importance in present days that it has given rise to two new philosophical theories. There are the theories of personalism and existentialism and are much in vogue in Europe and America.

(4) *Economic Environment.* The economic environment is a part of both the physical environment and social environment. It refers to those economic goods and material things which surround the individuals and are meant to provide them the comfort and convenience in life. Thus it consists of all the economic apparatus like houses and roads, lands and gardens, domestic animals, machines, stores of manufactured articles and in short all such material facilities that bring men on the high level of civilization. Economic order is, in other words, an order of everyday life which man has built up for the satisfaction of his needs through the application of economic laws. The social significance of the economic order is that it is based upon the principle of division of labour that is on the specialisation of functions of the groups and the areas. This leads to the interdependence of not only of individuals but also of groups and of nations. Economic environment is also important for the fact that it determines the life and character of society. The closeness of their relationship was clearly proved when the Industrial Revolution was followed by remarkable degree of transformation in the existing social order. It is in view of this fact that Karl Marx propounded the theory of Economic Determinism of Social Change.

(5) ***The Social Environment.*** The social environment is constituted by the society of our fellowmen in so far as they affect us. Society has an influence not only on the physical and economic life of man but above all on its mental and moral development. It is the most pervasive of all the environments and very necessary to the life of the individuals. It is so vital a phenomenon that the life of the individuals can be totally and even fmally explained in terms of society. This type of environment also affects our artificial environment to a large degree and but for the co-operation of society, the development of art, science and technology would not have been possible. It has exerted a great influence on our psychological life as well. Thus social environment has become a very important factor in the working of social order. It is identifiable with the whole mass of social culture and is,

therefore, synonymous of the way of life around the people. That is why every important aspect of social life, *i.e.*, sex relationship, ownership, comradeship, the exchange of services, and goods is ordered, supported and controlled by the different elements of social environments. These elements include customs, traditions, laws, modes of thought and forms of knowledge and belief which form man's social inheritance.

There is indeed great sociological significance of this type of environment, but even then for some unknown reason it is found omitted in many of the modern works on sociology.

(6) *The Outer and Inner Environment.* Maciver has mentioned the outer and inner environment of social life. He says, "In his incessant environment. This man-made environment has a twofold character, an outer and inner aspect." These aspects are called the outer and inner environment.

The outer environment consists of the physical modifications of nature, including our houses and cities, our means of transportation and communication, our comforts and conveniences the whole apparatus and machinery of our civilization. It includes what some anthropologists have termed our "material culture". This physico technical structure or a part of it would endure for some time if the society itself perished, as is evidenced by the remaining monuments of past civilization. But this is not true of the other aspect of the social environment.

But, on the other hand, the inner environment is society itself and endures only so long as the society endures. It consists of organizations and regulations the traditions and institutions, repressions and liberations of social life, of what we collectively name the social heritage. For every member of society this system is just as much a part of the environment as are the outer conditions of life, except that his adjustment to it is not of the same inexorable character, not being imposed by natural law.

The total environment, then, *(i)* an outer environment in various ways modified by man, in the centres of modern civilization and *(ii)* a inner or social environment to which man is adjusted through conscious response and habituation. It is not worthy that the distinction between these two aspects of the total environment is essential in the analysis of social reality. But it must also be remembered that the two are always interactive. For man is constantly changing to satisfy his never-satisfied wants, both the outer and inner environment both his physical and social worlds.

However, a close study of various types of environment reveals that those are not isolated phenomena. On the other hand, they act and react upon one another in a large measure. It may also be mentioned that just as environment influences man, even so man influences environment. In this way, it is clear that there is an interplay between the different types of environment and there is also an interplay between man and his environment. Referring to this fact Pascual Gisbert writes, "All these types of environment are so intermixed in their action that at times it is not easy to distinguish one from the other. As to their effects on individuals or society, it is so difficult to find out how far the influence of each of them extends that the attempt to do it is a perpetual challenge to sociology and philosophy".

Effect of Environment on Social Life

While discussing the different types of environment every effort was made to bring out their effect but the matter is so important that something more of it needs to be said here separately. It goes without saying that environment plays a significant part in the determination and regulation of the human affairs as well as social phenomena. To quote in this context the words of Maciver and Page, "Environment is embedded in each and every sphere of life, it does the work of initiating, encouraging and discouraging man's powers, it is the softness of his speech, it makes minute changes in his structure. And not merely this it resides in him, it is etched on his mind and muscles, it functions in his blood....it cannot be separated from life. The environment is the warp and woof which constitutes the living cloth of society."

Furthermore, every change in a living creature involves some change in its relation to environment; and every change in the environment also brings some change in the life and ways of the organic being our environment is our habitation in the completest sense. In its totality, as relative to any group, it is a factor of great complexity. Every difference of environment means a difference in the habits of the people and in their ways of living. On the other hand, the habits and the ways of living of the people, in so far as they differ, create for them a different environment, a different selection of it within it, and a different accommodation to it through a process of constant selection and constant adaptation. In this way the moving equilibrium of life is maintained in a diversified society.

Environment, Life and Human Society

The correspondence of life and environment is amply illustrated in the case of social groups. Just as every region of a country is in some respects different from every other, so also are the inhabitants of each region. The difference among the people of various regions is in some degree relative to the environment in which they respectively dwell. It is a matter of common observation that as people change from country to city, from agriculture to industry, from mountain to plain, from hot to temperate climates they become adjusted to the new conditions undergoing a process of change as their environment changes. It is obvious that a well-to-do group has a different outlook from a poor one, a coloured urban group from a white one, and a professional class from an artisan class. The correspondence between life and environment is visible in the character and organization of both small as well as large groups. Whether it is a large group like community and nation or it is a small group like family, the influence of environment is manifested in every case and under all circumstances. The revelation of the manner in which the environment moulds and is i self modified by the life of the group is one of the chief achievements of the sccial science, It is sure that from the ancient times men have observed certain rough correspondences between broad physical conditions and modes of living. For example, the inhabitants of tropical regions exhibited characteristic differences from those of temperate or of Arctic regions. This is why in their physical features and in the living ways the Indians are typically different from English people. But in the recent times these observations have been gradually refined and elaborated into a sysrematic form. The relationship between physical environment and social phenomena has been particularly brought to the fore-front in the knowledge and thoughts of the people by the findings of modern sociologists. No less progress has occurred in the field of enquiry of social and economic environment as well. Thus it may be said in the end that environment in the totality have proved to be a factor of everlasting importance in the social life of individuals as well as groups.

8

Social Distance in Society

Each human being has affiliations with his family, his caste, his village, his language group, his religious sect, his nationality and so on. This membership of one's group is basic to our existence. Otherwise we are purushapasus. We become human beings with foresight and understanding, because we are socialized by our parents, our relatives, our teachers and others. For a man, his parents, his birth place, however humble or exalted it is, his religion, his language all these are good. He is born into them. They are given to him. They are like the air that he breathes. He takes them for granted. Generally it is believed that the love of the parents, the neighbourhood and other groups is the result of the rewards. Because his family feeds him, looks after him and gives him security, he learns to love them. But according to Allport, "A child who has plenty of fun at a family re-union may be more attached there—after to his own clan because of the experience. But normally he would be attached to his clan anyway, simply because it is an inescapable part of his life. Few of our group memberships seem to be sustained by the pleasure they provide... it takes a major unhappiness, a prolonged and bitter experience, to drive us away from loyalties once formed.

Thus according to Allport we adhere to our own families, clans, castes, linguistic groups, ethnic groups because that is the ground of our existence. We came from there and that is the basis of our existence. Even when a person feels unhappy or miserable in his village or in his caste group he does not abandon it. A few years ago when the writer was at Harvard University, he met a Negro gentleman from a Southern American State. He spoke about the humiliations of the Negro in the South, about the handicaps, how his children were unable to move with the white children with equality. In contrast he said that his life at Harvard was so different. He was able to get a house in the midst of the white people. His children were mixing with the white children in the neighbourhood. This was an astonishing experience for him. He was a teacher. When asked why he does not give up his state and come and live in Harvard, he said that he could never think of giving up his home. This is a typical human situation. The persecuted group never desires to give up the place of its birth. Particularly so in a country like India where it is only in recent years that there is population mobility. Several Muslims who went to Pakistan when that state was formed now feel miserable that they are cut off from the neighbourhood where they were born and brought up. In a similar way the Indian who migrates from one state to another state in pursuit of a career always speaks with regret that he was unable to find a suitable job in the state of his origin. It is true that people migrate; but it is also true that they continue to have a love and a yearning for the place from which they came.

Thus the individual as well as the family tends to have a strong in-group feeling and so he will not forsake the group or migrate from the area. In every city in India we find that new localities are springing up with better roads, better houses and other facilities. Still we find that the old families with their ancestral homes in the middle of the city will not move out though they may be owning houses in the new extensions. The very same process that is responsible for the in-group formation is also responsible for the out-group formation and social distance. In our villages and in our towns we find that the more prosperous and more cultured groups live around the centre and as we go farther and farther from the centre we find that the less privileged groups construct their homes until at last the Harijans live at the outskirts of the village or the town. This was the old pattern. But in the new cities we find that with the rapid increase in population, extensions are formed and the homes of the middle class or of the upper-classes may be beyond the homes of Harijans.

Before proceeding further it would be useful to discuss some of the aspects of the problem of the formation of in-groups. As we have just now seen in a static society like in the village, kinship, status, sense of responsibility etc., are almost rigidly prescribed. But in a mobile society particularly in our cities, which are growing bigger and bigger, there is no such rigidity. Thus the nature and the composition of the in-group varies with the dynamic or the static character of the group as a whole. In a static group the membership of the in-group is more rigidly prescribed and so the individual cannot shift his membership to other groups. On the other hand in a more dynamic society where the group membership is not rigidly prescribed the individual may belong to a number of organizations. But, membership of certain groups is essential; for example, the child is regarded as a member of his parents' groups. So he belongs to the same race, caste, class, religion etc., as his father. When he grows old and particularly if he lives in a more mobile group he may escape from some of the memberships but not all. The boy who belongs to the barber's caste would have to take the barber's occupation if he lives in the village. If he takes up any other occupation he will meet with disapproval from his own caste group in the village as well as from the other caste groups. On the other hand if he goes to a school and obtains general education, and also obtains some professional education he may not take up his caste occupation. He may become a teacher or a doctor. Thus the status of an individual is of two varieties: *(a)* there is the ascribed status, which the individual gets because he is born in a particular family belonging to a particular group. *(b)* There is the achieved status depending upon the education of the individual, his ability, his character and achievements. As the society becomes more and more dynamic, the membership of the in-groups depending on achievement, will become more important and significant than the membership which is based upon his birth and upbringing. It may be said that one of the important aspects of the Indian Constitution is the stress on the achieved status in contrast to the stress on ascribed status, which existed for thousands of years in Indian society.

Thus, in the olden days membership of a small in-group like that of the clan was the most significant. With the development of society, membership on the basis of clan, class, caste, and so on become less significant and membership of the race, the nation or the commonwealth becomes more significant. We have already seen that the ancient Indian concept of the ashrama-dharma has taken note of this essential character in the development of an individual. In the Brahmacharya-ashrama the individual belongs to the group into which he is born and he conducts himself so that his potentialities find an expression. On the basis of his education and training he enters into a profession, marries and sets up a home. He now belongs to a larger number of in-groups depending upon his achievement. But finally in the Sanyasa-ashrama he gives up his affiliation to all the various in-groups and now becomes a member of the in-group which includes the entire humanity. So, for the Sanyasi there is no out-group whatever.

However, though the human beings in different countries and in different cultures are trying to outgrow the narrow limitations of the old formations, still they are unable to develop a world outlook. Ancient Indian thought itself had realised that very few individuals can rise up to the stature where they can look upon the entire humanity as an in-group. It is not possible for a whole group, which identifies itself and differentiates itself on the basis of colour, creed, or culture to develop this universalistic attitude. Consequenty, the fears, loyalties and rivalries have now been shifted from the primitive clan level to the modern ideological level. So whole groups of nations and races join together to form an ideological block which looks upon members of the other ideological block as members of the out-group.

We have to realise the in-group membership is not a permanently fixed feature. There are certain in-group memberships, which are permanent, but certain others are not permanent. For example, one's membership within a family is a permanent membership. Though the individual may migrate into other areas he will still have affiliation with the village in which he was born, with the family in which he was born, with the group in which he was brought up. These affiliations may be so strong that he may come back and settle down in his village after the age of retirement. It is possible that he may be disillusioned. There may be a conflict in him as well as between him and the other members of his family. Anyway this illustrates the strength of the affiliation. But the other in-group memberships may be given up more easily, and he may become a member of a new group depending upon his education, his interests, his wealth, his profession his status etc. In fact in a city there are so many voluntary organizations into which he can enter as a member. Each organization will have its own rules and regulations. If he is qualified he can become a member of these new groups or he may himself start a new group and get like-minded people to become members of this new group. So there is no end to the possibilities of change of membership. But the basic thing is that the in-group feeling, the sense of belonging, is a highly personal matter. One may be a member of an in-group socially but psychologically he may feel that he is not a member of that in-group. For example, a man may belong to a caste group but he may not like to look upon himself as a member of that caste. He may repudiate the entire caste system with all its implications. Similarly a man may belong to a professional group, but he may not like the work that he is doing, and the other colleagues in that profession. His interests may be in other directions. This may lead to a clash between his membership of a particular profession and his personal interests. For example, by profession a man may be an engineer but by interests he may develop affiliations with some artistic or economic or scientific groups. Such an individual will work as an engineer but his whole interest may be with a non-engineering group.

Nor is it necessary that an individual should have direct acquaintance with all the members of the in-group. He may know intimately the members of his family and some others in the in-group. He may know his classmates and his school fellows by personal contacts or merely by name. Other members of the in-group, whether it is of caste or class or nation, he may know only indirectly.

Thus, the feeling of belongingness to an in-group depends upon symbols and upon hearsay. No one can have direct knowledge of all the members of one's group. Still one feels a certain belongingness to one's religion and so there are close affiliations. Consequently when a stranger from another state or another country who belongs to the same religion writes to one, he may be received with great affection though probably that is the first and only occasion that these two members ever meet. Similarly, the child identifies himself with his family merely on the basis of hearsay. He may not have seen his parents much less his grand-parents and great grand-parents. The Hindu, when he offers oblations to his forefathers at the shraddha ceremony, he has to recall the names of his father, grandfather and great-grandfather and offer symbolic food to these pitrus, though he may never have had any personal contact with any of them. In this way the *shraddha* ceremony tries to make an individual feel that he belongs to a family with certain noble traditions. This makes him a member of an in-group with a past and with a future and thus makes him develop a certain attitude of responsibility to preserve it by good behaviour, by bringing up his children properly so that the fair name of his family is perpetuated and enhanced. Similarly, one cherishes one's caste membership on the basis of the symbols and the hearsay. The words he hears provide him just as authentic a ground for his life as do his daily experiences. By symbols one learns family traditions, patriotism and racial pride.

The in-group membership thus, is based upon the sense of belonging, the 'we' feeling. When all the individuals look upon themselves as members of that particular group, there is the development of the sense of belonging. However, we should not mislead ourselves that this in-group feeling is the same in all the members. History has shown, personal experiences show, that any group can be pulled down effectively only by the members of that same group. The bitterest enemy is not a member of the out-group, so much as a member of the in-group. It was the Greeks who gave hemlock to Socrates, it was an American who shot Abraham Lincoln, it was a Hindu who shot Gandhi. So, the mere fact of in-group membership does not imply that there is an undifferentiated uniform feeling of affiliation to every member of the in-group. The greatest hostility is between the people who love each other. No two people can become more bitter enemies than the husband and wife, or the brother and brother or sister, or the parent and child. So the mere fact of in-group membership does not imply that there is freedom from jealousy and rivalry within the group. The thief in a gang is more frightened that a member of the gang may betray him, than that a member of the police organization may discover him. Similarly the labour union, which is on strike is more afraid of sabotage from within, than of being crushed from without.

So we should not mislead ourselves into thinking that all the members of an in-group perceive each other in the same way and have love for each other. Rivalries and jealousies may lead to a good deal of hostility among the members within the group.

Sherif and Sherif have introduced the concept of Reference Group in order to explain differences within the group. They have defined the reference groups as "those groups to which the individual relates himself as a part to which he aspires to relate himself psychologically". Thus, within the in-group there is a reference group, which is warmly accepted by the individual and with which the individual wishes to be included or a reference group may be outside the in-group. For example, many educated Indians look upon the British, the Americans and other Western nations as a reference group. During the days before independence the ideal of a highly educated Indian was to send his child to England so that he could study there and become a small "Englishman". For example, Nehru had his high school as well as college education in England. Similarly, Aurabindo Ghosh had his entire education from the elementary stage to the college level in England. He became thoroughly Indian in his outlook after he returned from England and has written many books expounding Indian culture. Even after independence, there is a great deal of eagerness on the part of highly educated Indians to send their children to the convents conducted by the Westerners or by Indian Christian missionaries. As a matter of fact in many cities many convents have been established in the post-independence years because of this need. Similarly our large programmes of industrialisation are based on the American or the British model. So the out-group itself may serve as a reference group. Similarly a certain section of the in-group may serve as a reference group. In many parts of the country the Hindus of the other castes look upon the Brahmin caste as the reference group; particularly in the South, there is a double attitude towards the Brahmin group among the other castes: they want to imitate them and at the same time they are hostile to them. Similarly in the North, particularly in the cities like Lucknow and Delhi or in Hyderabad the reference group, were the Muslims. The Hindu would look down upon the Muslim but still imitate him in dress, customs and manners. Consequently we cannot agree with Sherif and Sherif that a reference group always implies a warm acceptance, which serves as a model. It need not necessarily lead to warm affiliations. As Freud pointed out long ago there may be an ambivalent attitude towards the reference group, or a complete identification. Many castes in the South have tried to elevate themselves by adding the word Brahmin to their caste name and by putting the sacred thread and reciting the gayathri at the dawn and in the evening. Such groups not only have the Brahmin group as the model but they also have love and admiration for them. There are also non-Brahmin groups, which have the Brahmin group as a model and at the same time are hostile to them. Among the former there may be, what Kurt Lewin has called, "self-hate" because they want to be like the members of the reference group, they may develop a hatred and contempt for their own in-group, their own caste. They may suffer from serious conflict because they would like to be incorporated with the reference group but they are forced to live as members of their own caste group and so they may tend to dislike the members of their caste groups.

Social Distance

As we have noted above prejudice is revealed in social distance. It is the distance at which members of a prejudiced group hold another group and its members. The concept of social distance was first used by the sociologist Park when he was describing the observed fact that the relative intimacy and understanding between the members of the different groups vary. In 1924 Bogardus developed a scale to measure social distance. He asked the respondents to indicate to which of the following steps they would admit members of the various groups in United States:

1. to close kinship by marriage,
2. to my street as neighbours,
3. to my club as personal chums,
4. to employment in my occupation,
5. as visitors only to my country,
6. to citizenship in my country,
7. would exclude from my country.

Thus Bogardus devised a list of statements, which represented the varying degrees of social intimacy or distance. He asked the subjects to indicate the classification to which they would willingly admit members of a given group. It has been found that throughout the United States people belonging to different racial groups have given a remarkably similar picture of social distances for the national ethnic groups, which compose the population of United States. Americans, irrespective of their ethnic group generally asserted that the English and the Canadians were the most acceptable people as citizens, as neighbours, as social equals, and as kinsmen. In other words all the various American groups have the least social distance to the English and the Canadians. On the other hand all of them agree to put at the other extreme the Hindus, the Turks and the Negroes. In between these two groups the Southern and Eastern European nations are placed. Now this general pattern of the social distance appears to be unaffected by factors like space and time and race in the United States. Students from all parts of the United States give substantially the same picture of the group of the various races. It has also been found that this social distance persists through time. Bogardus obtained the first measure in 1926 and the second measure in 1946. The respondents varied in age from 18 to 35 years and varied in profession, though the people from the skilled and the professional people were somewhat over-represented. He found" the population groups to which the great nearness was expressed in 1926... maintained this role for the most part in 1946... likewise the groups which were placed at the greatest distance in 1926 maintained this position with only one major exception, the Chinese in 1946. It is likewise true that the groups which occupied the middle positions in the, scale in 1926 were accorded similar positions in 1946". Hartley and Spoerl also found similar results in 1946 and 1951 respectively. Thus, we find the operation of the concept of reference group with respect to social distance in United States. Individuals irrespective of their race, income, education and occupation have the same pattern of social distance. The only difference is with respect to the position given by the minority ethnic groups to themselves, for example, the Jewish individuals would give the Jews a high place but for all the other groups they would give the same pattern as the reference group, namely, the White Protestant majority. In the same way an Italian or a Greek would place his group very high but would put all the other groups according to the prevailing pattern.

In 1951 the writer used a modification of Bogardus' social distance test among the students in Madras State. The respondents were asked to indicate to what extent they would admit Brahmins, Christians, Harijans, higher caste non-Brahmins, lower caste non-Brahmins, Muslims, Parsis and Sikhs to the following social relationships:

1. to kinship by marriage,
2. to take food in your own dining room,
3. as an intimate personal friend,

4. as a guest in your house,
5. as your neighbour,
6. as an acquaintance.

They were asked to indicate their preferences regarding each group as a whole and not with reference to any particular individual of that group. It was found that 107 subjects out of 591 (18.1%) indicated that they would admit anyone of the groups mentioned to any degree of social intimacy (10.8% women and 21.7% men), 80% of the students indicated varying degrees of social distance and 1.9% did not give any response.

On the basis of the number of times the various groups were admitted to the various social relationships the social distance was calculated. The greater number of "Yes" responses for the, group the nearer is the relationship to it and the smaller the number of "Yes" responses the farther the group. On the basis of the distribution of the preference responses has been drawn up indicating the social distances existing among the groups examined.

We find that each group ranks itself as the first in the order of preference. We further find that in general the higher caste non-Brahmins are given the relatively higher position by all the four groups. As regards the Brahmins we find that the respondents who are not Brahmins have given them a low position so that in the total preference they get only the third position. On the other hand the Christians get the second position in the group as a whole because they are given high preference by the Brahmins non-Brahmins as well as Muslims. All the groups, except the Christians, give a lower place to the Harijans, than to the lower caste non-Brahmin group. We find that Muslims are given the last place by the Brahmins as-well-as the non-Brahmins with the exception of the non-Brahmin women, who have given the fifth place to the Muslims. On the whole we find that the Parsis, the Muslims and the Sikhs are placed at the lower end of the scale. On social distance is given graphically. The method adopted was first preference and the last preference were fixed at the two ends and the intermediate groups were put in between. This helps us to see how the out-groups are spaced far away from the in-group in each case. We find that the next preferred group after the in-group is far away in every case except among the non-Brahmin men who give a relatively close place to the lower caste non-Brahmins.

Hostile Action

So far in our analysis of prejudice we have seen that there are two factors operating. We first took up the cognitive factor and showed how there will be a set of beliefs concerning the group towards which there is prejudice. We found that on the basis of the traditions in the group as well as on the basis of personal experiences certain stereotypes developed and we have seen that the beliefs expressed in these stereotypes are very persistent and that they resist any kind of a change.

Secondly, prejudice manifests itself in an attitude unfavourable to the other group. This is of the essence of social distance. The prejudiced group keeps the other groups at varying distances depending upon the intensity of the unfavourableness of attitude towards that group. Here also, personal experiences generally do not alter the social distance. Further, the group pressure will be so great that it is very difficult for an individual to give up social distance. If he gives up social distance, then he may himself be victimised by the group. This is why for thousands of years the social distance towards the Harijans and the lower caste Hindus have persisted inspite of the attempts particularly by Buddhism, Vaisnavism and Saivism and other such religious groups to discover saints among the Harijans and the lower caste Hindus. Still social distance as well as the stereotype regarding this group have persisted and are active even today in the villages, inspite of the articles of the Constitution, which are against the practice of any kind of discrimination.

We can now proceed to study the third aspect of prejudice, namely, action. Over and above the beliefs, which are enshrined in these stereotypes and the attitudes, which are manifest in social distance, under certain circumstances there will be hostile action towards the prejudiced groups. As we have seen above, neither stereotypes nor social distances necessarily lead to hostile action. Thus prejudice does not inevitably lead to hostility.

Allport has given five steps to describe the range of activities that issue from prejudiced beliefs and attitudes: antilocution, avoidance, discrimination, physical attack and extermination. While one may agree with the last three items it is a matter for doubt whether antilocution, expresses greater hostility or avoidance. The present writer would put avoidance first and antilocution second. The five degrees of action arising out of prejudice may now be briefly described.

1. ***Avoidance.*** Prejudice leads to social distance. Social distance not only creates a certain distance towards the group but when it is extreme it may lead to avoidance. Thus avoidance may be looked upon as the extreme expression of social distance. As Allport himself notes "the bearer of prejudice does not directly inflict harm upon the group he dislikes. He takes the burden of accommodation and withdrawal entirely upon himself". Thus, when we dislike a group we may try to withdraw from the group. This is a mild expression of hostility towards the other group while at the same time it is a manifestation of extreme social distance. However, this is a civilized way of expressing dislike. As we have seen above, the right kind of socialization should enable an individual to have a love towards all the various human groups. But if there is any failure in socialization so that this standard of conduct and feeling is not reached it is possible that the individual may entertain a prejudice against a group.

2. *Antilocution.* When we have prejudice against another group, we tend to speak against that group, particularly when we meet like-minded individuals. It is possible that we may speak against the others even when we meet strangers who have nothing to do with either of the groups. In the opinion of the present writer this is a more hostile action than avoidance because there is injury done to the other group by decrying that group in season and out of season. The Muslim League for instance not only formed itself into a political group against the Indian National Congress but started speaking against the Congress as well as the Hindus who formed the majority in India. We find a similar tendency even in the social relationships of individuals.

3. *Discrimination.* When the hostility is greater there may be discrimination. For example, the members of one group may prevent the members of other groups from employment. In some of the southern states of India we find such discrimination being practised among the various caste groups. So long as our cities and towns were small, and so long as there was not much pressure of the populations, the division of housing area worked satisfactorily. But with the increase in population the discriminatory practices became more pronounced. For example, because there was housing shortage and because the members of the Brahmin caste had houses in the good residential areas of a town or a city the other caste groups realised that there was a practice of discrimination. The present writer asked this question: "To which of the following communities would you let your house if it falls vacant: Brahmins, high caste non-Brahmins, lower caste non-Brahmins, Harijans, Muslims, Christians?" It was found that 43.6% of the Brahmins (188), 54.5% of the non-Brahmins (290) 61.1% of the Muslims (36) and 48.1% of Christians (77) asserted that they would let out the house to anyone. As against this 36.3% of Brahmins, 34.1% of non-Brahmins, 16.7% of Muslims and 6.8% of Christians asserted that they would let out the house only to the members of the same community. This practice of discrimination in the letting out of houses is one of the important reasons for generating caste tensions between the Brahmins and the other caste Hindus in the last few decades. This has lead to discriminations in employment. In many of the southern states of India there has been an attempt to reserve employment opportunities in the Government services to a very large extent among the non-Brahmin castes. This has extended also to the educational facilities. In the same investigation the following question was asked: "Should admission to colleges be on the basis of caste and creed?" "As we have already seen certain sections of the community took to western education right from its inception in the middle of the last century. But other sections for various reasons did not take to education at all or to education in the western style. This led to a great disparity in the educational level of the various sections. After the first world war all sections began to feel the need for education. Since the professional colleges and science colleges were few, while a large number sought admission, it was found that the backward castes could get admission only when there was special reservation for them.

In response to this question it was found that the majority of the group as a whole were against admission to the colleges on the basis of caste and creed. Only 17.3% of the group favoured it. The caste and creed breakdown revealed that 97.4% of the Brahmins, 65.9% of the non-Brahmins, 78% of the Christians and 55.6% of the Muslims were definitely against caste and creed being the basis of admission to the college. On the other hand 1.6% of the Brahmins, 24.1 % of the non-Brahmins, 20.8% of the Christians and 36.1% of the Muslims were in favour of caste and creed being the basis for admissions. The rest of the groups either favoured that caste and creed should be the basis for some time or did not give any response at all.

4. ***Physical Attack.*** There may be violence against the members of another group or against their property when there is heightened emotion. For example, during the 1930s and 1940s constantly there was violence and destruction of life and property because of the physical attacks in the communal conflicts. Similarly we find that in the 1940s and 1950s student-groups have been indulging in violent acts against the University property or the public property.

5. ***Extermination.*** This is the most extreme expression of hostility leading to a total extermination of the group as a whole. The Germans under Hitler tried to exterminate the Jews in Germany. Similarly during 1947-48 before and after partition in India the Hindus wanted to exterminate the Muslims and the Muslims wanted to exterminate the Hindus. This is the most violent expression of hostility.

The point that we have to bear in mind is that prejudice against a group or against an individual may lead logically from avoidance and antilocution to physical attack and finally to extermination. This is why indulging in attack against the group has to be restrained. If it is not restrained the continuous attack against a group will lead ultimately to physical action against the group and finally to extermination. So, the only way of ensuring against violence is to prevent antilocution and antilocution can be prevented only when there is positive resistance to hatred in the minds of individuals. It is difficult to practise love for other people and the humanity as a whole, but it is not so difficult to train ourselves not to hate other individuals and groups. If we do not hate we will not speak against them and if we do not speak against them we will not physically attack them.

Methods of Reducing Prejudice

Prejudice, thus, arises out of the formation of unfavourable attitudes. So the problem of controlling prejudice resolves itself into the problem of the change of attitudes. In a previous chapter we have discussed this problem about the change of attitudes. We may close this chapter by making a brief reference to some of the important features regarding this problem. In India prejudices towards castes, linguistic groups, and occupational groups, have been of very long standing. There have been attempts right from the days of Upanishads and Buddha to control prejudice in the social relationships. Several methods were adopted and are being adopted in order to control prejudice. We may briefly refer to some of these in this section and determine the value of these methods that have been employed.

It must be remembered that prejudices are formed over a long period of time in the life of an individual as well as in the life of a group. Prejudices are traditional and they are socially transmitted. Consequently the prejudiced attitudes are a part of socialization of the individual. This is the reason why a prejudiced individual hardly looks upon himself as prejudiced. He looks upon his behaviour as a normal "natural" behaviour. It must also be realised that prejudices are internalised social norms and so they have an anchorage in the ego system. This is the reason why it is very difficult for an individual to give up his prejudices. Because of this long process in the formation of the prejudice in the group as a whole as well as in the individual we find that any piecemeal attempt to control prejudice cannot have much of a success.

It is often asserted that if there are more contacts between the members of two prejudiced groups familiarity will bring about friendliness and appreciation of each others' values. But this is only superficially true. Increase in the number of contacts may reinforce mutual appreciation or mutual hostility. So it does not depend merely on the frequency of contacts. It depends upon the conditions under which the contacts are established. Even when the conditions are very favourable it is possible that the prejudiced individual may look upon the other individual as an exception and thus he may not permit any change in his attitude towards the group as a whole. Often times we hear remarks indicating that a particular person is a very good person and is not typical of the group at all.

In India attempts have been made to reduce prejudice by increasing the opportunities for education and employment for the socially handicapped groups. These measures have brought in their trail social injustice. When one social injustice is set right it is possible that another social injustice might be perpetrated. In the southern states of India while the non-Brahmins are getting facilities in admission to the colleges, as well as in recruitment to the services, this is operating against the Brahmin community. Because the children of various caste groups study together there is a greater tolerance today. But this should not mislead us into thinking that all prejudices are eliminated. While the operation of prejudice in one area may be eliminated it is possible that prejudice may continue to operate in other areas. For example, the child of a higher caste may mix freely with the children of lower castes in the school, in the restaurant and in other places. But when he goes home he may behave in a prejudiced way. This is because he is now accepting two sets of social norms. He behaves in school or college in a liberal way because that is the social norm at the campus. But when he goes home he may act in a prejudiced way because that is in conformity with social norm at home. We may refer to another aspect of the problem. In the last two or three decades in the southern states many castes and creeds started their own free hostels because the members of the lower castes realised the value of education in uplifting the caste. They readily came forth with donations, so that facilities are offered to the children of that caste to get, themselves educated. But this has brought about a greater prejudice to the out-groups. Particularly in the recent years the state itself has supported starting of a number of hostels for the Harijans, While the Harijan youth are getting facilities to get themselves educated, they are prevented from mixing freely with the youth of the other communities. Consequently attempts are now being made to see that there are no communal hostels, or at any rate no communal hostels are started by the state funds. The regulations are made so that about 10-20 per cent of the hostel admissions are reserved for the general community irrespective of caste and creed.

One of the important methods adopted to establish and perpetuate social distance is to have segregated residential areas. Attempts are now being made to see that there are no segregated residential areas. While living together in one residential area may lead to a reduction of prejudice, it must be realised that it may also lead to an increase in prejudice.

Attempts have also been made to eliminate prejudices by means of social legislation. In the Constitution itself it was laid down that in India no individual should be made to suffer on the basis of caste or sex. Mere social legislation itself will not succeed in reducing or eliminating prejudices. It must be realised that legislation has a very limited success to start with. Legislation can become socially effective only when it becomes a part of the social norm. The legal norm, which is not a social norm will be an utter failure. But it must be realised that a piece of legislation like the removal of the disability of Harijans has a long history behind it. Apart from what people like Buddha, Ramanuja, Basaveswara and other social leaders had done in this country, the work of Gandhi prepared the way for the social legislation.

Consequently we find that the only way of controlling prejudice is by bringing about changes in the social norms themselves. Prejudices against the Harijans will go only when such prejudiced behaviour is socially condemned. In other words, there should be a difference in social norm. What was the social norm should now become something against the social norm. When a Harijan becomes an administrative officer his social prestige automatically goes up. He is a highly educated man. He is a man with an influential and respected appointment. He is now a man with a big income. All this will make him a person with high social prestige. On the other hand when people become conscious of his caste, they may have a double attitude towards this individual. The Harijan Administrative Officer should now understand the conflicts in the minds of the officials as well as the citizens. So he should not be sensitive to some of these expressions and manifestations of the conflict in the minds of the others. By ignoring them and being insensitive to them he will help the people to have a greater admiration for him. If, on the other hand, he becomes very sensitive he may find that he gets into more trouble and his life may become miserable. As Sherif puts it, "Lasting and consistent changes in attitudes toward out-groups can be expected (1) when individuals become psychologically related to a new reference group with differing norms toward out-groups or (2) when the norms established in the individual's present reference group are changed". This is where Gandhi had a very great insight into social behaviour and thus was able to succeed in bringing about a reform, which resisted for thousands of years. The Congress Party, which was nationalist became the reference group for the country as a whole. Leaders coming from various castes with high prestige because of their wealth and education and because of their renunciation and sacrifice shed all their prejudices against Harijans and treated the Harijans as brothers and respected members of the community. Identification with this reference group was able to transform the behaviour of the other groups, and this is one of the imporportant reasons why we find that in the cities and towns of India untouchability, and other discriminatory practices against the Harijans are practically dead. It must, however, be realised that the members of the higher castes particularly the Brahmins, are now very liberal in their outlook towards the Harijans.

●●●

9

Rural and Urban Community in Society

Introduction

Every person is born not only into a family but also into a community. At first he is not made aware of the Community. But in course of time he becomes fully conscious of it. To began with he develops contacts with neighbourhood but afterwards one by one he comes to be involved in intimate relation with other forms of community like the village, city, the region, the nation and at last the world at large. Thus as Bogardus writes, "His ideas of the Community begin with the neighbourhood, but untimately his thinking about community reaches out to include sections of the world group." As a matter of fact, a Community is a social group with some degree of "we-feeling" and living in a given area. To develop real community of spirit it is necessary for all members of a community to participate and to acquire of a sense of belonging. A community may be limited to a specific area or it may extend to all who commune together in the fellowship of similar attitudes and values.

The most important and the most general of the human communities are the rural and urban Communities. But there is a sharp difference between the city and village life though with the expansion of urban influence on this village, this difference is becoming more and more a matter of degree.

However, in spite of the recent trends of urbanisation the villages still retain many of their traditional features and present a sharp contrast with the urban life. To put it in the words of Maciver and Page, "One of the broadest and most revealing of all social contracts is exhibited by the differences of urban and rural life. This contract is one of social environment. It is also one that permits us to distinguish between two broad types of Community organization. The city is an environment created by society, in which for the purposes of community living many aspects of the natural environments are modified or entirely eliminated. Under rural conditions social attitude and social institutions present characteristic differences from those developed within a city." In short, the main points difference between the two types of communities can be discussed in the following manner.

1. Rural Community is more Custom-ridden than the Urban Community. The first difference between the two is that rural community is more tradititional and custom-loving than the urban community. In the rural community the force of traditional mores and the bonds of family solidarity are more dominant than in the urban community. The sense of group responsibility which tend to be more and more dissolved in the growth of the city prevails in village life. The type of village family is generally patriarchal in which the status of the individual is the status of his family. In rural community the individual holds a subordinate place to the family. All the questions of the individual *i.e.*, his marriage, religion, recreation, occupation etc. are determined by family traditions. Any deviation from the· established family traditions especially in sex matters, is regarded an offence against family unity and hardly tolerated the life of all men and women is merged in family life. Thus family dominates individual's life in village community. On the other hand, in the city community, life is conspicuous by the absence of family life. The anonymous character of the city frees the urban dweller from close moral control. Social control becomes the activity of specialized agencies. Family control is lessened on the individuals. Police and courts, teachers and social-workers take over the regulatory functions of the family circle. If an individual violates the family customs, he is not socially boycotted by the urban community while in the rural community he has to abide by family discipline and tradition. It may also be noted that the urban life is more regulated by the State than is the case with rural life. Thus in a city as opposed to the village the mores and folkways least counted on to handle the social situations.

2. Unlike Urban Community, the Village Community is Marked by Primary Contacts. Secondly, a great distinction prevails between the two social systems regarding the nature of contacts. A village community is marked by immediate contacts between its members. It is quite common to find persons in a village Community helping one another, and sharing the joys and sorrows of one another. In the village every body is, known to every body and there are personal contacts among all the rural inhabitants of a particular area. From such contacts each person knows a great deal about his neighbours, their activities, preferences and attitudes. Written contacts are less important than a word of honour. Crime in village community is rare and there prevails an atmosphere of comparative peace and social harmony. The rural life is characterised by corporate feelings and things are, done by mutual understanding. In city life, on the other hand, nearness counts much less. The inhabitants of a city hardly know each other. Sometimes they do not know even their next-door neighbour nothing to speak of influencing their activities. In big cities like Mumbai, Delhi and Kolkata people living in the lower storey do not know the people living in the third or fourth storey of the same building. There prevails atmosphere of indifference and callousness in a city. Thus it is obvious that while rural life is marked by primary contacts, the urban life is characterised by secondary contacts.

3. As Against City Life the Village Life is Marked by Simplicity and Uniformity. Thirdly, the two communities are not identical with regard to the ways of life of their respective inhabitants. Life in a village community is simple and uniform. There are few ambitious men and fewer excitements. The villagers lead a uniform life tilling land and rearing animals. Their standard of living is lower than that of the town people because the means of earning money are limited. They view land as the most substantial of all heritages. The poor turning rich overnight or rich being reduced to beggary in one day are cases unknown in the village. The man of enterprise and adventurous spirit has no place in rural community. The city dweller becomes indifferent to extremes of all kinds. Indeed the distinction between public and private, between what is shown and what is concealed is much sharper in the city it is the public behaviour that the city regulates and the private behaviour that it ignores.

4. City Life is More Specialized than Village Life. Another contrast between city and community is concerning the modes of production. In the village as a rule, only a predominant type of occupation *i.e.* agriculture prevails. Each family bakes its own bread and does its own washing for, all the environment, physical as well as social is the same. The city on the other hand is the place for different kinds of people. All the sections of society *i.e.* the semi-skilled workers, the skilled artisans, the paper experts, the technicians, the artists, the bankers, the teachers, the social reformers and many others alike live in every city. It is heterogeneous group of people engaged in various pursuits. "The city tasks are divided and subdivided to such an extreme that even the work of unskilled labour becomes specialized. The trend in the urban life is clearly in the direction of a larger percentage of specialized work leading to a multiplicity of organizations, economic and social. The residents of a city become affiliated with a number of organizations catering to their needs. Thus it is obvious that the city life is specialized in nature while the rural life is of general character.

5. Condition of Women in Cities Better than that in the Villages. One more contrast between the two communities pertains to the conditions of woman. It is a matter a common observance that the general conditions of the woman in cities is decidedly better than that in the villages.

6. Social Mobility in Urban Community is Greater than in the Rural Community. Social mobility is an essential characteristic of urban life while rural life is not marked by this trait to such an extent. This is to say that there is open society in urban areas but in the rural areas the society is closed one. The city requires and promotes great social mobility. It lays emphasis on achievement rather than the ascription of States. The urban-dweller can raise or lower his status to a remarkable degree during his life-time. The caste element in social stratifiction is minimized. Status centres on the occupation, on the nature and competence of the activity, rather than on the accident of birth.

Specialization in the city has also influenced the life of woman. According to the recent census report the number of woman in every big city has increased considerably. The fact is that the city offers more and more opportunity for woman to advance in life. But on the other hand, no such facilities can be available to them in the villages. The woman in the city areas enjoy an air of independence while in the village they are still slaves to men. There they cannot find any independent Job to do and thereby to earn their own living. Therefore for their financial needs they have to depend on men and to keep busy in doing of house-hold affairs. But such is not the case in the cities where the woman can find a good number of profitable things to do and to get freedom from burdensome duties of house-hold. If the social life had remained predominantly a village life, woman would have been the drudges in the household. Industrialization and specialization have brought the woman to workshop and factory. They have entered into the wider life, which has altered their outlook and habits and liberated them from the exclusiveness of domdsticity. To quote Maciver, "The individualization of woman has been fostered by urban life. And the resulting freer reciprocity of relationship between men and women, as individuals is exercising and will doubtless continue to exercise since the process is still advancing a significant influence on the whole structure of society."

7. Presence of the Contrast of Qualities. The city community evokes in man the qualities, which stand in sharp contrast, with these demanded by rural community. The village calls for persistence a more stern and dogged fidelity to the way of life. The villagers in constant contact with nature become a devotee of nature. Since the forces of Nature are beyond his control and reckoning, they becomes superstitious and religious. On the other hand, the city requires alertness and quicker responses to changing situation. The city-dweller is more tolerant in the matter of religious belief, tastes and opinions. The city is ruled by impersonality of law and the caprice of fashion. In a rural community the rural moral codes are fixed and strict. Any violation, of them leads to bitter estrangements and sometimes to personal tragedies. In a rural community there is much of mutual aid while in the cities people are self-centered and hardly care for others. There is an atmosphere of kindliness and brotherhood in the rural areas. But in an urban community there is no strong "we-fealing" and the people do not like to identify themselves to the area as a whole. Thus the people of urban areas are individualistic in their outlook whereas the people of rural areas are collectivist in their attitude.

It is clear from the above facts that there exist several points of difference between rural community and urban community. Both the social systems have some distinctive features, which forms the basis for their mutual contrast. However, in the present time under the force of urbanization and industralization these differences are shortening and there is taking place much of assimilation between the two communities. They have started acquiring the good points of each other and the result is that it is very difficult to draw a marked dividing line between the rural and urban communities. Thus in the end it may be said that there do exist points of difference between rural and urban life with a trend towards urbanization and the liquidation of traditional rural system.

Village Community in India

India is rightly called the land of villages. The bulk of her population lives in villages and they play a vital role in the socio-economic life of this country. There is no other country in the world else than India having so much rural leanings and maintaining the traditional character of social life. According to recent census about 78% of the people in India inhabit in the villages. The number of big cities is very small and mostly the villages are of small size inhabited by a few 100 persons. The Indian villages are of typical character having very little of urban touch. The people in general in the rural areas do agriculture or such other professions having link with agriculture. They observe their old customs, Keep faith in religion and maintain the highest degree of social life. The Indian villages are unlike the western villages in many ways. It means that the Indian villages have their own distinctive features, which are not found elsewhere and the most important of these can be mentioned here in the following way.

1. ***Isolaton and Self-sufficiency.*** The Indian villages have been known for their isolation and self-sufficiency. Almost till the middle of the 19th century, the villages in India were more or less self-contained, isolated and self-sufficient units.

The inhabitants of the village had very little to do with the people outside. All of their essential needs were satisfied in the village itself. Agriculture was the main stay of rural population. People either tilled the land or did such professions as were related to agriculture. All the articles of general use could be produced in the village itself. Each village had a number of shops, some artisans and a good many menial workers who satisfied all the household and professional requirements of the villagers. They could easily do without outside help. Thus in short, it was more of a society within itself. However, changing political and economic conditions are putting an end of to the isolation and self-sufficiency of the Indian villages. The rapid development of the means of transport and communication has broken the barriers between the village and city. The former is now socially and even economically connected with the neighbouring city or town. Political parties have made villages the centre of their activities as much as the cities.

2. *Conservatism.* One more significant fact about the Indian villages is that they bear a strong mark of conservatism. The inhabitants of the village are strongly attached to old customs and traditions. Their outlook is primarily conservative and they accept changes with extreme reluctance. They love old ways and are less eager to follow the advice of zealous social reformers regarding their marriage and other customs. Referring to this feature of Indian villages Sir Charles Metcalfe is said to have remarked thus, "They seem to last where nothing else lasts. Dynasties tumble down; revolution succeeds revolution. Hindu, Pathan Moghul, Marathe, Sikh, Christians all the masters change in turn, but the village communities remain the same".

3. *Peace and Simplicity.* Another important feature of an Indian village is the atmosphere of simplicity calmness and peace prevailing therein. In the village there is no noise and little sophistication. The humdrum activities of modern civilization are rarely seen there. Though occasionally a car or a bus rolling along the rural kutchas and pucca roads may be seen there but on the whole, life in the village moves with traditional quietness and peace. The villagers lead a simple life eat frugally, dress simply and live in muddy-walled houses completely lacking in the trappings of modern civilisation. But here also the old order is yielding place to a new one. The muddy walled-houses are giving place to well-designed buildings. Fashion is making its in-roads in the life of young men and women of the village. However, this change is gradual and slow.

4. ***Strong-bold of Caste System.*** Rural life in India is composed, by caste grouping. Caste largely determines function, status and occupation as well as opportunities and handicaps for an individual. There is a system of social distance and pattern of superior and inferior relationship. All administrative functions are generally divided according to castes. Thus, in rural areas social life is determined by caste. It also determines ideals, pattern of life and role of a leader. In this sense rural life is traditional, regulated by its laws of social conduct.

5. ***Religious Domination.*** In comparison to urban life, there is greater predisposition of religion in rural life. This is .the case almost in all the countries, but India leads them all in this matter. The Indian villages are the strong-hold of religious activities. Here religious outlook dominates intellectual, emotional and practical life of the people. Even forms of art and ethical norms etc. represent the mentality of rural life. The urban people are growing secular in outlook but in the villages religion is still a motivating force. The rural folk leads, its life both personal and social in accordance with the dictates of religion of the respective communities. It is on account of the influence of religion that the rural people are still tradition-loving, conservative and narrow minded in their outlook. It is right that like other features this mark of

Indian village life is also losing ground under the force of modern influences. But on the whole the change in the sphere is comparatively slow and less radical.

6. ***Poverty and Illiteracy.*** A very glaring and depressing feature of Indian villages is the poverty and illiteracy of the village people. They are generally poor with low income. They have to take simple food and wear coarse clothes. The pressure on land is high resulting in fragmentation of holdings and poor productivity. Besides poverty the village people are steeped in ignorance and illiteracy. The opportunities for education are meagre in the villages. The village school is generally in a poor condition and lacks facilities for education. Due to illiteracy the villagers cannot improve the agriculture or supplement their income by other means. Poverty is thus the cause and effect of illiteracy and backwardness of the villagers. However recently the need has been realised for rural reconstruction. The Governments, both of the Centre and the States have launched schemes for liquidating illiteracy and removing poverty of the people living in the villages. Agricultural production is becoming more and more mechanized and agricultural products are fetching high prices. The net result of all these modern changes is that the Indian villages have made good deal of improvement in the financial field.

7. ***Local Self-Government.*** The villages in the ancient India enjoyed a considerable measure of autonomy or self-government. The villagers managed their own affairs through the 'traditional institution of Panchayat. The Central Govt. had neither the will nor the means for interfering with the self-govt. of villages. But with the advent of Britishers in India and their introduction of a highly centralised system of administration the importance of Panchayats began to decline. Their judicial powers were taken over by the British courts and the officers were appointed to look after the administrative affairs of the villages. This change produced unpleasant results.

However, with the attainment of freedom now efforts are being made to revive the old Panyhayat system and make Panchayats play a dominant part in the work of national reconstruction.

8. Control of Primary Institution. In rural India, the control of primary institutions is greater than secondary institutions. Among these institutions family and caste council are most important. Family serves the purpose of a school and recreation centre. Besides, it welde the rural life into a homogeneous and egoistic unit and strengthens solidarity and co-operation. Thus there is greater discipline and interdependence in village life.

Types of Community Organization

Human communities can be classified on the basis of many different criteria. A large number of classifications of them have actually been made and they have been found useful for different purposes. A very broad and familiar classification is based on the size and density of the population. In terms of this fact we classify communities as neighbourhood, village, city, region and world community. In this connection Davis writes, "In classifying communities one may use four inter-related criteria. They are: (1) the size of population (2) the extent, wealth, and populousness of the hinterland (3) the specialized functions of the community and (4) the kind of organization the community has. These criteria enable one to distinguish between various kinds of primitive communities, between primitive and civilized and between rural and urban communities. Here, we are concerned mainly with rural and urban communities.

Features of Village Community

It is believed at all hands that the,'village is' the oldest permanent community of man. According to Kropotkin, "We do not know one single human race or one single nation which has not had its period of village communities." To quote Bogardus, "Human society has been cradled in the rural group." The villages have been in existence ever since human beings started leading a settled life. But from time to time there had occurred a change in their basic tenets. For example, there were two peculiar features of village community in the primitive societies. These were the part played by kinship and its collectivist bus is. The chief marks of medieval village communities were feudalism and the commonness of general life of the rural folk. But in the modern rime the village community has undergone remarkable changes. Industrialization and urbanization are the main forces which have tended to shape the rural life. The rural society cannot be free from the influences of modern industrial and urban society. There has been a powerful shift of population from rural to urban areas. But all the same a large mass of population still lives in the villages. For instance, in India 78% of the entire population is even these days living in villages. This may also be true of many of other countries. Thus Bogardus is right in maintaining that human society began in rural groups, developed to the level of civilization in rural groups and in cities supported by a rural hinterland. Human society has been cradled in rural group.

It is right that under the force of current influences rural community is fast changing but still it has tended to retain some of its traditional features. In them there might have occurred here and there some changes but not to the extent of their vanishing point. Some of these distinctive features may be mentioned here:

1. ***Semi-Isolation of the Rural Family.*** The most obvious feature of the rural community is the relative isolation of the country life. It is not an isolation of the individual, but usually of the homestead or groups of homesteads a to a great extent, it is the semi-isolation of the family. It so happens in the rural communities that family supplies the greater part of the

economic and social needs of its members. The necessities of common toil and reciprocal services strongly corroborate the ties of family relationship. To quote Maciver and Page, "It is often observed that in sparsely settled areas famities are frequently at strife with one another, a consequence of the intense and exclusive cohesion in the rural family. Its attitudes and its morals are apt to be predominantly familiar. It tends to grow-centered and to a large extent psychologically self-sufficient."

2. *Narrow Mindedness.* It is often seen that the members of rural community suffer from narrow-mindedness. They are rigid in their outlook and comparatively uncompromising to the outside influences. The rural folks are more attached to their family customs and ways. They have rarer contacts with the outside community and this fact tends to sharpen in the mind of the country-dwellers the contrast between their ways and those of others and to confirm them in their own followings and beliefs. They have neither the opportunity to cultivate an altitude of broad-mindedness nor the temptation to become busy seekers after new things. Customs rule over them and for fashion they have little use. Their ways are fixed for them and their vicissitudes are mainly those associated with the natural sequence of the seasons and with the stages of their own life span. Despite the recent changes in rural life the rural population, in average, still continues to be more convention-ridden than the urban population.

3. *Predominance of Primary Relationships.* Another characteristic of rural life is the predominance of primary relationships. If the contacts of the semi-isolation country-dweller with the outsider are infrequent and impersonal, those with the members of his immediate household and rural neighbourhood reveal the intimacy and non-categoric characteristics of primary relationships. His social existence consists predominantly of face-to-face situations, and his associates are whole persons with whom he directly co-operates or directly conflicts. His limited rural community, the details of which and the member of which he knows so well. is often itself a primary group.

4. *Simplicity and Frugality of Living.* Simplicity and frugality of living is another characteristic feature of rural life. It is the direct result of the rural areas being pre-dominantly agricultural units. "In this connection Maciver and Page write, "The rewards of the farmer's toil are rarely bountiful, especially of the small-scale farmer. If the rewards are somewhat speculative, it is usually between the limits of penury and a modest livelihood. In bad years he falls into debt; in good years he does little more than recover. If he is a proprietor he is still a manual worker than to that of property owners". "The rural folk is tempted to simple and frugal living partly because of its low income and partly because of its keeping over busy in work. Thus these are in short, the elementary factors that distinguish, in general, rural from urban life. Together they form a community environment, which profoundly influences the social responses of the country population. As to the fact whether or not Indian village is a community the issue is thoroughly discussed in the following question.

5. *Pre-dominance of Agriculture.* Agriculture is the main-occupation of the villagers and it has more or less become a distinctive feature of rural life. The rural people, in general, do agriculture or such other professions, which centre round agriculture. Therefore, agriculture has become a backbone of rural economy. To quote Maciver, "The principle occupation of the country man may be hunting or fishing, as in many primitive communities. But pre-eminently it is farming involving the raising of crops and of stock." This pre-dominant occupation of agriculture has a number of attributes, which impress themselves on the mentality of the countrymen and are reflected in his social life. They often become hard working, God-fearing, lovers of Nature, attached with land and simple in their ways. It is right that in the present time other types of occupations like trade and industry are finding way into rural areas, but even then agriculture remains a primary occupation.

Main Features of Urban Community

The urban community is just the opposite of rural community. Generally by an urban area we mean an area with a high density of population. It must be large in area and thick in population. Both the elements in their absoute character are the pre-requisites of a city. Normally both in the matter of population and area a city, is much bigger than a village. Even in their social sides they are markedly different from each other.

1. ***Namelessness.*** The urban groups have a reputation for namelessness. By virtue of its size and population, the city cannot be a primary group. The inhabitants of a city do not come into primary contact with each other. They meet and speak without knowing each other's name. Although superficial manners of politeness and mutual convenience evolve in the city, they are mechanical. The city dweller treats the strangers, he meets, as animated machines rather than as a human being. A person may live for several years in a city and may not know the names of fraction of the people who live in the same city area.

2. ***Class Extremes.*** Class extremes characterize urban community. In a city are found the richest as well as the poorest people. Similarly there live in an urban area the people rolling in luxury and living in grand mansion as well as the people living on pavements and hardly getting two meals a day. The best form of ethical behaviour and the worst racketeering are both to be found in the citizens. Superior creativeness and chronic unemployment are alike urban features. Thus it is obvious that the city is the home of opposites.

3. ***Homelessness.*** Homelessness is another distributing feature of city community. The house problem in a big city is very acute. Many low class people pass their nights on pavements. The middle class people have but insufficient accommodation, a room or two and that also on the sixth or seventh floor. The child does not get any play space. The city environment puts a premium on childlessness.

4. ***Energy and Speed.*** Energy and speed are the final traits of a city. People ambition work at a tremendous speed day and night, which stimulate others also to work similarly. Stimulation interest, and imulation are endless. People indulge in too many activities and inconceivable efforts which ultimately eat their nerves and kill their energies. Cities may be called consumers of population. The consumers of population in the sense also that due to congestion insanitariness and unhealthiness they adversely affect the health of the inhabitants. It may be of interest to note that death-rate in rural area is lower despite the fact that rural areas spend very little money on public health while the cities spend much and in cities the facilities for preserving health, such as hospitals and medical specialists, are many and excellent. Sickness rate is higher in cities. There are more cases of insanity in urban community than in the rural one. Thus it is on the basis of these features that a sharp contrast is said to be existing between the rural and urban communities. This contrast is one of social environment and also of general life. It is by virtue of these features that even in the present dynamic age the two sets of communities are able to maintain their entity.

5. ***Social Heterogeneity.*** The city is more heterogeneous than the village. It has been the melting pot of races, peoples, and cultures and is a most favourable breeding ground of new biological and cultural hybrids. It has not only tolerated but rewarded individual differences. It has brought together people from the ends of the earth because they are different

and thus useful to one another, rather than because they are homogeneous and like ·minded. The personal traits, the occupations, the cultural life and the ideas of the members of the urban community vary widely than those of the rural inhabitants.

These are, in short, the main features of Indian rural life. But in the modern time a good deal of changes are taking place in the Indian villages. They are being equipped with the means of modern life. Rural reconstruction is one of the pious goals of the Government. of India and it is making all sorts of possible efforts to achieve this goal. The villages are being linked to the cities by the roads. Schools and hospitals are being established in the rural areas to provide the rural population, educational and health facilities. In place of muddy-houses good buildings are being built in the villages. There has occurred a great change in the manners, ways and thinking of the people and the ties of caste-system, conservationism and religious bigotry are fast losing ground among them. From economic point of view also they are much better than before. Thus the Indian rural life is presenting a new look and the forces of urbanization and industrialization have helped to bring about this transformation.

●●●

10

Group Structure Psychology

Groups are products of interaction. This is generally overlooked when we are dealing with groups, which are already well established like the family, the church, the state and the political party and so on. But, when we are studying informal groups we will see the processes underlying the formation of groups. This will help us not only to understand the properties of the group but also to understand the way in which the individuals find their place as members of the group. We can see these processes operating when a number of individuals are faced with a problem for which they do not have any ready-made solutions or established ways of behaviour. It is under such circumstances that we can see the way in which a group is formed. In the recent years a number of studies have been made on informal groups of adolescents in street corners. Further experimental studies have also been made in order to find out how a number of people who were brought together form themselves into a group. Thus we must distinguish between the informal groups and the formal groups.

Formal and Informal Groups

We are members of a number of formal groups. We are citizens of our country with its own Constitution. We belong to a particular State with its own governmental organization. We also belong to our family, which has its links with several generations, which could be identified and our family is a unit of our caste and creed. We may also be members of our college organisations. Probably we may be members of a number of other social service organizations or cultural organizations. Now all these organizations have been existing for some years or even centuries. Each group has got its own norms and as members of those organizations we have a particular status with other individuals having a similar or other kind of status. Now we have seen how each person is socialized as a member of each one of these groups and how we accept the beliefs of the groups to which we belong and conform ourselves to the opinions of the particular group. We have also seen how we develop attitudes, which are in consonance with the other members of the group to which we belong. Thus, in these formal groups most of the norms are pre-ordained. These norms are defined independently of the person who occupies the position.

On the other hand we are also members of a number of informal organizations. We develop friendships and the friends as a group meet in a very informal manner. For example, when the college association arranges a tea party we meet as members of a formal group but within this formal group we have our own informal group. We sit with our close friends at the tea table. If, by force of circumstances we are unable to sit with our friends, and if we have got to sit at another table, we feel a little uncomfortable. The other members also may feel uncomfortable. Still all of us are members of one formal group, of a particular association. Thus, there is a close relationship between the informal groups and the formal groups. A formal group has a number of informal groups within it. Similarly every informal group is linked with some formal group. In the formal group our roles are specified. We have to behave according to the expectations of the group. On the other hand, in the informal groups we can develop our own roles congenial to each person. For example, at a tea party the members around each table will behave in a very free way indulging in a number of jokes and. laughter. Probably the time has come for the meeting to start. The President of the organisation may make a sound and call the meeting to order. Suddenly all the members will become quiet. Their attention is directed towards the main table at which the President of the organization is sitting and now the whole group becomes formal and starts its business. We have relatively more freedom as members of the informal group whereas we are constrained to behave in a particular form as members of the formal group.

Sociologists have made a number of studies about the small informal groups. Elton Mayo of the Harvard Business Group studied the behaviour of small groups in industry. The sociologist Moreno studied role relations in small groups. Kurt Lewin and his associates Sherif and Bales and others have conducted experiments on small groups. We have now considerable literature about the behaviour of individuals in informal groups.

As we have seen above formal groups may have long history involving several generations. Informal groups are more transitory. But, it must be realised, that several large organizations have had their beginnings in informal groups. A number of worldwide organizations like the Masonic Club or Rotary Club or Lions Club, all started as informal groups. With time and because of the purposes, which these informal groups were fulfilling they became formal groups. The Mysore State Adult Education Council, which is a vast organization today, started as an informal group with a few enthusiastic students and teachers in the Mysore University Union in the 1930s. Secondly, the interaction in these small groups is very intimate. There is face-to-face relationship and communication. On the other hand in the more formal groups the communication may be only through mass media. It may be a statewide or countrywide or worldwide organization. So we can learn about what the other people are doing only through mass media like the newspaper or special newsletters and so on. A vast machinery has to be moved in order to bring about even a slight modification. For example, any change in the law of the state would involve probably about a year's work or more. On the other hand in the small groups there is considerable amount of flexibility. The state, for example, may be faced with a critical situation and so it has armed itself with the power of passing an ordinance which may be later on made into an act after the Legislature considers it. We have already seen how in the formal groups there are compelling structural properties. Each individual will have his own status and role clearly defined. In the informal group the status and roles are in formation.

We find informal groups starting automatically among the children of the nursery school, among the children in the village streets. There are small friendship groups and play groups. These groups may develop structural properties with time. Several of the football teams started as small informal groups and have now developed themselves into large organizations. In the schools and colleges we find a number of informal groups, cliques, and friendships.

We may now describe briefly the importance of the study of the small informal groups, the interaction and the reciprocal relationships of the individuals in the small groups. We can observe them and specify the problems as well as the activities of these small groups. This helps us to study the way in which the group is formed and how it is stabilised. We can also study the changes in these informal groups and how they disintegrate. We can understand the process of group formation as well as the process by means of which the individuals affiliate themselves and identify themselves with the groups. We can specify the conditions under which the group is formed and its effects upon the individuals. Thus the whole process of group formation can be brought within the scope of actual observation. Apart from this methodological reason for the study of these small groups, as we have seen above, informally organized groups are very important in social life. They prevail at all ages of the life of an individual and they are there in all groups.

The Essential Properties of the Small Informal Groups

Before we discuss the essential properties of small informal groups it is necessary to bear in mind some basic conditions underlying group formation. As we have seen above when two or more individuals come together there is interaction. It is on the basis of this interaction that the group may be formed. Secondly, this interaction should involve communication. Thus interaction and communication are the basic conditions for the formation of a group. But it must be realised that these are not sufficient conditions for the formation of a group. Neither mere interaction nor mere communication by themselves are necessary and sufficient conditions for the formation of the group. We can now proceed to study the essential properties of small informal groups.

Sherif has indicated that four properties are essential in the formation and functioning of small informal groups. These four properties are:

(1) *Common Motives.* Informal organization of groups can arise only through the interaction of individuals with common motives. The boy in a street corner may learn on the basis of interaction and communication that there are common motives. It is this, which leads to the formation of a group, which may endure for a short or a long time. The village boys who have brought their cows for grazing may join together to organize a game of marbles or they may join together to invade the neighbouring garden and steal some fruits. Food, recreation and entertainment underlie many of the informal group formations. Similarly the students in a hostel may form themselves into a small group when they know that their neighbour has got a basket of food from his home or a jar of pickles. They may invade his room and make him share his food with them. This may even lead to further activities like a boy writing to his home to got packets of food for the whole group. Similar activities are reported to happen among the prisoners. In the villages and sometimes even in cities, the common threat of burglars may bring about an informal organization of night watchmen who will, go from street to street in the night. The whole group is involved and excited over their duties. Particularly individuals facing some uncertainties or insecurity in their social ties will somehow meet each other. In a political party groups may be formed because of certain threats or deprivations. They may organize themselves so that they can even pull down the leader of the Legislative party who is the Chief Minister. "Therefore common motives conducive to interaction necessarily imply that the individuals perceive, even though dimly, that others also face the same problems and that cooperation with them has some relevance for the problem, even if only that of providing mutual solace". It is possible that the cooperation may not lead the group to achieve its ends. If the group is confronted by obstacles which it is not possible to overcome then, it will disintegrate. It is only when it succeeds that the group becomes strengthened and continues to exist for a longer time. The "ingroup" feeling may develop. This in turn may lead to new motives and new goals. The sense of belongingness may provide a sense of security and importance.

It is a familiar fact that a number of well established organizations came into existence first as informal groups. Recently several colleges, liberal as well as professional, have been started in India on the basis of such informal groups. Retired engineers who have not been able to get their sons admitted into an engineering college or retired medical men or retired teachers in a similar situation may call for an informal meeting and when they find that several individuals are ready to respond and cooperate they may join together and form themselves into a committee and start colleges. Similarly new religious movements were started because of the sense of dissatisfaction of the few with the defects of the existing religious organizations. So we find that deprivations and threats serve as common motives to bring together a number of individuals so that they organize themselves to achieve those goals. As we have seen, once a group is formed other goals may be set up and so the group becomes an enduring institution.

(2) ***Differential Effects of Intercommunication of Members.*** When individuals interact with each other they perceive the other people as unique individuals with certain abilities or disabilities. As Asch puts it, the final outcome of interaction with others and of the perception of their actions, motives and emotions is that we come to know persons as having particular unique individualities. The individuals in the course of their interaction understand in a more or less definite way the intellectual and character qualities of each other. This leads to differences in attitudes towards each other. It is possible that due to a sense of belonging and a sense of security certain new aspects which, neither the individual, nor the members of the family of that individual had ever suspected, may now come to full light. Unsuspected characteristics of planning, ingenuity, perseverance, capacity to endure suffering for the benefit of the group as a whole, may all emerge. It is in this way that informal groups bring out the hidden talents and aspects of our personality. This is why there is a difference in the behaviour of the individual in the gang as compared with his behaviour at home. Parents are often astonished and similarly teachers when they find that the youth show evidence of new characteristics when they are in a new group. It is possible that these new experiences mayor may not lead to a perseveration in the

individual. It is possible that the individual may accept that kind of behaviour only in that particular group and this may not be transferred to other situations of his life.

(3) ***Formation of Group Structure.*** When individuals with common motives interact with each other for a fairly long time, then a group structure will emerge. The differential effects of interaction well bring about certain expectations and if those expectations are fulfilled by the individuals then there will be hierarchical status within the group. One individual may become the leader of the group because of his talents and his courage. He may assume leadership and the group may accept him as a leader. If the individual succeeds in leading the group to undertake some cooperative work then his position as a leader becomes stabilised. This also leads to role-taking by the various individuals. When the individuals cooperate with each other to attain a common goal this cooperation leads to differentiation of functions and coordination of efforts. Each member will do something, which he is capable of doing efficiently. For example, when half a dozen boys gather together and go for a picnic each will take his own role. One may get a few stones and setup an oven and get some firewood and start the fire. Another may take on the role of a cook, a third may become an assistant to the cook, the fourth may clean up the whole place and get some leaves to eat with. In this way there will be role-taking by the different individuals which leads to cooperation and successful attainment of the goal. To quote Sherif, "In its broadest sense, group structure refers to a more or less stabilised system of inter-dependent relationships (status and role) among individuals according to their respective contributions to interaction toward a common goal. These relationships are interdependent and reciprocal, linking a given individual to every other individual in the group in certain definite ways (roles). In terms of the individuals respective contributions in various capacities relevant to the

tasks, problems, or goals significant in the interaction process, reciprocal expectations are stabilised for each member in relation to other members. These stabilised expectations for behaviour in the group define the roles of the group members".

(4) ***Formation of Group Norms.*** Side by side with the group structure the group norms will emerge. These norms will regulate the behaviour of the individuals. Gradually certain approved ways of behaving will develop and the members who conform to these approved ways may be rewarded while those who do not conform may be punished. Recognition and praise, or ridicule and scorn, will reinforce these group norms. Norms may also develop regarding the behaviour of the members of the group towards those who are not members. This will lead to social distance. The group norms develop because of the expectations, which arise out of interaction of the members of the group.

For mere togetherness situation to develop into a group situation, the interactions among the individuals must continue for a fairly long time. So, time is a very important condition for the formation of the group. Further, the group formation occurs after a series of episodes. When the individuals join together at varying intervals and engage themselves in the group activities then the group becomes knit together.

Status Stabilisation in Informal Groups

Sherif and his co-workers produced two groups experimentally and studied the status-stabilisation in these two groups. They found certain characteristic ways in which the statuses stabilise themselves in the course of interaction over a period of time. They found that those members who contribute effectively towards the goals of the group emerge into the foreground. Thus from a situation where there is no status difference, gradually through the process of interaction they found that the individual or individuals who are very active by their words and deeds assume the leadership status. The group as a whole accepts these individuals as leaders. At the other end those who are quiet participants assume the bottom position. In the course of time the members who are in the middle assume varying positions in the hierarchy so that after a time, after a series of episodes of successful working to attain the goals of the group, statuses stabilise themselves and the group structure takes shape. They also found that there is a good deal of struggle for the "lieutenant" position near the leader. We find that there are some common features in the two groups particularly with respect to the emergence of the leader and the members in the bottom position at the first stage and the development of the positions of the sub-leaders a little later on and the finalisation of the middle and the lower middle statuses in course of time so that every member has a particular status and position in his own group.

Whyte's Study of the Street Corner Boys

He studied the formation and function of informal groups in the slum areas of a big city. The children, the youth of the slum area, are looked down upon by the families who live in more respectable quarters in the city. They live in very poor homes. They are not looked after by the parents, because probably both of them will have to work from dawn to dusk to get the wherewithal to support the family. These children do not go to schools nor do they have work. Whyte studied the unemployed and money-less young men who were around 20 years of age. They gravitated towards each other to obtain recreation, entertainment, recognition and security. Their sense of deprivation of biological as well as psychological needs leads them to meet and interact with each other. In the course of interaction there is the group stabilisation with hierarchical arrangements of the statuses. In the group studied by Whyte there was a conflict between the leader and the lieutenant. When the lieutenant was able to defeat the leader several times the lieutenant became the leader. The whole group centred around him. Whyte found that the man who is able to plan escapades and entertainments, who is physically strong and shrewd becomes the leader. It was also found that once a hierarchy is formed the member of the group with the higher status has to lead a more strict life because there are several expectations placed upon him. For example, the leader has to be very generous in spending money when he is in the group. On the other hand, he had to observe very strict rules in securing money for himself. This is a typical phenomenon in all groups. The higher the position of the leader the greater the need for self-discipline. Unless he is strict with himself he cannot be strict with others. Unless he observes the social norms scrupulously he cannot punish the others for deviation from the norms. Whyte found this in the informal groups of the street corner boys. Similarly, thieves have very strict codes among themselves, and the leader of the thieves, like the leader of the respectable citizens, must have greater self-discipline. It was also observed that the group activities usually originated from the leader of the group. Further the leader encouraged suggestions from the other members, which involved activities in which the leader himself excelled. On the other hand, he would discourage the suggestion, which involved activities in which he did not excel. This is again a very important observation regarding inter-relationships between the leader and the followers and the types of activities in which the given group engages itself. This is how the leader is able to enhance his authority and prestige because he gets the group to undertake activities in which he is very good and so can lead the group to success. Whyte also observed that the group structure involved a system of mutual obligations. It is in this way that the group was not only well-knit as an in group it also developed a certain set of norms which regulated activities of the group as well as the behaviour of the individual members within the group. Whyte also found that there were all kinds of frictions within the group for status. When the members with high status did not fulfill the expectations or when the individuals pursued goals, which were not conducive to the goals of the group, there were frictions and conflict between the members. This might lead to a disintegration of the group. Whyte also found that the conflict may arise from outside when the group is unable to withstand conflicts with the other groups or with the society at large, there would be friction and mutual bickerings, fault finding etc. Another major factor of disintegration of the group was when a member of the group got a job or got married. When a member got a job he was unable to devote his whole time for the group activities as previously. So among these unemployed youth, as individuals obtained employment, the group would disintegrate. This indicates in a negative way the function and significance of the informally organized gang. It serves a very significant purpose so long as the young man is unemployed and is unmarried. In other words because the young man has no work to do, no responsibilities and hence no sense of importance, no social recognition, he gravitates towards the street corner gang, which gives him satisfaction for all these needs. It is in this way that the informal group provides the members with a feeling of importance, belongingness and security. On the other hand when these needs are achieved by employment and by marriage he gives up the membership of the group. So merely telling the boy or the young man not to join the street corner gang, or speaking about the evils which arise out of this membership, will not lead him to surrender his membership. It is only when opportunity is provided for the individual to obtain what the street corner gang gives that it is possible to dissuade him from being a member. This is as far as the individual is concerned but as far as the group is concerned the best way is to get the group to undertake activities which are in line with the social norms of the group as a whole and which will also provide for the needs which the individuals feel that they are deprived of.

In the particular group that Whyte was studying he found that the group disintegrated when the leader, who was the "soul of the group ", gave up something in which the whole group was very enthusiastic. The leader announced that he would stand for election in a political party. The whole group was enthusiastic about this. Suddenly he announced that he was withdrawing from the elections. The boys had no knowledge of the circumstances, which led to the leader's withdrawal. Their faith in him was completely shaken up. They suspected that the leader withdrew from the elections after making a bargain with the rival. This was a big shock because they never-expected this behaviour from the leader. The intensity of the shock experienced is proportional to the level of expectations. This led to the disintegration of the group and the leader who was so powerful in knitting the members together became a powerless individual. He lost his 'magic '. The members did not care for him.

Experimental Production of Group Structure

In America, on the basis of the field study such as that of Whyte regarding the spontaneously organized small groups some social psychologists have developed a hypothesis, which they have tried to test by means of experimental studies. We can now summarise the work of Sherif and his co-worker, who conducted an experiment to produce conditions conducive to the formation of groups. They tried to test the hypothesis whether individuals who have no established relationships with each other will form themselves into a group if they are brought together to interact in activities with common goals. To test this hypothesis Sherif and his co-workers brought together 24 boys of about 12 years of age who were as homogeneous as possible with respect to age, sex, education, religion, socio-economic status etc. They also took care to see that there were no previous bonds of friendship or hostility among these individuals. Clinical tests were made in order to see that there were no "problem children" in the group. The boys came from Protestant families of lower middle class with similar education. The experiment was started in summer in an isolated campsite. The nearest town was eight miles ·away. The first stage lasted for three days. The individuals were given maximum freedom to choose their friends, their activities, their rooms in the camp and so on. Thus this period was planned to study the techniques of spontaneous or informal group-formation among these boys who had not known each other previously. The four participant observers who noted down the behaviour of these individuals found that there was spontaneous formation of clusters and emergence of leaders in specific situations.

Observations of the second stage, was started by deliberately splitting up the group into two groups. The friendship groups developed at the first stage were deliberately split up. The second stage lasted for five days. The two groups chose two different bunk houses where they lived and they went for hikes and other parties in opposite directions. It was found that at the beginning some boys showed resentment at being separated from their new found friends. It was, however, later found that these two groups developed well-defined in group organizations. It was further found that the most popular person became the leader. It was also found that in each group there was another person or persons who were quite powerful though they were not popular. But these powerful persons yielded to the overall leadership of the popular person. As the group structure was formed members developed positive attitudes towards each other and norms were stabilised. Each group chose its own colour, its own group name, its own signs and so on. It was also found that each group had it own methods of praising and punishing. At the end of this stage socio-metric choices were again obtained in informal interviews. This revealed that there was a big difference between the choices at the end of the first stage and the choices at the end of the second stage. With the two groups of the second stage as the frame of reference, it was found that while at the end of the first stage 35% of the friends came from the in group and 65% from the out group, at the end of the second stage 90% were chosen from the in group and only 10% from the out group. Living together as an in group for five days considerably changed the friendship formation among these 24 boys. In the third stage, which lasted for five days the two groups were pitted against each other and it was found that during this stage negative inter-group attitudes were developed.

Social Factions

We can now proceed to a study of the relations between groups. Historians, sociologists and psychologists have always been interested in the study of inter-group conflicts. We can differentiate between two kinds of group interactions: *(a)* Interactions between two different groups like, for example, the Hindus and Muslims, the white and the coloured people, the Brahmins and non-Brahmins, the Maharashtrians and Gujaratis and so on; *(b)* there are also conflicts between two sub-groups within a group. We have the notorious factions in the villages, group formations within the political parties and group formations within associations. In this section we shall attempt to study the basic principles involved in inter-group conflicts and hostilities of these two kinds.

As we have seen above a group is a social unit with individuals who stand in more or less defined interdependent status relationships with one another and which possesses explicitly or implicitly a set of norms, which regulate more or less the behaviour of the individual members. By the term "inter-group relations" we refer to the relations between two or more groups. As we have seen these groups may be within an in-group. There may be group identifications within the group itself. The main thing is that the individual should be conscious that he is a member of a particular group, that he reacts with another individual whom he regards as a member of the out group. However, it must be realised that these groups, which we studied are not isolated and independent social units like the tribes studied by anthropologists. They are sub-units within a large group or within the nation. Consequently the properties of these sub-units are determined by the nature of the larger social units of which they are a part. It will be profitable to study the relations between small groups so that we can study the behaviour and attitudes of specific individuals in a concrete fashion.

As we have seen above the study of inter-group behaviour has, its roots in the work of historians. Several factors have been singlled out and emphasised in accounting for the inter-group behaviour. For example, some have emphasised the cultural differences as very important factors. Differences in national character have been stressed as a very important reason for bringing about inter-group conflicts. Others have placed major emphasis on the role of leadership. The significance of individual motives and frustrations with the ensuing displaced aggressions have also been emphasised by some scholars. In a broad way we may say that inter-group behaviour is the outcome of *(a)* internal factors like motives, attitudes etc., in the individual members and *(b)* external factors like the situational, the organizational, the socio-economic etc. It must further be realised that all these various factors are operative as interdependent factors in producing social conflicts.

●●●

11

Psychology of Social Control

It is very essential for the life and progress of every society that there should prevail in it perfect harmony and order, its members should live with a sense of discipline and there should prevail perfect social equilibrium. It is expected of the individuals to observe social conformity and abide by the accepted ways of society. The society in order to enforce its rules and ways on the individuals keeps some degree of control on them. This control in popular usage is known as social control. Every society in order to survive and progress exercises some form of social control. This term 'social control' has come to acquire a great role in the general working of human society. This term has been variously defined by sociologists and some of these definitions may be given here.

Definitions

To quote **Park** and **Burgess**, "What we ordinarily mean by social control is the arbitrary intervention of some individual official, functionary or leader in the social progress."

In this connection **Brearly** writes, "Social Control is a collective term for those processes and agencies planned or unplanned, by which individuals are taught, persuaded or compelled, to conform to the usages and life values of the groups to which they belong."

According to **Maciver** and **Page**, "By social control is meant the way in which the entire social order coheres and maintains itself how it operates as a whole, as changing equilibrium.

Ogburn and **Nimkoff** say, "The pattern of pressure which a society exerts to maintain order and established rules is known as its system of social control."

In the words of **Gillin** and **Gillin**, "Social control is that system of measures, suggestions, persuations, restraints and coercion by whatever means including physical force by which a society brings into conformity of the approved pattern of behaviour a subgroup or by which a group moulds into conformity its members."

To put it in the words of **Paul H. Lands**, "Social control is a series of social processes by which individual is made group responsible, by which social organization is built and maintained... by which personality is formed through socialisation."

The view of **R.G. Smith** is "Social control is the attainment of ends through collective conscious adaptation of means to those ends."

Mannheim defines social control as, "the sum of those methods by which a society tries to influence human behaviour to maintain a given order."

Roucek has used the term 'social control' "for those processes and agencies, planned or unplanned by which individuals are taught, persuaded or compelled to conform to the usages and life values of groups."

Lunderg has defined, "Social control as designating those social behaviours which influence individuals or groups towords conformity established or desired norms."

Thus in view of these definitions social control may be defined as any influence which the society exerts upon its members for the purpose of providing the welfare of the group as a whole. It operates on three levels group over group, the group over its members and individuals over their fellows.

Ingredients of Social Control

When the working of the process of social control is taken in view, it unfolds a number of its elements.

There are broadly speaking three main elements of this process. Social control is an influence, the influence is exercised by society and it is exercised for common good. This fact will become more clear by examining these points in greater detail.

Firstly, as has been said above social control is an influence. The influence may be exerted through a number of agencies and means; which are commonly known as the means and agencies of social control. These include public opinion, coercion, social suggestion, religion, appeal to reason or any other method. There occurs a variation in the extent of these forces of social influence. But at all times some of these are certain. Other means of similar kind keep on operating for exerting social influence on the individuals.

Secondly, the influence is exercised by society. It means that group is better able to exercise influence over the individual than individual. This group may be the family, the church, the State, the club, the school, the trade union-variable factors. Sometimes the family may exercise more effective influence than the State and sometimes it may be quite otherwise. Similarly, the influence of the club may be more effective than that of the church. There are innumerable agencies of social control and the effectiveness of each agency depends largely upon the circumstances.

Thirdly, the influence if exercised for promoting the welfare of the group as a whole. The person is influenced to act in the interest of others rather than in accordance with his own individual interests. Social control is exercised for some specific end in view. It is not aimless. The aim is always the welfare of the whole. The individual is made conscious of others' existence and their interests. He is made to adhere to the appropriate social ways. Due to inadequate socialization he behaves in typical ways; he is bound to conformity with the typical by the pressures of social control. In a word, he is made social. According to **Gurvitch** and **Moor**, "Social control can be defined as tire sum total or rather the whole of cultural patterns, social symbol, collective spiritual meanings, values, ideas and ideals, as well as acts and processes directly connected with them whereby inclusive society every particular group and e very participating individual member overcomes tensions and conflicts within themselves through temporary equilibrial and take steps for new creative efforts."

Social Control Vs. Self-Control

Social control differs from self-control because the latter is from within while the former is from without. When an individual controls himself, his impulses not because of a certain coercion exercised by some other individual or group, but because of his own will and self-realization he said to have practised self-control. It is individual's own attempt to guide his own behaviour in accordance with some previously developed ideal, goal or purpose.

One may exercise self-control either for one's own gain or for other's gain. For example, when a person gives up drinking because it affected his health, he exercises self-control either for one's own gain, but if he gives it up because his family is not financially sound, he has exercised self-control for the gain of the family. The essence of self-control is that it is always the result of one's own inner realization or feeling little influenced by others authority. If it is not so, it will be transitory and will last so long as one is under the influence of others. But if self-control is out of one's own realization, it will be permanent and real. Referring to the distinction between self-control and social control. H.C. Brearley writes, Social control, should be distinguished from self-control, although the two are closely akin. Social control refers to the individual's attempt to control the behaviour of others in accord with his wishes, while self-control refers to the individual's attempt to control his own behaviour in accord with some previously developed ideal, goal or purpose. This goal is of course usually determined by the values and folkways the group to which the individual belongs. In a sense, then self-control is derived from, and is a form of social control." In view of these facts some points of distinction between the two can be noted here.

Firstly, self-control is a sort of self-restraint whereas social control is a pressure or influence. Secondly, self-control follows from within whereas social control comes from outside. The social control is always exercised by outside agencies. Thirdly, self-control aims at individual good but social control is always directed to secure social good. It may be that sometimes self-control is also meant to promote common good, but largely it is individualistic in nature. Fourthly, social control is exercised by society with the help of a number of agencies. But self-control is always the result of self-motivation and self-exercise. Lastly, self-control may be regarded as a prelude to social control. It trams the human mind to admit of larger sanctions for higher purposes. Thus it may be said that social control is the whole of which self-control is a part. H.C. Brearley is of the opinion that for convenience, consequently, social control and self-control are to be separated, but their close relationship needs to be recognized."

Social control should not be confused with personal leadership. When one person tries to control the behaviour of others, he is usually thought of as exercising leadership rather than social control. But, when he gathers a group of followers who join with him in endeavouring to influence the conduct of a larger group, he is acting as an agent of social control. In addition, it should be noted that leadership is sometimes used as a term of approbation for those whose attempts at social control are in harmony with one's own wishes or life values. Some, what similarly, propaganda may be termed to indicate the speaker's disapproval of some effort at social control. As a precise term, propaganda is preferably used to mean a form of social control that is believed to be prompted by some concealed motive.

Purposes of Social Control

The purposes of social control according to Kimball Young are : *(i)* to increase the regularity of human behaviour and *(ii)* to make possible greater predictability, stability, and continuity of social life. These purposes may possibly guide unselfish social scientists, but most men who endeavour to control their fellows indicate little altruism or perspective in their efforts. Often they merely struggle to increase the acceptance of the modes of conduct that they themselves prefer. This preference may be based upon childhood training insight derived from life experience or the desire to exploit others in order to gain power, economic, personal or political. Social control it is true, often perpetuates the accumulated wisdom of men long gone, but only rarely are living men and women cognizant of the significance of the cultural patterns they transmit or modify. Some reformers and exploiters do seem aware of their purposes and aims, but most of them either lack insight or conceal their true motives by good reason in the form of altruistic rationalizations. Examples of such rationalizatians may easily be observed in radio or newspaper advertising.

In longtime perspective of course, the social scientist can note that the efforts of men to obtain greater acceptance of their own values and patterns of living do result in a greater regularity and predictability of social behaviour. The assumption, however, that men in general are concerned with the advantages of regularity or predictability of conduct is difficult of acceptance without also assuming that the average man possesses a high degree of insight and social understanding.

As a matter of fact, it is difficult to know and classify the motives of the agents of social control, for example, it is difficult to understand the motives of parents who endeavour to train their children in outmoded patterns of conduct. It may be either because of unfamiliarity of the new patterns of conduct or it may be because they think that what proved good to them will also prove good to their children or they may be acting primarily from habit or distrust of the new modes. Likewise, it is difficult to ascertain the motives of a teacher who makes an attack upon the prevailing folkways and life-values. Thus, classification of the motives or purposes of the agents of social control is not easy. However, these purposes may be roughly classified as *(i)* exploitative, motivated by self-interest *(ii)* regulative, based upon habit and desire for behaviour of the customary types and *(iii)* creative or constructive based upon social benefit.

Custom

Custom is one of the most powerful and most common means of social control. It has existed at all times and in all societies dedicated to the task of maintaining social order. Shakespeare has called custom "a tyrant", Montaigne "a violent school mistress," and Bacon "the principal magistrate of man's life." All these utterings serve to indicate the control potential of custom. Disobedience of custom brings social disgrace. Custom has great utility from the social standpoint. It is a kind of social necessity. Several sociologists have given their observations about the term custom.

According to **Maciver**, "The socially accredited way of acting are customs of society."

Bogardus, writes, "Customs and traditions are group accepted techniques of control that have become well established, that are taken for granted and that are passed along from generation to generation."

In the words of **Ginsberg**, "Custom has usually been interpreted in accordance with the psychological laws of habit. It has been regarded as a way of behaviour which has become general in the community and has come by frequent repetition to be performed quasi-automatically."

To quote **Davis**, "Custom is a broad term embracing all of the norms classified as folkways and mores. It connotes long established usage and is, therefore, frequently contrasted with what is new."

Custom refers primarily to practices that have been oft-repeated by a multitude of generations practices that tend to be followed simply because they have been followed in the past. The term is, therefore loser to folkways than to mores, but it tends to convey the traditional, automatic, mass character of both of them.

Nature of Custom

It is generally seen that underlying and sustaining the more formal order of institutions and associations there exists and intricate complex of usage or modes of behaviour. Thus there are accepted procedures of eating, conversing, meeting folks, wooing, training the young, caring for the aged, almost infinitum. The socially accredited way of acting are the customs of society.

We conform to the customs of our own society, in a sense "unconsciously" for they are a strongly embedded part of our group life. They are so strongly embedded, indeed, that we frequently make the error of identifying our particular customs with the only correct ways of doing this or that or even with human nature itself. This situation throws up a large number of problems, which demand the attention of all the sociologists.

Distinction of Institution and Custom. The difference between a social usage or custom on the one hand and an institution on the other is essentially one of degree. Institution implies a more definite recognition. We would call the marriage feast an institution, but various courtship practices are better named customs. Marriage itself is an institution and not a custom. Institutions have external insignia, marks of public recognition, which customs as such do not require. We sometimes hear that our institutions are being undermined, but this charge is rarely made with reference to our customs.

This suggests another difference. The term "institution" stresses the impersonal factor in social relationships. When we speak of customs we think of the accepted ways in which people do things together, in personal contacts. When we speak of institutions we think rather of the system of controls that extends beyond personal relations. This system of controls is the bond between the past and the present and between the present and the future, linking men to their ancestors, their gods, and their descendants. Thus we do not usually become too seriously concerned with say, the changing customs of courtship or dress or recreation But consider how some persons are disturbed by what may appear to be threats to "property" or "marriage" or "free enterprise" the institutions which ramify into the greater organizations of political, economic, and religious life.

Interrelation of Customs and Habits. In common parlance custom is often used as coterminous with habit, but there are vital differences between the two habit is personal phenomenon while custom is a social phenomenon. A custom is formed on the basis of habit gaining the sanction and influence and therefore the social significance, which is peculiar to it. Customs are social habits, which through repetition become the basis of an order of social behaviour. In this connection Ginsberg write, "Custom in fact is not merely a prevailing habit, but also a rule or norm of action. The rule is supported on the emotional side by two sets of forces. There is, firstly a sentiment or group of emotional disposition attaching to custom as such, and condemning its breach. In this sentiment there is a rational element, the recognition, however vague of the importance of order, and the necessity of knowing what to expect and what is expected in given situation. Round these there cluster the social feelings; and the obedience of customary rules is one of the most elementary ways in which the individual responds to the cell of social life and realizes his dependence upon the group."

Customs are the long established habits and usages of the people. Wherever there is a widespread habit there is a corresponding custom as well. According to **Lundberg**, "They are those folkways that persist over relatively long periods of time so as to attain a degree of formal recognition and so as to be passed down from one generation to another." Habits precede and create customs, though there may be certain customs which presuppose no habit, for example, the custom of forming the queues and the custom of widows wearing weeds as a sign of morning for their husbands do not have any habit to serve as their basis. On the other hand, many customs may give rise to habits and be supported by them; thus the custom of taking meals at a certain time may create the habit of eating only at the appointed time even when one is alone. Thus customs create habits and habits create customs. The two though distinct are indirectly related in social life. This process of customs determining the habits and the habits in turn determining customs is a significant aspect of social organization.

Object and Purposefulness of Custom

Some thinkers who feel that customs have no proposefulness. They attach element of irrationality to them and look upon them as the agent of conservative thoughts and practices. Emphasising this fact **Mc. Dougall** writes in these words, "The ends and purposes of many customs are lost in the mists of antiquity. In some cases perhaps, the ends have been never clearly defined in anyone man's mind. The custom may have arisen as a compromise of fusion between diverse customs, or through some purely institutive mode of reaction or through some perverted imitation of some foreign model. But however and for whatever purpose instituted, a custom once established, the practice of it always becomes in some degree an end in itself and men are prepared to maintain it, often at great cost of effort or discomfort, long after it serves any useful end." But it is not fight to express this out-right opinion about toe customs that they are meaningless and they serve no useful purpose. If we go deep into the genesis of the customs we would find that the charge of irrationality to them is not valid. It may be admitted that there are some customs and practices adopted by men, which cannot be justified on any utilitarian or ethical grounds. In India a number of such practices may be seen among all the communities. Thus sprinkling water on some stone or any other inanimate object or giving food to it, offering 'Shradhs' to dead, giving up journey because a cat has crossed the path and such many other practices may be said to be irrational but all of the customs cannot be said to be irrational. The root of the difficulty is that modern minds consider only those acts rational, which can be logically proved and are calculated acts.

In this connection mention may be made of the customary acts like man saluting the flag of his country, the son touching the feet of his parents in the morning the people entertaining their relatives and friends on a festival, the Hindu woman taking meals after the husband. If one gets psychological satisfaction or social praise by following a custom, these are sufficient rational grounds for following it.

The prevailing beliefs and the realities of life lead us to the conclusion that no single rule can be laid down about the origin and existence of custom. Many customs have taken birth and survive to satisfy the fundamental needs of man, especially those connected with his self preservation, tendencies, sex life, procreation and the like. Some of the customs have been learnt by imitation from other people and many of them came as adjustments to changing situations. Many a custom still remain even though their usefulness has long ceased to exist. They are obeyed more spontaneously prevail, they are the strongest ties in building up a social order. But it must be noted that customs, which appear to be irrational are sometimes reformed or even abolished due to the deliberate thought of the people concerned. In India many customs of Hindus have been abolished by statute while others have been greatly reformed as a result of preachings of our social reformers.

Today the educated class also of Indians does not follow many customs of the ancestors. Owing to the women's emanicipation movement in India there is a growing tendency among the women to give up many of the customs followed by them previously. The result is that the customs, which were once very prominent are no more in use

While assessing the utility of customs we must keep in view certain basic facts. Thus as **Gisbert** writes, "In custom, like in any other norm, we must, distinguish the content from the form. The content consists in the things that are prescribed; the form in the way in which they are prescribed, or in the sanction attached to them. Thus what is peculiar to custom is that the matter prescribed has a social interest that concerns the community at large and is upheld by its members even by coercive means. But as to the matters prescribed there is a great deal of variety. Religious rites, economic operations, moral precepts, magical actions, and purely social observances connected for instance, with marriage ceremonies or Public festivals have unequal value before the human mind and their violation weighs quite differently on man's conscience. Certain rules have no religious sanction attached to them; no fear of punishment visits their breach; the stigma of public opinion or moral blame falls only lightly on the transgressors."

These facts point to the truth that social life is unthinkable without customs. They are the warp and the woof of social life. Customs are the channel through which social life flows. The life of the primitive people in particular is custom-ridden. Ginsberg aptly portrays the place of customs in these words, "The obedience of customary rules is one of the most elementary ways in which the individual responds to the call of social life and realizes his dependence upon the group. Long before kings started making laws, they ruled their people in accordance with customs. Custom is not only the king of men, it is also the king of kings." According to Maciver, "Custom is a group procedure that has gradually emerged, without express enactment, without any constituted authority to declare it, to apply it, to safeguard it." Common acceptance sustains custom. The social character of custom is revealed by those customs, which cannot be practised but collectively, for example, the various celebrations on the occasion of birth, marriage and death when people come together and by participating in a common occasion stimulate the social consciousness of one another. It is in this way clear that, on the whole, the customs are neither irrational nor purposeless. They are a great social force, which help in the regulation of social lire. They have been proving useful in the primitive as well as modern society.

Social Role of Customs

It is undoubtedly true that custom is most genuine channel along which the flow of social life runs especially among preliterate peoples. This requires that certain actions, thought to be conducive to the good of the group, be performed by all, or at least by large numbers of individuals. This is what gives to custom that degree of presumptive goodness on account of which it is followed by everybody with a certain degree of spontaneity strengthened by the habits which have been built round it. This assumed goodness confers on custom that emotional value whose force is mostly felt when custom is broken. Such a violation is taken as an insult and offence against the group whose outlook on life, its hopes, and ideals are reflected in its custom, especially when these take upon themselves a religious or sacred character. The violation in this case is not only a challenge or a crime, but also a sacrilege calling upon the people the vengeance of the gods.

The giving and taking in which social life consists is characteristically expressed in the ambivalent character of custom made up of spontaneity and coercion. Spontaneity or agreement with the group, hardly offers any serious problem for the individual but when the performance of a custom becomes difficult for him or he has a judgement of his own as to the functions that it performs, or the greater good that it prevents, then the painful giving of social life weighs heavily on him as when the modern Indian, who no longer believes in caste taboos. if often made to observe them by social or family pressure. Habit, being an individual affair, is free from this predicament; but the life of society cannot be ruled by habit alone. If man were not social, this would suffice, but as he demands by nature the company and co-operation of his fellowmen, custom must be present with all its assets and liabilities the former preponderating over the latter.

Referring to the social value of customs McDougall beautifully writes in these words, "The first requisite of society and the prime condition of social life of man, was in the words of Bagehot, a hard crust or cake of custom. In the struggle for existence only those societies survived which were able to evolve such a hard crust of custom, binding men together, assimilating their actions to the accepted standards, compelling control of the purely egoistic impulses and exterminating the individuals incapable of such control." It is thus clear that custom is an important means of controlling social behaviour. They regulate social life especially among illiterate people to a great extent and are essential to the life of a society. Custom is obeyed more spontaneously because it grows slowly.

Another function of custom is that it is the repository of our social heritage. The language, which the infant unconsciously endeavours to utter, the songs with which he is daily lulled, his ways of reacting to events, the occupations with which he later on grows familiarized his recreations and games, the mythology and forms of worship that he follows- all are offered to him in and through customs. The power of developing culture is inborn in man, as mind or the power of thinking is but its accomplishments and varieties are not born with him. They are acquired and transmitted from generation to generation through custom or tradition.

It may also be said in this connection that customs are universal and they are not confined to any particular area or a set of people. There is no country or community wherein customs are not found. In some communities they are regarded so sacred that their violation cannot be even thought of. The society wishes us to follow them. In primitive society adherence to custom was the general rule and so it is even today among the aboriginal-tribes. Even though in India with the spread of western education the observance of customs has loosed, still the old women folk of the country continue to observe them. They weep when they meet their relatives after a long absence and weep at the time of the departure of their daughters, during marriage ceremonies. The Morries of New Zealand rub noses with each other as an expression of their love and the women of Pulawat Caroline Island walk in a stooped position in the presence of men.

Major Social Codes

Social life is a complex affair. A large number of problems and issues are involved in it. It is not easy to conduct and regulate it. The problem of human relationship is especially intricate one and it needs some definite ways and rules for its regulation and keeping in order. There is a great need of enforcing social conformity among the members of society. This work is done by the social codes. The term social code is a very wide phenomenon and it includes both legal and social rules. The important social codes which are used as the means of social control are folkways, mores, customs traditions, conventions, religion and morality. These means can suffice for simple and traditional societies. But with the dawn of modern complex society these means have to be supplemented by the laws. Therefore law has also become a part of social code. In the modern times the legal rules along with customary rules do the job of maintaining social order and conformity.

Place of Law Among the Means of Social Control. It has been admitted at all hands that in modern civilized societies customs tend to loosen their hold. The result is that laws are enacted by the state to control the individual. The transition from custom to law is just a part of the general rationlisation in modern society. According to Malinowski, "The fundamental function of law is to curb certain natural propensities to hem in and control human instincts, and to impose a non-spontaneous, compulsory behaviour—in other words, to ensure a type of cooperation which is based on mutual concessions and sacrifices for a common end. A new force different from the innate spontaneous endowment must be present to perform this task." Law is endowed with compulsory character and this attribute of it is the result of several causes.

Firstly, there is the fact that law is a social rule and like all social rules it has at times an aspect of compulsion.

Secondly, there is the influence of the growth and expansion of society. As the members multiply, the problems, which confront society increase in magnitude and complexity to such an extent that it becomes no longer possible for the average citizen to encompass all their aspects and to perceive the justice of the measures or decisions taken. This is usually left to specialized bodies, which are thought competent to decide on the merits of a case. Meanwhile it is only left to the ordinary man to obey the law, taking for granted that it is sufficiently justified and worth of inconvenience that its observance brings with it.

Thirdly, it consists in the further complication of social relations, which takes place in an industrial society because of the growing division of labour, differentiation of functions and expansion of communications with other communities.

Finally, there is the growth of individualism by which men do not assent to law unless the reasons for it are sufficiently apparent to them, but as these are hardly ever so, especially in times of emergency when secrecy and swiftness of action are required, the law which bas to be observed and has behind it the compulsory machinery of the State takes upon itself more than ever a strong compulsory character. This was long ago referred to by VICO when he wrote, "The certainty of laws involves an obscuring of reason, in so far as in them reasons supported by authority. And this makes us experience the laws as hard to obey, and yet we are constrained to obey, because of their being certain."

Meaning of Law. The term law has been variously defined by the eminent thinkers.

Kant defined law as "a formula which expresses the necessity of an action."

In the opinion of **Duguit**, "Laws are the rules of conduct which normal men know they must observe in order to preserve and promote the benefits derived from life in society."

In the words of **Krabbe**, "Law is the expression of one of the many judgments of value which we human being make, by virtue of our disposition and nature."

In this connection **Mannheim** writes, "Law is a body of rules which is recognised, interpreted and applied to particular situations by the courts of the State."

Ross opines, "Law is the most specialized and highly furnished engine of social control employed by society."

Austin defined law as, "the command given by a superior to an inferior." He says, "Laws properly so called are a species of command. But being a command, every law properly so called flows from a determinate source or emanates from a determinate author."

To quote **Maciver** and **Page**, "Law is the body of rules which are recognised, interpreted and applied to particular situation by the courts of the State.

Thus it can be said in view of these definitions that law means the code upheld by the State, which because of its inclusive applicability, is thus a guardian of society itself.

In the light of foregoing facts two views can be taken of law. In a wide sense, it includes all the rules of conduct observed by men as a matter of habit. In a narrow sense, it may mean the body of rules, which are recognized or made by the State and interpreted by the courts of the land. Custom becomes law when the State is prepared to enforce it as a rule binding on citizens. To avoid the confusion between custom and law we should use the term 'law' in the narrow sense. It stands for rules enacted or at least interpreted and enforced by special agencies of the State and such a meaning of the law points to a number of its basic features.

Firstly, laws are the general conditions of human activity prescribed by the State for its members.

Secondly, law is law only if enacted by a proper law-making authority. It is a product of conscious thought; planning and deliberate formulation.

Thirdly, law is definite, clear and precise.

Fourthly, law applies equally to all without exception in identical circumstances;

Lastly, the violation of law is followed by penalties determined by the authority of the State.

Difference between Custom and Law. It goes without saying that although both custom and law are used as the means of social control, yet they are not identical and may not be confused with each other. Maciver and Page have beautifully explained the distinction of law and custom in these words:

"Custom, too has its own distinctive nature. Whereas law is often made, and is always applied, by the definite power of the State, custom is a group procedure that was gradually emerged, without express enactment, without any constituted authority to declare it, to apply it, to safeguard it. Custom is sustained by common acceptance. No special authority prescribes the raising of the hat to ladies or tipping in restaurants or dating on Friday evenings or fireworks on the Fourth July. Customs are the most spontaneous of all social rules and often the most compelling. But they are sanctioned not like law, by organized coercive authority, but by a wide variety of informal social pressures. Customs are so intimate that, until we reflect on it, we do not realize how they attend nearly every occasion of our lives, how our actions from morning till night, from youth to old age, are custom-regulated. In all sorts of ways, through chance, trial and error, experience, particular modes of procedure are devised, are followed and imitated and unobtrusively are accepted in the social mores. And often just as unobtrusively customs fade and disappear, again with our formal abolition and without recognition by any but those who recall the "good (or bad) old ways." A close study of this statement reveals the following points of distinction between custom and law.

Firstly, law is explicily and deliberately made by the definite power of the State whereas custom is a group procedure that has gradually emerged, without express enactment. It comes into being and continues in operation without any constituted authority to declare it; to apply it and to safeguard it. Custom emerged spontaneously without any guide or direction. But law is consciously created and put in to force at the moment of its enactment. In this way it is clear that law is a make, while custom is a growth.

Secondly, Law needs a special agency for enforcement while custom does not need any enforcing agency. Law is applied by a special agency and is sanctioned by organized coercive authority. Custom does not need any special agency for its application, it is enforced by spontaneous social action, No physical penalty visits a violator of the Custom. The State will not punish any body who violates in custom.

Thirdly, law is specific, definite and clear. One can know what the laws of the land are. But custom on the other hand, are not definite or clear, they are not codified in any single book so that it becomes difficult to know all the customs of the land.

Fourthly, law can readily adjust itself to changing conditions; whereas customs cannot be readily changed. Customs are relatively fixed and permanent. At times of crisis a law can be immediately enacted to meet the emergency. A sudden change cannot be brought about in custom.

Thus law is more flexible and adaptable than custom. The former can be introduced, amended or abolished with relative ease, whereas to reform or adjust the later is an arduous task.

Fifthly, customs fade and disappear without formal abolition and without recognized authority. Just as formal enactment of law is necessary for it to come into effect, so its formal abolition also is necessary to stop its binding influence.

Sixthly, law is more idealistic than custom. It is the offspring of mind and directed to aims, which are far above the actual practice of society. Custom is the product of experience and mainly concerned with daily routine of life. Law reforms the customs and abolishes those, which are out of tune with the changing conditions. For example, the Hindu Code Bill seeks to reform and abolish many of the Hindu customs regarding marriage, divorce and succession.

Lastly, law generally deals with matters, which are vital to the life of society whereas the subject-matter of custom is more ordinary and familiar. The customs are observed in addressing persons of authority or taking meals or celebrating festivals and they do not rise above the common place. But the laws are passed for creating a national institution *e.g.*, establishing a welfare State, abolishing zamindari system; and nationalising the banks, all of which deeply affect the social structure. Thus it may be said that custom also applies to comparative small number, while law applies to large numbers. A large nation could not maintain itself with custom alone; it is law that keeps it montly together.

Social Role of Fashion

Fashion is an important means of social control. It determines our speech, opinion, belief, recreation, dress, music, art and literature. Herbert Spencer regarded fashion as a leveller of custom. Maciver defined fashion as "the socially approved sequence of variation on a customary theme." Gabriel Tarde described fashion as the, "imitation of contemporaries." According to Lundberg, "Fashions are folkways that survive for only a short time." In the words of Ross "Fashion is a series of recurring changes in the choices of a group of people which, though they may be accompanied by utility, are not determined by it." Fashion implies certain habits upon which fashionable change flourish. It is a compromise between desire for novelty and desire for conformity. It is a transitory accepted change on a permanent line of behaviour. Thus wearing a nylon sari, putting on high heeled shoes, having, bobbed hair, playing cricket using painting to decorate the drawing room and going in pair are all examples of fashion. It is a characteristic feature of modern society and the people in general cannot escape its touch.

This term has been explained by Maciver and Page at length in these words, "By fashion we mean the socially approved sequence of variation on a customary theme. The variations of fashion occur in a more or less regular sequence—the 'cycle of fashion,' as it is sometimes called and fashion specially affects those aspects of the cultural factors which are regarded by the group as being in themselves relatively indifferent to basic values. Fashion applies to such matters as opinion, belief recreation, dress, adornment of all sorts, house decoration and furniture manner of speech, popular music, literature and art. In these areas fashion does not wholly supersede custom, but rather supplements it. Thus there is in every period a customary type of dress, such as trousers for men, or of fiction, such as the novel, or of song writing, such as the ballad, on which fashion rings its changes. By its continuous of the type, fashion may, of course, undermine the customary factor and prepare the way for a new one. Moreover the attitude associated with fashion tends to weaken the attitude that clings to custom."

Changing Nature of Fashion. When fashion is compared with custom its changeful nature becomes quite apparent. In this connection Maciver says, "Custom differs from law in the spontaneity of its origin and the immediacy of its sanction. Custom differs from fashion by reason of the more enduring character of its prescriptions, its closer relations to the intimate life and temperament of the group, and its traditional quality".

Fashion is definitely anti-traditional. It controls those aspects, which are apt to escape from custom's hold. The changefulness' of fashion is illustrated in the extreme by facts and crazes that bring rapidly to forefront for a time a certain entertainer or a particular version of "the game" or a special mode of greeting one's friends, only to be forgotton almost as quickly. In the field of dress there are general types of garments, which are prescribed by custom for particular occasions, such as weddings or funerals or sports, or for particular seasons or for particular times of the day; while within these types the changing modes and styles are regulated by fashion. In recreation, certain games, such as football, basketball, tennis, baseball, and bridge, have become a part of our customs of recreation, but within each of them the fashions change from time to time and from place to place. So in numerous other areas of social behaviour, fashion determines the fugitive varieties of the custom-prescribed general type.

Sometimes, however, the trend of fashion exhibits continuously the same direction. In this case the influence of some underlying factors is revealed, and the fashion may at length undermine the custom which at first it merely variegated. Thus the long range trend in women's fashion in dress has led to the obsolescence or disappearance of certain garments which were previously prescribed by custom—a reflection of major changes in the status of women, the sex, mores, and other factors. The same influence have been at work in determining the direction of the fashion in sports, apparel, generally from more or less, which in turn has helped to bring about the change from "bathing" to swimming and that from "lawn tennis" to the modern vigorous game.

Difference between Custom and Fashion

Various sociologists have contrasted fashion and custom. Herbert Spencer regarded fashion as a leveller of custom and especially of customary distinctions between social classes. He thought of fashion as gaining ground when custom declines and associated both tendencies with the growth of industrialization. Gabrial Trade defined fashion as the imitation of contemporaries and set it in contrast to custom, which was the imitation of ancestors. But neither of these views is wholly satisfactory as revealing the relation of custom to fashion. It is a relationship of significance in the study of both social structure and social change. Referring to the points of distinction between custom and fashion Gisbert observes in these words, "Fashion is a transitory accepted change on a permanent line of behaviour. It usually affects custom by supplementing and completing its role, but not by superseding it. The object of custom is more important for social life than of fashion, which is generally concerned with more frivolous and superficial matters.

Custom is more spontaneous, impersonal and enduring. Fashion is more artificial, individualistic and changeable. The former is usually transmitted from generation to generation; the later hardly lives the life of a flower. Custom is followed because it always has been followed and better satisfied our tendencies to conform to the part. Fashion, on the: contrary, is followed because it never before has been followed and better satisfies our desire of breaking with the past. Paradoxical though it may seem, evanescence is the life of fashion and permanence its demise; if fashion survives, it ceases to be; it becomes custom." Keeping in view these facts we can draw following conclusions regarding the main points of distinction between custom and fashion.

Firstly, custom is enduring while fashion is changeable. Custom is transmitted from generation to generation, and is customarily followed from time immemorial. Fashion on the other hand, is short lived and hardly lives a decade. Time is the very essence of fashion. The style of dress that seems so beautiful today will appear ridiculous a few years hence. If fashion survives long, it in fact, ceases to be a fashion.

Secondly, custom is spontaneous whereas fashion is artificial. Custom grows in society by itself and followed as a matter of habit but fashion is created and followed with a purpose in mind.

Thirdly, custom stands for sociality but fashion for individuality. Custom is followed by all the members of a community and this universal following creates social bonds between them. Fashion is started by somebody and somebody has to be last to adopt it. When it becomes universal it loses its novelty and gives place to a new fashion. By following a custom an individual seeks to identify himself with the rest, whereas by following a fashion he seeks to distinguish himself from the rest.

Fourthly, custom is concerned with important matters, whereas fashion is concerned with frivolous ones. In other words, we may say that Custom pertains to things that cannot change because they are important. Fashion stresses the change itself, not what changes. For example, in the field of dress there are general types of garments prescribed by custom for particular occasions, such as weddings, mourning or sports, or for particular seasons; while within these types the styles are regulated by fashion.

Finally, fashion frequently grows where custom breaks off. If divorce becomes a fashion, society may be said to be heading for disaster. If the use of contraceptives becomes a fashion the future of the family may be doomed, when fashion takes the place of morality the solid pillars of social life are shaken.

Creators of Fashion. Manifold are the ways in which fashion originates. Sometimes it is the aristocracy or the selected few who start a 'new look' and others gradually follow suit. Sometimes it is a political or social movement, which starts a fashion, as the Gandhi cap or the wearing of Khadi in modern India. New fashions are also designed by agencies especially devoted to this as the Parisian centres for ladies dress fashion. On other occasions new fashions are artificially introduced by business firms in order to popularise a product by associating it, for instance with some famous personality or film-star until the public grows weary and another new fashion is started.

The flexibility and pervasiveness of fashion have also their limits and conditions of which the most important are the moral ideas and the material conditions of society. Thus a fashion, which makes light of certain values that are held high by people in general has no chance of success, it may even provoke vigorous reactions. Another by which its followers are exposed to the cold in winter and to the heat in summer can hardly make any headway unless it has some compensatory features as an increase in prestige or health.

Fashions are prone to take with the public in periods of optimism and prosperity, democracy and freedom as an outward expression of activity and life. On the contrary, poverty, depression, dictator regimentation tend to reduce the range and frequency of fashion. One of the most important functions of fashion is, that it facilitates social change by providing a transitional stage from one custom to another. The cake of custom is hard to break, but the introduction of fashion tends to mollify its rigidity and the belief in its importance; while, at the same time, it prepares the minds for a change so that this may not come suddenly enough to disturb the social order.

It may finally be added that the social sanction of fashion is usually mild. By not following it one may be held as old fashioned or an old crumb. But it also has its counter-sanction as those who too readily take to fashion are liable to be dubbed as green and light-headed.

Social Role of Fashion. A question is often asked as to what role fashions play in society. The question is important as we find people often groaning under the tyranny of fashion. Fashion promises no utility; it makes no appeal to reason and being a fugitive and transitory deviation has little effect on the major trends of social change, yet it has a strong hold over the people. It is because of the following points of social significance contained in the fashions.

●●●

12

Family of Social System

It is a well-known fact that family is found everywhere and it is concomitant with group life. Society and State derive from a circle of intermarrying families banded together to satisfy their basic needs. Sociologically and historically, the family may be viewed as a group consisting of two or more parents and their children. Such a view suggests itself because there have been great variations in the number of parties entering into the marriage union. Although the family is universal, no particular form of it is primary or inevitable. Like all other institutions, it is a social product subject to change and modification. In. response to varying conditions, different forms of the family have appeared from time to time. But in the present day world Patriachial family organised under the system of monogamy is most prevalent isntitution. In such a kill-group that it is both an association and institution and very essential to the life of society.

FUNCTION OF FAMILY

Main Functions of Family

It is an open secret that family plays an important role in the life of society. There is no other human group that dominates the life of the individuals, more than family. It is in the light of this hard fact that, Maciver says, "Of all the organizations, large or small, which society unfolds, none transcends the family in the intensity of its sociological significance. It influences the whole life of society in innumerable ways, and its changes, reverberate through the whole social structure. It is capable of endless variation and yet reveals a remarkable continuity und persistence through change." The family occupies a vital place in the working of social order and it is so because it performs certain characteristically significant functions. Davis has characterized the main social functions of the family in four divisions. These are reproduction, maintenance, placement and socialization of the young. It also performs individual functions but these are the corollary of its social functions. However, Davis has said, "From a sociological point of view we are mainly concerned with the social functions and consequently we stress the four functions mentioned here as being the core functions with which the family is always and everywhere concerned. There may be great variation from one society to another in the precise manner and degree of fulfilment of theee functions, but the four mentioned above seem to be the ones which universally require a family organization."

Lundberg has also mentioned a number of basic functions of the family. In them he has included the regulation of sexual behaviour and reproduction, care and training of children, co-operation and division of labour and primary group satisfactions. Besides, there are many auxiliary functions as well. Maciver divides the functions of the family into two categories. They are the essential and non-essential functions of the family. Under the essential he includes three functions *(i)* Stable satisfaction of sex need. *(ii)* Production and rearing of children, and *(iii)* Provision of a home. Under the non-essential functions he mentions religious, educational, economic, health and recreation, which he says have now been transferred to specialized agencies in society. In short, the various functions of the family can be mentioned in the following way:

Essential Functions of Family

The essential functions of the family are those functions, which it has to perform exclusively. They can neither be shared with any other group nor they can be delegated to any other association. They are the functions, which in every age and in any form the family must perform and there can be no deviation from them. Some of them are: *(i)* Satisfaction of Sex need and *(ii)* Provision of a home *(iii)* Production and rearing of children. They are in a way the primary functions of the family, for the doing of which some sort of family group has ever to remain in existence. This fact is aptly testified by Reuben Hill in these words, "Family life is probably more than a social habit. The family may be viewed as a device for solving certain fundamental problem, which must be faced by any group of people who live and work together in a society. As a problem-solving device it has simplified the social life of many of its members. Through it sex partners are sorted out and their sex drives are harnessed and linked with the love sentiments to weld together conjugal units into which children can be born, cared for and reared to adulthood. Within it all the basic elemental needs are met and kept from becoming individual problems, which if left unsolved might demand collective action. It simplifies life to live in a family and that is true for adults as well as for children. Certain basic needs of affection, intimate response, recognition, personality, expression, growth and security are met through the family which are not met satisfactorily elsewhere." In view of these facts the important essential functions of the family can be explained in some detail in the following manner:

(i) Satisfaction of Sex Need. This is the first essential function, which the family performs. Satisfaction of sex instinct brings the desire for life-long partnership among male and female. The satisfaction of sex instinct makes for normal personality. If sex instinct is suppressed, it may produce personality maladjustments and disrupt social relations. The modern family can satisfy this instinct in greater degree and in a better way than the traditional family. In the old family the sexual act was combined with reproduction and the fear of pregnancy as a result of intercourse prevented the couple to satisfy their sex urge. But in modern family the task of sexual satisfaction has been eased by the invention of contraceptives and other methods of birth-control. It has now become a primary function of the modern family. According to Reed, "The fundamental function of the family is to regulate and gratify sexual needs. Manu accepts sexual satisfaction besides production as the aim of family. Vatsyayan also regards sexual satisfaction as the primary objective of the family.

(ii) Provision of Home. The desire for a home is a powerful incentive for men as well as women after marriage. Man after the hard toil of the day returns home where in the midst of his wife and children he sheds off his fatigue. Though, in modern times there are hotels and clubs which also provide recreation to the man but the joy that a man feels within the congenial circle of women, parents and children stands far above the momentary pleasure. Which is provided by club and hotel. In spite of these re-creative agencies the home is still the heaven and sanctuary where its members find comfort and affection.

(iii) Production and Rearing of Children. The inevitable result of sexual satisfaction is procreation. The task on race perpetuation has always been an important function of the family. It is an institution par excellence for the production and rearing of children. The function of child-rearing is better performed today than in the past because now more skill and knowledge are devoted to the care of the unborn and new-born children. The infant death rate has shown a market declare. In the achievement of this result specialized agencies like nursing child welfare centres have come to the aid of the family. A close study of the available statistical data reveals that the number of illegitimate children is falling down, the practice of prostitution is vanishing away and the number of marriages is increasing rapidly. It is a pointer to the fact that the function of procreation of race is only performed through family. In most human societies of the world the child is believed to be the nucleus of the family. Procreation perpetuates the family. It increases the population of the country.

(iv) Protection and Care of the Young. It is another essential function of the family and it may be said to be a corrollary of its sexual and procreative functions. According to Groves the protection and care of children is one necessary function of the family. The human child is the most helpless and weak being. A family is needed in order to maintain its existence and to ensure its coordinated and balanced development. Its balanced development is achieved with difficulty and that too with the care of the parents and other family members. It is right that in the modern age this function of the family is losing much of its past significance and it is being handed over to the subsidiary agencies. But all the same it still continues to be one of the essential functions of the family and the Indian families are particularly known for this function.

(v) Provision of Psychological Satisfaction and Security. Another fundamental and universal function of the family is to meet the psychological needs of its members. Ogburn has included affectional functions in the necessary or vital functions of the family. According to Groves it is the functions of the family to provide opportunities for the establishment of intimate relations. Burgess and Lock have written, "Mutual affection is becoming the essential basis of marriage and family:" The individual receives affection, sympathy, love and psychological security in the family. The relations between man and woman in the family are not exclusively physical. Profound conjugal affection for each other is generated in husband and wife by working together in the family and by sharing each other's joys and sorrows. An all around development of individual is not possible in the absence of family love. The family has an important part to play especially in the development of the child's personality. Ralph Linton has written that merely the satisfaction of bodily needs is not sufficient for the proper development of the infant.

Non-Essential Functions of the Family

The non-essential functions of the family are those functions which it performed in the traditional society but which it is giving up one by one in the modern times. These functions are being either delegated to the subsidiary agencies or they can be shared with other groups. They are no longer the exclusive function of the family but still in some societies the family is associated with them in some form or the other. The Indian society is one such example where the family despite so many modifications and being placed under limits has been laying its claims on the so-called non-essential functions along with the essential functions. Some of the non-essential functions of the family can be enumerated in the following order:

1. ***An Economic Unit.*** A very important non-essential function of the family is that it serves as an economic unit. In the traditional family most of the goods for consumption were made at home. The members of the family were all engaged in the family occupation. The ancient Hindu joint family served as a sort of mutual insurance society. It was a unit of production and the centre of economic activities. However, in the present time the importance of family as an economic unit has been lessened because most of its economic activities have been taken over by some outside agencies. The members of the modern family do not work together as they did in the old family. They are engaged in different activities outside the come. Moreover the family has not even remained

the unit of production as most the goods for consumption including even the food are purchased ready-made from the market. But with all these shifts in the family as an economic unit, it has not been reduced to a passive body. This is to say that the old pattern has not been destroyed, it has been merely changed. In the family one or the other profession is still carried on though of a different sort and in a different atmosphere. In the West the family might have lost much of its role as an economic unit but in India it still to a certain extent continues to perform this traditional function.

2. ***Centre of Religious Activities.*** Another non-essential function, which the family performs is of a religious character. It is a centre for the religious training of the children who learn from their parents various religious virtues. In the old family, different religious practices like idol worship, yagya, religious discourses and sermons by pandits were carried on which made the outlook of the children religious in India. The modern family, however, does not observe religious practices and has become secular in outlook.

3. ***Centre of Education.*** One more function performed in the family is the education of children. The family is an important education agency. The child learns the first letters under the guidance of parents though today he learns them in a nursery-schoo1. The traditional family was the centre of vocational education because the children from the early childhood were associated with the family task. The modern family has delegated the task of vocational education to technical institutes and colleges. But despite all this the role of the family as a center of education has not vanished completely and in a somewhat modified form it still continues to perform some of the educational functions. For instance, it is even now in and through family that the people learn their social habits and moral virtues. It is in no way an in significant function for which the Indian families are conspicuously known and popular.

4. *Guardian of Culture.* The family keeps the culture of society, alive. It moulds its members according to the social culture. The children are educated in the various aspects of culture from their infancy. The family creates such an environment for them that they learn to live and behave in acccordance with their culture. The elderly members of the family impart training in matters of conduct, thinking religion and ethics etc. to the children. The family is aptly described as the maker and guardian of Culture.

5. *Centre of Recreation.* The old family provided recreation to its members. They used to sing and dance together and visit the family relations. In modern times family relationship is individual rather than collective. The present forms of recreation such as bridge tennis carrom and movies, provide for only individual or couple participation. Moreover, recreation is now had in club or hotel rather than in home. In this way, there has also occurred a shift in the recreational functions of the family. However, it needs be said that in countries like India having close ties of ancient culture the family is still acting as a centre of recreation at least in the rural areas.

It is clear from the foregoing facts that there has come about a great change in the functions of the family whereas about a hundred years back the family was more of a community, it has become today more of an association. The very importance of the family has been loosened. It is no longer a home for recreation of its members, a school of education for children or a centre for their religious training. Many family duties, which were performed formerly by the parents have now been transferred to external agencies. The functions of a modern family are very much limited both in their number and extent. Even the task of procreation has suffered a setback. Of course the task of satisfaction of sex need is better performed, by modern family. In short, the family has lost some of its former: functions. It is to be, however, remembered that though there is a loss of functions the family is not going to perish. There are certain functions for this performance of which no human society can do without family. Thus it may be said in the end that despite its structural and functional changes, the family still plays a significant role in social strength and social solidarity.

FAMILY AS A SOCIAL SYSTEM

It is customary to regard family as a social system. In fact there are many kinds of social systems and these are composed of variety of elements. So far as family is concerned, it fulfils many of the conditions, which go to make it a social system. It is for this reason that family is characterised as being a perfect social system and this notion fully holds good at least in the case of joint family. Defining social system Talcott Parsons writes, "The social system is composed of the patterned interaction of members. It consists of interaction of a plurality of individual actors, whose relations to each other are mutually oriented through the definition and mediation of a pattern of structured and shared symbols and expectations." Similarly C.P. Loomis is also of the opinion, "Socialogists frame of reference is inter action, characterised by patterned social relation that display in their uniformities social elements articulated by social processes, the dynamics of which account for the emergence, maintenance and change of social system."

When these observations are applied on family, it becomes clear that the family is contained in a number of elements, which are found in every social system. These are some of those elements of which most family groups consist and on the basis of which family is entitiled to be called a social system.

1. Status. Every family consists of a number of persons and all of them have a certain status. This status of the members of a family is normally determined on the basis of age and sex. But sometimes learning and occupation also have some effect in this matter. The status of parents is always higher than that of the children. Similarly in a family sons enjoy better status than daughters. Status helps in making gradation in the position of the different members of their family and their social relations are determined in accordance with their position. Since father's status in the family is the highest of all, he is authorised to perform all the family responsibilities. The eldest son being next in importance to his father automatically obtains the same position after his father's death.

2. Role. All the members of the family perform a certain role and it is by this means that the working of the family is made possible. The roles that the different persons perform are determined and conditioned by the status that they hold in the family. In fact every status has a correspondent role attached to it. Role is the outward manifestation of the status and, thus both of them go together. Every member of the family while performing his role keeps in view his status in the family and does the things accordingly. The role maintains the balance of status system and thereby keeps intact the structure of the family. Since, there are a variety of status differing from person to person, so there are a number of roles varying from person to person according to his status. For Instance, the role of parents in the family is quite different from that of the children but it needs be said that the functioning of the family can go well only if all of its members perform their respective roles properly.

3. Privilege. In a social system every unit is gifted with a certain kind of privileges. These privileges also go with the roles that they perform and the status that they hold in a social structure. It is through the enjoyment of privileges that a unit is enabled to do its responsibilities nicely under all circumstance. It is this element that gives stability and continuity to a social system. The samething can be said in the case of family as well. The members of the family are always in the enjoyment of certain privileges according to their status. It is by the exercise of these privileges enjoyed by the members that structure and functioning of the family remain intact.

4. Necessities and Aims. Every social system consists of the needs, aims and ends of the people. They are related to the level of cultural and economic progress of the society. Sometimes they are also concerned with the social development of the people. Men have some basic needs and the fulfilment of them is the chief aim of a social system. For realization of these aims a social system has to set before it its certain ideals and ends. In this way needs and alms play a vital role in the efficient working of any social system. Family as a social system is concerned with fulfilling some-physical and social needs of the people. There are some basic needs like sex impulse, procreation of race and the provision of home, which cannot be met elsewhere except in the family. These needs aim at ensuring good life to the people. It is right that in the modern times many of the functions of the family have been taken over by some other associations, but all the same there are some primary functions which must be performed in the family in all civilized societies.

5. Sanctions. The sanctions determined by the social values and Ideals play in important part in the field of human conduct. The social sanctions make a distinction between what is right and what is wrong in the activities and behaviour of the individuals. Society permits its members to do certain things and forbids them to do others and thereby lays down a standard for the general conduct of its members. The members are allowed to do only those things, which are beneficial for the life and stability of the social order. In this way sanctions also help a lot in the strengthening of a social system. They maintain discipline and orderly conditions in it. This element is found in abundance in the working of the family as well. There are some set rules and codes of behaviour which are binding on the members and which they cannot ignore easily. Thus the family as a social system depends largely for its life and sound working on a set of rules, which operate in the form of social sanctions. The more active and forceful are these social sanctions, the more solid and the longer lasting will be the structure of the family. This is why in the past families were more integrated and well disciplined because there was more force behind the social sanctions.

6. Power. In every social system there exists a supreme power which acts as a controlling figure in it. It, on the one hand, resolves the conflicts of different units and on the other, keeps intact the unity of that social system. The family as a social system vests its supreme power in the father or husband who supervises and controls the activities of other members. There can be no challenge or disobedience to the command of the head of the family. Only such families last long in which there is unity of command and a well-knit controlling power.

7. Ideal Principles. The family, as a social system, derives its life out of the inter-relations and inter-actions of its members. Every member of the family has a special function to do and a particular role to play for its well-being. There is great need of making. It certain that all the members of the family do their part well. For this purpose there exists some ideal principles. These principles maintain solidarity and balance in the family. These principles are in the form on unwritten maxim and are based on common consent. They are so vital to the social life that they cannot be set aside easily and in their absence a good family life cannot be made possible.

8. Sentiments. Sentiments occupy an important place in a social system. The sentiments especially influence collective life. It is under their influence that an individual gives preference to collective interest over his own individual gain. They develop general working patterns of different groups, which afford stability and uniformity to a social system. Family as a social system gives expression to a number of sentiments. The chief among these are a sentiment of love, the sentiment of co-operation, sentiment of sympathy and the sentiment of respect. These sentiments form the be all and end all of family life.

Thus it is clear from the above facts that family is truly a social system because it contains most of the basic elements of a social system. It is right that in the modern times family is undergoing great changes. As a result of this fact it is feared that family may not lose in course of time, its character of being a social system. But such doubts appear to be unfounded because there are so many elements of social system, which cannot vanish from family. Thus in the end it can be said that family is definitely a social system with this much exception that it has been more apparent in a joint family.

Difference between Family and Society

There is a general agreement on this point that both family and society are not only natural but also necessary for mankind. They are very old organizations which have been working since the time immemorial and which are bound to exist till the unknown future. It is neither possible nor desirable to challenge this assumption. But despite all this they cannot be viewed as identical terms. There exists a broad and clearly visible line of distinction between them.

To begin with, the first mark of distinction between them is the flame as is between the whole and a part of a thing. Society is the collection of different communities, associations and institutions while family is one of them. It is an association and also an institution serving some of the basic needs of the individuals. In this way society is the whole of organizational pattern of human relationship of which family is a component part.

Secondly, from the structural point of view society is much bigger than family. The family is a small kin-group, which consists of father, mother and their children and in some cases it may contain some other close relatives. But on the other hand, society is a large organization, which is composed of several families and clans. Thus family may be said to exist within society and not society within family.

Thirdly, from the standpoint of their origin also a distinction is drawn between them. Many sociologists are of the opinion that the first and the primary unit of human organization in this universe is family and not society. The family later on developed and assumed the form of society. In this way, society is the developed form of family and family in the matter of origin is regarded as prior to society.

Fourthly, the membership in a family is always limited and definite but this is not the case with society. The members of a family always live in that very family and they cannot change their family affiliations at their own sweet will. But there is no such limit on the members of a society. People can change their membership of society at their own pleasure. They may leave one society and join another and they are under no check in such changes. Thus while the membership of a family is natural and inborn, the membership of society can be in some cases the work of human wishes and efforts.

Lastly, from the view-point of their functions and nature, the structure of the family is becoming more and more simple day by day while the structure of society is becoming increasingly complex. There used to be in the past huge joint families, which have now become small simple single families. On the other hand, with the passage of time the society is constantly growing in bigness of size and complexity of structure. However, despite all these differences the two organizations must always work simultaneously and live together.

DIFFERENCE BETWEEN MODERN FAMILY AND TRADITIONAL FAMILY

Family is a very old social group. It has been in existence since long times. It is older than society and as old as human life itself. But despite all this, it is not a static institution. It is always changing with the march of time. It is for this reason that the structure of the modern family is not the same as it was about a century ago. In order to emphasise this fact, J. Rumney and Joseph Maier observe, "Although the family is universal, no particular form of it is primary or inevitable. Like all other institutions, it is a social product subject to change and modification." Similarly Nimkoff and Ogburn also write, "The family has changed a good deal in the past and has assumed many different forms and functions. The family has proved to be a very resilient and flexible institution. Despite radical changes in form and functions, the family has continued to exist in every society known to us. It should be clear from these facts that family is undergoing constant changes. As a result of this the modern family has become much different from the ancient family. In short, some of the main points of difference between them can be shown in the following way.

1. Replacement of Joint Family by Single Family. To begin with a fundamental difference between the modern family and the ancient family pertains to its size. In the ancient societies joint family system was the order of the day. There used to be families of very big size consisting of the members of many generations. Not only parents and their children but also the families of their brothers, grand parents and the widow daughters of the same family used to live in one house. Such family group was like a social unit and many a time the number of its members exceeded even a hundred, but in the modern times single-family system has become the order of the day. Now joint families have broken up and their place has been taken over by single families. The modern families are quite small in size consisting of parents and their small children. Even the grown up children after their marriage separate themselves from their parents and establish their own families. At present the number of membership in a family hardly exceeds ten persons or so. This process of the disintegration of joint families and in its place the establishment of single families first began in the west and now it has spread all over the world.

2. Modern Family no Longer a Social Unit. Secondly, the traditional family was regarded as a social unit, whereas the modern families have become individualistic in outlook. In the ancient times all the members of a family lived at one and the same place and they were bound together by a thread of the commonness of residential and social conditions. All the physical and social needs were fulfilled in the family and there was no necessity of any outside agency to interfere in the human life. But such is not the case in the modern families wit the disintegration of joint family system. The family in the modern time has lost. Its character as a social unit. The people have become more Individualistic In outlook than they think of common interests. Now even the members of the same family live scattered at different places and do separate occupations. Emphasizing this fact Gisbert writes, "The family has somewhat relaxed as a closely knit social unit and has opened the door to individualistic tendencies and outlook. The husband now has to leave his home for a living and work at a specified time and place and under conditions prescribed by others."

3. Change in the Position of Women. Fourthly, an important point of difference between the traditional and modern families relates to the position of women. Formerly, the women occupied a very low position in the family. They were just slaves to men possessing none of their own individuality. They had no rights nor any freedom. They had to carry out the dictates of the male members of the family. But now her position has changed altogether. In modern famdy the woman if not the devotee of man but an equal partner in life with equal rights. The husband now does not dictate but only requests the wife to do tasks for him. She is now emancipated of man's slavery. She can divorce her husband as the husband can divorce her. She can sue the husband for her rights and likewise be sued in turn. Thus the position of the women has changed in the family with the changing times.

4. Economic Independence of Women. Fifthly, a very important feature of modern family is the economic independence of women, while such a thing was not found in the traditional family. Previously, women were dependent on men for the fulfilment of all their needs and wants. They had no independent economic resources of their own to support them. They were confined within the four walls of the home and all their basic needs of food, clothing and shelter had to be met in the family by men. Women could own neither property nor could they hold any occupation. Marriage was a compulsory bond .for them, which they had to undertake for the fulfilment of economic, needs. But now the position has changed altogether. Women in modern family have attained an increasing degree of economic dependence. It is not only the husband who leaves the home for work but it is also the wife who goes out of doors, for work. The percentage of women employed outside the home is continually on the increase. They are now property-owners as well as wage earners and do not want to lag behind men in any way. This economic dependence has largely affected the attitude of modern woman. Formerly, she had no choice but to find a male partner who could marry her and support her economically. She now does not feel helpless before man, settles matters with him in terms of her own right. She is not a slave of the man who provides her with food, clothing, and shelter but she can now earn her own living. Such a feature did not mark the traditional family.

5. Decline of Religious Control. Seventhly, while the traditional family was religious in outlook, the modern family is secular in attitude. The religious rites of the traditional family such as early prayer, yagya etc. are no longer performed in modern family. Marriage also has become a civil contract rather than a religious sacrament. It can be broken at an hour. The authority of religion over the conditions of marriage and divorce has markedly declined. Divorce is a frequent occurrence in modern family. In traditional family it was a rare phenomenon.

6. Decreased Control of the Marriage Contract. Marriage is the basis of family. In a traditional family the parents contracted the marriage. The marriage ceremony was based on the principle of male dominance and female obedience. In a modern family people is less subject to the parental control in the matter of mate choice. The partners themselves do not settle the marriage and it can be undone at their own will.

7. Abandonment of Non-essential Functions. Lastly the sphere of activities of traditional family had been much larger than that of modern family. The modern family has given up a great many functions, which were performed by the traditional family. These functions have now been taken over by specialized agencies. According to Jay Rumney and Joseph Maier, "Compared with the family of medieval times the functions of the modern family are few. All but gone are its economic, educational, religious and protective functions. They have been transferred to the State, the Church, the school and industry." Not only this much but many of the traditional tasks of the household such as cooking and baking, cleaning and washing are also performed outside the household by specialized agencies. In this way while the traditional family performed both essential and non-essential functions, the modern family is concerned with the doing of essential functions.

8. Modern Family no longer an Economic Unit. Sixthly, the traditional family was an economic unit, which the modern family has, ceases to be now. The traditional family was all at once a production and consumption unit. It was self-sufficient in economic needs. All the active members of the family were employed in the family occupation. All the articles of consumption could be prepared at home. There was no cause of depending on outside agencies for the sake of economic gratification. But the modern family does not possess such a character. It is no longer a self-sufficient unit. The members of the family have to seek outside help for finding a suitable occupation. It has also ceased to be a unit of production because most of the articles of daily need are now obtained from the market. In this connection Gisbert has aptly remarked, "The modern family is no longer the Economic unit that it was in the Middle Ages where production, distribution and consumption developed in the home as a self-sufficient unit in an agricultural and handicraft economy. It would be misleading to say that the family is losing its economic functions, but it is certainly transforming them considerably."

It is clear from the foregoing facts that the family has been subjected to profound modification of an economic, social and biological nature. The modern family is no longer the economic and self-sufficient unit. But despite all this it may be said, that the family still remains a strategic social institution. The loss of its functions and the change in its structure has not destroyed its basic position. Thus it may be said in the end that the modern family has considerably changed from the traditional family, but this process of change has been all at once the result of changing needs and current circumstances.

CHANGES IN THE MODERN FAMILY

It is a well known fact that change is the Law of Nature. There is no human organisation on social institution which has remained uniform and static at all times and under all circumstances. It has to move and change with the changing conditions, or it is apt to become obsolete and go out of existence. This rule is fully applicable on the age-old institution of family as well. The family as it is now is much different from what it was a few generations ago. Several changes have taken place in its nature and structure with the result that it has undergone an overall transformation. Whereas about a century back the family was more of a community, it has become today more of an association. According to Ogburn and Nimcoff, "The family has changed a good deal in the past and has assumed many different forms and functions. The family has proved to be a very resilient and flexible institution. Despite radical changes in form and function, the family has continued to exist in every society known to us."

It points to the fact that in the recent times many changes have occurred in the family and some of them may briefly be mentioned here.

Referring to some of the changes occurred in the modern family and the forces bringing about them Davis writes, "Modern civilization characterized by an elaborate industrial technology, a high degree of urbanization, and a great amount of geographical and social ability, has sheered away the extended kingship bonds.. The role effective kinship group is now the immediate family and even this unit has lost in size and function. True, the immediate family has gamed in importance by being freed from the control of extended kindred, but it has declined in importance in other ways."

It is clear from this statement that in the modern time a large number of changes have occurred in the organization and working have the family and several factors has been operating to bring about these changes. Some of the more important changes in family life need be mentioned here in order to reveal its present position.

(i) To begin with, the joint family system is declining and in its place single-family system is coming into prominence. Unlike the large family of traditional society the modern families are small in size. They consist of the husband, wife and their minor children. This is of course the first and the fundamental change that has occurred in the structure of family.

(ii) In the modern time there has occurred a change in the mutual relation of parents and children. The control of parents over their children has lessened a great deal and now the family discipline is not as tight as it was in the ancient families. The children have become less obedient to their parents and they are very particular about their freedoms and rights.

(iii) There has taken place a change in the mutual relation of husband and wife in the family. Unlike old times women have become independent and self-reliant in many ways. Now that the women have gamed equal fights with men, their mutual relationship has undergone much change. Mowrer has correctly written of modern woman that 'she is no longer the drudge and slave of other days.'

(iv) The modern family is no longer a permanent association. It is precarious and can be rendered void at any time. Marriage has been reduced to a mere social contract, which it is not difficult to break in the event of even the slightest friction. According to Maciver, "The Modern family in comparison with the ancient and medieval families is very weak and unstable."

(v) There has come about a good deal of change in the extent of family functions. Many of the functions which family

performed previously are no longer under its care. They have been transferred to several external agencies. The family has ceased to be an economic as well as social unit. When compared with the family of medieval times, the functions of the modern family are few. All but gone are its economic educational, religious and protective functions. They have been transferred to the State, the church, the school, and industry.

(vi) The modern family is under less religious control. It has been replaced by legal control. With the decline of the Influence of religion the family morals have also become comparatively loose. The modern family has become secular in outlook and it has given up many of its religious activities.

(vii) The rigidity traditionally associated with marital and sexual relationships no longer characterizes the modern family. The use of contraceptive and means of birth control has rendered the size of the family very small. There is not much affinity among the blood relations of the family. In this way the relations in the family have become more formal and mechanical in Nature.

Lastly, the family seems to be coming on the verge of disorganization. The number of divorces is on the increase. The control, which the family exercises over the individual is being lessened rapidly. Thus the family has undergone a good deal of transformation in the present century.

Factors Responsible for Changes in the Family

It is clear from the foregoing facts that a large number of changes have occurred in the structure of family. This process has not completed yet and is liable to continue till indefinitely even in the unknown future. There is not one but many factors which are working at the root of all these changes.

Referring to some of these factors Jay Rumney and Joseph Maier write, "The modern family which is still essentially patriarchal in character has been shorn of much of its power. The State is tending to become a super-parent, having arrogated to itself much of the patriarch's authority. Profound economic changes since the Industrial Revolution have deprived the family of its economic functions as a unit of production. It is now mainly a unit of consumption. The new economy, requiring the use of womanpower opened up new occupations to women, they became economically in dependent of their husbands. The political and economic emancipation of woman as well as periods of prolonged unemployment undermined the authority of the father, especially if his earnings were surpassed by those of his wife and children. A new morality emerged in conflict with the traditional moral standards. Large families became rare. Urbanization led to a wide dissemination of contraceptive knowledge. The small independent if it, consisting of parents and one or two offspring became the rule. Thus, lit short, some of the causes and factors of family changes may be explained in the following order.

1. Impact of Industrialization. The first important factor bringing about changes in the structure of family has been the force of industrialization. The Industrial Revolution substituted the power machine for the manual tool. As new techniques of production advanced they shelved the old family of its economic functions. New factories with heavy machines have been set up which have taken both the work and the workers out of the family. Now cloth is produced not on the family handloom but in the textile mill. Thousands of workers who are drawn out of home are required to work in the factory. Not only males but females also have begun to go to the factory for work. The work of women has become specialized like that of men. They instead of being busy with the multifarious tasks of the family have started going to workshops and factories for work. As a result of it women have become as good the earning members of the family as men. This earning power of the women has made them free from dependence on men. In this way industrialization has greatly affected the character of modern family. 'The family' as Maciver says, "has changed from a production to consumption unit."

2. Decline of Religious Control. The modern family has become secular in its outlook because of the decline of the force of religions. Marriage has become a civil contract rather than a religious sacrament. It can be broken at any time. The authority of religion over the conditions of marriage and divorce has suffered a great decline. Divorce is a frequent occurrence in modern family while in traditional family it was a rare phenomenon. Religion has been a great uniting and solidifying factor in the, family. And with the loss of its force the family is bound to undergo disintegration.

3. Effect of Urbanism. An inevitable result of industrialization has been the, growth of urbanism. Urbanism has materially affected not merely the size of the home but also the essentials of the family life. It has substituted legal controls for informal controls and has brought the family into competition with specialized agencies. The result is that many of the family functions have been taken over by the external agencies. For example, the educational, health and recreational functions of the family are now performed by schools, hospitals and recreational centres respectively. Under the joint force of industrialization and urbanization the family has ceased to be a social as well as economic unit. The joint family system is vanishing and in its place the single-family system is becoming the order of the day. It has even affected the mutual relations of the different members of the family. To quote Davis," It has forced individuals to co-operate with countless person who are not kinsmen. It has also encouraged them to join special interest groups thus drawing them out of the unspecialized and heterogeneous family with its wide sex and age differences." In this way urbanism and industrialization have caused considerable modifications in the structure of family.

4. Effect of Changing Mores. The mores concerning family life are constantly changing and this factor has. Also greatly affected the organization of family. Now the mutual relations of different members of the family have undergone remarkable change and it is all the result of changing mores. According to Maciver and Page "The basis of husband wife relationship in the family is no longer domination but co-operation". Previously everywhere, the wife was dominated by the husband and so the family stability survived because of the unity of command. But with the removal of this dominance the family organization has been exposed to powerful perils. Thus as a result of all these factors the family organization is not stable and it is undergoing quick modifications. But notwithstanding all these facts the family still continues to be a strategic social Institution.

5. Social Mobility. The critics are of the opinion that social mobility has cut still deeper into the family organization. In so far as individuals improve their class status by virtue of their own achievement rather than by birth, an intrinsic function of the family is lost to it. In this connection Davis writes, "In a completely open society where all vertical positions were filled purely by individual accomplishment, there could scarcely be a family organization; each family member would tend to find himself in a different. Social stratum, from the others, and the invidious sentiments thus brought into the family circle would prove incompatible with family sentiment." The organizations of the family can remain intact only if its members feel dependent on it for their personal advance in life. If this requirement is fulfilled by some external factors, it adversely affects the family organization. This is exactly what is happening in the present society. People do not feel themselves so much? Attached to family because so many external factors are on their disposal to help them in their individual development.

SOCIOLOGICAL SIGNIFICANCE OF THE FAMILY

The family is by far the most important primary group in society. Historically it has been transformed from a more or less self-contained unity into a definite and limited organization of minimum size, consisting primarily of the original contracting parties: On the other hand it continues to serve as. a total community for the lives born within it, gradually relinquishing this character as they grow toward adulthood. The family more profoundly than any other organization, exists only as a process. Referring to the sociological of the family Maciver and Page opine, "Of all the organizations, large or small, which society unfolds, none transcends the family in the intensity of its sociological significance. It influences the whole life of society in innumerable ways, and its changes reverberate through the whole social structure. It is capable of endless variation and yet reveals a remarkable continuity and persistence through change. Thus, in short, family is the first and foremost organ of society and this fact can be proved by the following arguments:

1. Universal in Character. The family is the most nearly universal of all social forms. It is found in all societies, at all stages of social development, and exists far below the human level, among a myriad species of animals. Almost every human being is or has been a member of some family. There is no other social group that can equal family in this matter.

2. Formative Influence. Family is also significant because it exerts the profoundest formative influence on the life of the individuals. It is the earliest social environment of man's life and plays a vital role in moulding it. No other organization can compete with family in this respect. According to Maciver, "In particular it moulds the character of the individual by the impression both of organic and of mental habits". Its influence in infancy determines the personality structure of the individual. It is largely from his parents that the child receives his physical inheritance and mental training, on the basis of which he leads the whole of his life. It is well-said by a critic, "To be well-born is to possess the greatest of all gifts. To be ill-born there is nothing which this world can offord that will be adequate compensation for the lack of good heredity." Thus family has come to surpass all other social organizations in the matter of formative influence on human personality.

3. Nuclear Position in the Social Structure. Family is the nucleus of all the social organizations. Frequently in the simpler societies, as well as in the more advanced types of patriarchal society the whole social structure is built of family units. Only in the higher complex civilizations does the family cease to fulfill this function, but even in them the local community, as well as its divisions of social classes tends to remain unions of families. One of the first definitions ever given of a community made it "a union of families" and for the local community the definition, with some qualification, still holds today.

4. Performance of Basic Functions. The significance of the family as a social institution may be measured by the number of basic functions it performs. Compared with the family of medieval times, the functions of the modern family are few. All but gone are its economic, educational, religious and protective functions. They have been transferred to the State, the church, the school and industry. Notwithstanding the loss of functions, the family remains a strategic social institution. It is our parents that first cure us of our natural wildness, and break in us the spirit of independency we are all born with. It is to them that we owe the first rudiments of our submission and to the honour and deference which children pay to parents all societies are obliged for the principle of human obedience", writes Mandeville. In addition to performing this all-important function of socializing the individual, the family regulates sexual relationships, provides for the affectional needs of its members, makes possible the prolonged care, which children require and transmits the values of the culture. It remains a powerful agent of social and political control and economic differentiation. Children generally stay in the social class to which their parents belonged. They inherit both the property and the cultural advantages, which its possession offers.

5. Proper Organization of Society Dependent upon Family. Proper social organization largely depends upon sound organization of families. If in a particular society families disintegrate, that society can never be safe and sooner or later it is found to meet its doom. This is why at all times one major cause of social disorganization has been family disorganization. Families develop the characters of the members of the society. In the opinion of ADLER, a man's role in the family determines his role in society. There is no exaggeration in calling family a cornerstone of society.

6. An Important Agency of Social Control. Family is an important agency of social control. Family controls sex passions in society. A strict control over sex relationships is necessary for maintaining the order otherwise society will disintegrate. In all cultures, family exercises some degree of control over the unmarried members from falling into bad habits. No parents would like their children to adopt the career of crime. The children under the influence of their parents drop bad habits and learn good habits. In the making of great men families have always played a major role. In this way the making of a good citizen in society depends upon the parents.

7. Family is the Conveyer of Culture. The family not only moulds character and personality of the individuals, but it also imparts its culture to them. It is while living in the family that the child acquires knowledge about the culture of society. It is an efficient vehicle for the transmission of culture from one generation to another. It is a very good socializing agency that makes the people social and cultured beings According to Deway and Tufts, "The family is a social agency for the education and protection of the race." It is through family that the individuals come to know the customs, traditions, social values and cultural background of their community. Family provides them knowledge and understanding of the past and thereby prepares them to live well in the future. Thus in all these ways family plays a vital role in the field of preservation and transmission of social culture.

8. Family is Vital to the Process of Socialization. Another point of significance of family is that it plays a vital role in the process of socialization of the individuals. Merrill is of the opinion that family is an enduring association of parent and offspring whose primary functions are the socialization of the child and the satisfaction of the members. It is in the family that child learns all good and human qualities like sincerity, sympathy, self-submission, consciousness of responsibility and so forth. It is the character developed in the family, which helps the child in becoming an important and responsible member of society. F. J. Wright was quite correct in saying that in every family, the child gets an opportunity for free expression of thoughts and developing his entire personality. It has been conclusively proved that the proper development of the child is impossible without a good environment in the family. The tendencies and habits, which he acquires in the family remain with him for the whole of his life. It is in view of this fact that Freud says, "The view-point of a child towards the senior in the family determines his attitude and viewpoint towards the elders in society." Thus it is obvious that 'family is the cradle of social virtues and no other social group contributes more than family in the process of socializing the individuals. Confucious remarked quite correctly that if you want to improve society, improve its families. Society will improve automatically when the families improve."

It is clear from the above account that family is the most important social institution. No other human organization can overshadow it in the matter of sociological significance. This fact is true not only from the structural view-point, but also from the functional stand-point. There are some functions of the family, which no other group can undertake successfully. There are some clear uses of the family, which no one can derive from any other group. Without family the process of socialization would remain incomplete, the task of preserving and transmitting culture to posterity would be half done and there would be no organization to safeguard their social and cultural values. Its significance also lies in the fact of its being the oldest and universal human organization. It is even the parent of society whose structure is raised on the foundations of family. If family were to vanish, it would expose the whole human race to the horrors of complete decay. The present changes in the family need not be taken to mean the signal of its possible downfall in the future; it is rather a process of its adjustment to the current needs and the changing times. Family in the past has remained an indispensable social system and it is sure to continue as such in the future as well. Thus on account of its strategic position the family more than any other group exerts persistent, intimate and far reaching influence on the habits, attitudes and social experiences of the people. It plays the foremost role in the formation of personality. It occupies a key place in social organization.

●●●

13

Psychology of Social Change

The study of social change in modern India is a vast enterprise, which requires that the same problem areas are explored not only from multi-disciplinary but also from multi-ideological perspectives. This entails fruitful communication and exchange between scholars following not only different disciplines but different, and sometimes conflicting, ideological approaches. It must be explicitly recognised that no single approach has answers to all the important questions nor has it the monopoly of all the useful insights. There is no master-key to all the secrets of the social reality and the belief that there exists such a masterkey is the product of ignorance, intellectual inertia, or vested interests. One should also make allowance for diversity of perspectives even within one or the other seemingly homogeneous intellectual approach. For instance, there should be scope for diversity of interpretations of social reality even within the framework of the common approach, which is labelled Marxist.

Countries of the Third World should avoid in this respect reproducing some of the negative features of the intellectual history of the Western and the Communist worlds. The lack of intellectual appreciation of conflicting approaches and ideologies has been an important feature of the Western world specially during the cold war phase, and of the Communist world during the Stalinist era. It took sometimes the form of a total conspiracy of silence against dissident ideologies and approaches, and sometimes even of their suppression, through non-intellectual means or naked coercion. Old habits of thought die hard and social science can be free from them only by tolerance of dissent and vigorous battle of ideas.

The practice of either open or veiled coercion in the realm of ideas should be rejected because there can be no science without free scope for divergent, even opposite, points of view. There could be no Marx without a Hegel and there could be no Weber without a Marx.

The creation of a cultural environment in which diverse schools of thought can contend with each other may contribute to scientific development in another way. An individual scientist or a group of scientists may begin their study of a problem with a bias for a definite ideological standpoint. But the very process of research, if it is pursued freely, has its own inherent logic. Scientific enquiry, much to the astonishment of that individual or that group, may ultimately force a modification or a rejection of that approach rather than provide its confirmation. Reality after all is much bigger than any school or system of thought. The Third World in this way provides a testing ground for many established approaches and theories. In course of time it may also throw up common approaches and perspectives on fundamental questions relating to study of society and social change 10 the contemporary period.

It should be noted that the developmental experience of countries of the Third World has already been serving as a dissolvent of many ideological cleavages and many established conceptions of the Western world about them (*i.e.* Third World countries). However, this developmental experience has not received adequate attention from social scientists. It has not yet become the basis for re-evaluating, or empirically verifying, the dominant approaches, theories and hypotheses about developing countries. Many of these intellectual frameworks originated during the colonial period but they have continued to influence social science research even after overt political colonialism ended.

Old intellectual orientations have thus become more sacred than the facts of life and there is no serious attempt to readjust the former to the latter. In fact, there is an attempt to ignore the latter in order to escape an agonising reappraisal of the former. The severest indictment of many studies of social change based on these intellectual orientations is that they do not show any awareness of the intrusion of colonialist or conservative ideology into their studies. These social scientists, therefore, are not adequately scientific in their method and approach.

It must be recognized that the analysis of society by a social scientist cannot be expected to be wholly free from biases derived from the social milieu. A social scientist is free from value biases not in the sense of having or not having biases but only in the sense of being ignorant or aware, being less or more aware, of his value orientations. Objectivity in scientific analysis, therefore, is related to the degree of awareness of the existence of value orientations and of their nature. Further, in order to ensure that objectivity is not seriously hampered by value biases, it is necessary to proceed at two levels. Firstly, scientific enquiry must also be focused on the question of values, especially on the questions of the social basis of divergent and conflicting valuations. Secondly, a social scientist must consciously expose himself to various facets of reality. Further, he should not merely look for facts, which support his standpoint or hypotheses. It should also be his scientific duty to look for facts, which do not support or corroborate his hypotheses.

It is our firm conviction that a serious intellectual effort at both these levels—at the level of sociological enquiry into values and at that of painstaking investigation into realities of developing countries since their emergence as independent countries—will contribute greater depth and authenticity to the scientific analysis of social change. It may also reduce the ideological hiatus between social scientists. As a result of this process students of social development may in coming years distinguish more between the scientific and the non-scientific rather than between the radical or non-radical, liberal or non-liberal approaches. By explicitly recognising the influence of ideology on scientific study and by exposing the social roots of various ideological approaches, social science may rise above ideologies and present a synthesis of vital elements of different and conflicting ideologies. In this way the light-bearing mission of social science is bound to be fulfilled to a much greater extent than before. And by performing better its light-bearing function, social science may emerge as a unifying rather than a divisive force. It may play a much greater role in promoting a cognitive revolution in the case of countries of the Third World than it did in the case of the Western world where the social sciences originated.

Why the study of social change raises the value problem much more sharply and why ideology colours scientific analysis much more in this sphere than in other spheres is also a point, which deserves to be explored. It should be explored as part of the general question why in the contemporary setting the value problem has re-emerged as a crucial issue is all spheres of scientific analyses pertaining to economics, politics, sociology, culture etc.

The value problem in the social sciences is again inseparable from the value crisis affecting countries like India. The roots of this crisis lie deep in the historical background of externally imposed rather than autonomously induced social change or modernisation. The contrast between countries such as Japan and India is relevant in this context. In Japan social change was the consequence of voluntary and critical borrowing from the Western world. In the case of India social change was not a consequence of the natural cultural contact between the East and West. Here the Western impact came mainly *via* colonialism. By depriving the Indian people of their autonomy, colonialism converted modernisation for them into a process controlled by outside forces rather than by forces within Indian society. In fact, by converting the traditional ruling class into the social base for colonial exploitation, colonialism created a deep inner schism within Indian society. The native ruling groups were alienated from the people and they ceased to be a force responsible to their own society. The value problem, therefore, could not be resolved within the colonial context. In order to resolve it, it was necessary first to put an end to colonialism. Thus, even though colonialism did not create the value problem, it was responsible for accentuating it.

It should be remembered that all late-comers to the process of modernisation are faced with the value problem, or the problem of defining the content of modernisation and of selecting the paths to modernisation. There is thus no escape from the value problem for developing countries. The main point is whether this problem is continuously resolved by these countries as politically sovereign societies or that 'choices' are imposed on them by more powerful countries which have deprived the former of their political sovereignty. In the case of such dependent countries the modernisation process gets perverted because it is deliberately adapted to the needs of the dominant countries. It ceases to be genuine modernization. It is only artificial modernization. Such a society becomes neither genuinely traditional nor genuinely modern.

The end of colonial rule closed the chapter of externally-imposed modernisation; it opened the prospect of moderniation as a conscious and creative process for many countries including India. The value problem, however, has not been fully clarified largely because some of the basic assumptions of the colonial era have continued in disguised if not naked forms in order to clarify the value problem, it is necessary to identify these old assumptions which obstruct a creative approach to this problem. It must be recognised that colonialism generated two major tendencies on the value plane both of which emanated as defence mechanisms to the colonial impact; the traditionalist ideology which sought an escape in glorification of traditional society and the 'modernist' ideology which sought an easy escape in wholesale Westernisation. Social scientists studying social change have seldom undertaken any systematic analysis of these ideologies and their social background. As a result, scientific analysis itself has often tended to be coloured by partisanship of this or that ideological orientation.

According to the 'modernist' view, the West is the model to be emulated by the late-comers to the historic transition towards an industrial society. Thus, the capacity for change or progress has generally come to be equated with the capacity for re-producing the Western type of social institutions and values, which are interpreted as an ideal framework of a modern society. Even colonialism from this standpoint is presented as a modernising agent in societies like India, which had failed to advance autonomously towards modernity.

In a nutshell, the implication of most of the 'modernist' approaches is that for the developing world the meaning as well as the path of modernisation has been pre-determined as it were by the examples of the Western (or the Communist world). When Karl Marx observed that the country that is more developed industrially shows to the less developed the image of its future, he was recording a fact which appeard valid for his times. But later the non-Western patterns of modernisation in Japan and Russia exploded the myth of the Western pattern as the ideal pattern for late-comers to the modernisation process. The example of these two countries clearly demonstrated that in the case of late-comers 'capacity for change' should not be equated with the capacity for reproducing the Western pattern; it should in fact be equated with the capacity for innovation of new patterns or paths by the developing countries. But the right lessons have not been drawn even from the Japanese and Soviet cases. If for some modernisation meant following the Western path, for some others it became equated with the Japanese or the Soviet paths of economic development. Studies of social change have suffered very much from such ethnocentric bias and the absence of a truly scientific approach. This is not a mere academic lapse but a great practical handicap for the planners of social change. Such modes of thought have led people both in the realms of thought and action to exaggerate the liabilities rather than the assets, the resistances to change rather than the potentialities for change, in the developing countries. Prejudice has also assumed the form of overlooking or even dismissing new experiments in change as, for instance, the Chinese experiment. Here is a typical case of value orientations hampering perception and anticipation of new possibilities and perspectives of social change in the non Western world. Since economic development constitutes an important aspect of social change in backward countries this bias is most marked in the failure to take note of new features contributed to the industrialisation process by the developing countries.

Alexander Gerschenkron, one of the very few social analysts who have contributed valuable insights into these new features, makes this very clear in the following passage:

> "What makes it so difficult for an advanced country to appraise properly the industrialisation process of its less fortunate brethren is the fact that in every instance of industrialisation, imitation of the evolution in advanced countries appears in combination with different indigenously determined elements. If it is not always easy for the advanced countries to accept

the former, it is even more difficult for them to acquiesce in the latter. This is particularly true of the institutional instruments used in carrying out industrial developments and even more so of ideologies which accompany it. What can be derived from a historical review is a strong sense for the significance of the native elements in the industrialisation of backward countries".

It is this 'strong sense for the significance of the native elements' which is lacking in the existing approaches to the analysis of social change in developing countries. This is particularly so in the absence of painstaking investigation into their development experience during the last quarter of a century. The literature on under-development pertaining to India and other countries often tends to suggest as if no economic breakthrough is possible in these countries without a change in their social structures in the direction of Westernisation.

In the very recent period Subhayu Das Gupta has again raised the pertinent question whether the Hindu ethos can meet the challenge of change in India. He seems, however, to be convinced that the emergence of the Western spirit of individualism is a necessity if India is to successfully cope with this challenge. Even though dealing with the vital question of traditional ethos and challenge of change, Das Gupta does not take pains even to mention Japan, the most dramatic case of change without social and cultural Westernisation. Japan's case casts doubt on the facile association between individualism and modern economic development as typified by the Western model.

"Some observers might regard this spiritual legacy of Old Japan as a gloomy spectre which haunts and inhibits its present. But here again, the anomalous, the accidental and the outmoded has been turned to good purpose a weakness, if you like to call it that has been transformed into an advantage. Much of the stress and shock of industrial life, its ugly clashes of jostling interests, have been cushioned by the old habits of thought. Individualism has its virtues and awards, but not in a peasant family whose tenuous bonds can often be maintained only on the pittance remitted by a daughter working in some textile mill. Or again, the old feudal sense of clannishness has been modified to embrace the whole nation so that it has served at moments of great national crisis to forge a spirit of national unity which all the tawdry theatre of a Mussolini or a Hitler cannot so effectively cope. Writing over twenty years ago Veblen commented pithily upon this interval between the borrowing of Western industrialisation and its full psychological acclimatisation and termed it Japan's opportunity."

Having raised the question of the Japanese pattern, it is also pertinent to ask what are the lessons of this pattern for the Third World today. There is no doubt that the resilience and readaptation of Japan's traditional social structure in the context of her transition to a modern economy shows that the social requirements of modern industrialisation have not been identical for all countries and for all historical periods.

But is it proper to conclude from the Japanese experience that in every backward country the traditional institutions and values are capable of readjustment to the requirements of economic development?

It must be noted that the traditional ideology, which is not averse to economic development but would insist on achieving it with minimum interference with the traditional institutions and values seeks to derive support from the Japanese case in many developing countries. How far the social structure of ex-colonial countries like India allows for a repetition or reproduction of the Japanese path of modernisation? How far is the repetition of this model consistent with the social and political forces, which have been released during more than a century following Japan's emergence as a modern nation? These are the pertinent questions raised but not resolved by the traditionalist ideology. These questions, however, have not yet been systematically pursued. Some advocates of the 'modernist ideology' have, however, doubted whether 'traditional society' has the potentiality to promote modern economic, social and political development. But the weaknesses of the modernist critique of traditionalist approach to Indian development .are threefold. This critique tends to regard the traditional society as more survival-and-security-oriented than growth-oriented though this contention is not based on scientific data-based analysis. The fact that India's traditional social structure is markedly different from the type of structure which is associated with economic and social progress in the Western world is regarded as enough evidence for the contention.

This approach had considerable fascination for the modernist elite in the past but it is possible now to re-evaluate It in the light of the recent experiences of transplanting Western institutions in non-Asian environment. It may be noted that far from being the vehicles of growth oriented value systems these institutions under different conditions turned into the opposite *viz.* into vehicles of survival and security-mindedness.

It is necessary to have a much deeper analysis of the Indian social structure and the factors influencing it than what has been provided either by the traditionalist or the modernist ideology in the past. In this background the third basic weakness of the modernist approach is its failure to analysis the nature of the colonial impact on the Indian social structure and to distinguish between the qualitatively different character of traditionalism of the Indian society before and after the colonial impact.

There has been a tendency to characterise the Indian social structure as 'conservative' or hierarchical without analysing the role of colonialism in shaping this conservative or hierarchical character of Indian society. In fact, the roots of this conservatism are traced by some scholars entirely to Indian tradition and values without any reference to the colonial impact and the response of the Indian people to it. Any exploration into the colonial impact would reveal that deepening conservatism of the Indian society was a natural reaction to the traumatic shock of the colonial impact and to widespread insecurity and uncertainty associated with it. It must be remembered that the major social problem facing India then was not that of growth and progress. It was that of survival and security under the tyranny, oppression and uncertainty created by colonialism. Considered from the real needs of the Indian society during this crisis period, the 'conservative' social structure did fulfil a positive function: it served as a massive shock-absorber.

In order to reorient a society from a psychology of survival to a psychology of change and development, it is necessary to alter the conditions of insecurity and uncertainty. For, if these conditions remained unaltered, the authority of the old institutions and values will remain undiminished. In the following passage Louis Dumont draws attention to the fact that:

> "The desire for security and the old loyalties carry the day against whims for independence. One could find no better demonstration to date how powerless are modern education and social and political transformation to overthrow the traditional system."

Dumont is, however, not very illuminating when he interprets this phenomena in terms of the unchanging nature of the traditional (caste) system without going deeper into the pressures and compulsions of the total social situation, specially the material circumstances of a given period. The failure to analyses Indian social institutions and values with reference to the economic, political and cultural history of different periods is a source of distorted conceptions of Indian society in the case not only of Dumont but of several other scholars as well. At the root of many of these misconceptions is again the value bias—a compulsive orientation to consider India and other backward Asian countries as inherently hierarchical or traditional and, therefore, stubbornly resistant to change.

Here then are a few examples of how explaining social change is linked with the value problem and how a scientific approach to values is necessary in order to provide a meaningful understanding of social processes relating both to the past and present. It is also necessary that a scientific treatment of values may ultimately force a rejection of many well-established interpretations of social change. It is further necessary to indicate that an assessment of present trends and future potentialities may be facilitated as greater clarity is achieved about the relation of values to analyses of social change on the basis of re-evaluation of past history.

If it is conceded that modernisation is a creative rather than a fixed concept and that it follows no pre-determined paths, then one should also concede the prospect of new patterns of modernisation in countries of the Third World and the possibility of 'non-Western countries bypassing Western stages to new forms of development'.

If these possibilities are conceded, then social scientists must continuously look for new features in the development process of developing countries. They must also evolve new categories and concepts so as to comprehend these new features. They must attempt radical departures in the spheres of social thought and theory. In fact, instead of trailing behind events in the under-developed world, they must evolve new theoretical orientations, which may help in going beyond post-mortem analysis and towards anticipating and predicting change.

W.F. Wertheim has aptly indicated the consequences flowing from the attempt to understand the changing realities of the Third World with out-of-date conceptual frameworks:

> "The interesting thing is, however, that to a certain extent in Asia the so-called fundamentalists are the real innovators. This is equally true of Mao Tse-Tung, the Leninist fundamentalist. In opposing some aspects of Western 'modernity' or Soviet 'modernity' for that matter they are really searching for new paths of progress. In this process of trying to find novel solutions they may even succeed by bypassing quite a few institutional patterns, which we 'Westernisers' or 'European Marxists' consider essential in modernising a society. If we are not aware of this... we might soon be outdone by their greater inventiveness; and our type of modernism might be turned by this lack of adaptation and empathy into a new kind of traditionalism."

It should be stressed once again that many features of Western development including capitalism represented a penalty, which the West had to pay for being first in the race for modernisation. Must the countries of the Third World necessarily have to reproduce these features in order to evolve a modern identity? Must they necessarily pass through the capitalist ordeal in order to outgrow their economic backwardness? Why should modernisation be conceived as a new kind of tyranny involving compulsory movement towards predetermined paths and conformity to rigid moulds of thought and practice, leaving no choices and no alternatives? Why should modernisation involve transition from the old to the new cage? To raise these questions is to plead for a fundamental reappraisal of the normative assumptions in studies of society and social change. Why is it that these value questions are not sharply posed and their implications for choices of the paths of social change are not seriously explored? Why is modernisation presented as a fait accompli rather than a creative challenge involving choices and innovations?

Before making some observations on the inter-relations of the value question and the class structure, it is also necessary to comment briefly on the traditionalist approach to the question of values in countries like India. Indeed, any discussion of the value question is wholly inadequate or incomplete without reference to the traditionalist standpoint. If the basic deficiency of many anti-traditionalist approaches is an uncritical and unhistorical denigration of native social structures, the traditionalist view has been guilty of the opposite tendency, *viz.* an idealisation of the past as the Golden Age and of Tradition as an ideal and immutable scheme of things valid for all times. The traditionalist standpoint is basically a defensive standpoint; it is not creative and forward-looking. Both the traditionalist and the anti-traditionalist orientations reflect a failure to understand the nature of the challenge facing ex-colonial societies after their liberation from colonial rule. If the former is based on the premise of Indian exceptionalism, the latter derives its alleged validity from the idea of universalism and superiority of institutions and values of the developed countries. Therefore, if the former seeks a return to the past the latter tends to interpret development as a transfer of institutions and ideologies from the advanced to the backward countries. Both are simplistic and erroneous approaches.

The view that the traditional society needs no fundamental change to meet the demands of changing times is as fallacious as the opposite view that these demands can be met only if traditional society is replaced by a society of the Western (or Soviet) type. It is not accidental, therefore, that the more strongly these anti-traditionalist views get identified with the idealisation or the universalisation of the Western (or Soviet) type of society, the more aggressive is also the articulation of a traditionalist ideology upholding the superiority of native culture and its validity for all times.

The intellectual inadequacy of these approaches is that both represent a flight from reality and from real challenges. The traditionalists in particular fail to see that the basis of the pure traditional society which they cherish has been undermined by the colonial impact; and that the attempt either to look for a traditional society where it does not exist or to revive it leads one into a blind alley. Traditionalism, despite its outward appearance of aggressiveness, reflects basically a timid approach to the value problem. It evades the painful task of sorting out the basic issues connected with value choices in response to the changing demands of life in the modern world.

It should be noted that the native vested interests when threatened by the forces of change construct the myth of reviving tradition and the Golden Age. And in this venture they try to capitalise on the deep-seated fear of change expressed by the most numerous and the most characteristic social stratum of the old society *viz.* the peasantry. Traditionalism thus solves neither the moral nor the practical problems facing the peasants in the context of change. But it should not be overlooked that, having lost the old world without gaining a new one, peasantry stands in a Trishanku like position, suspended in a void; it is thrown in a state of melancholy and hopelessness. And traditionalism with its false promise of stability may have enormous fascination, howsoever temporary, for peasants exposed to the stresses and strains of involuntary modernisation.

The throw-back from the process of Westernisation into diverse forms of traditionalism in many developing countries only confirms our point how Westernisation (or pseudo-

Westernisation) and traditionalism re-inforced each other. The challenge of traditionalism cannot be met through borrowed modernity *i.e.* pseudo-Westernisation. It can only be met by grappling with the challenge of change on the plane of all-round innovation and creativity, with due regard especially to peasant interests.

And this takes us to the role of the class structures of developing countries in thwarting the process of renewal in the realm of values.

The roots of unresolved value dilemmas in developing countries lie deep in their class structures. It should be remembered that these structures emerged not as a result of organic growth but as a consequence of forcible imposition from above, during the colonial period. They have continued though in a modified form even after the achievement of independence.

These class structures have been responsible for a deep schism between the upper and the lower classes. This schism has its ramifications in all spheres—the economic, the political, the social and the cultural. Since the days of colonialism the upper classes in countries like India have formed deep ties and allegiances with the upper classes of the western countries. Even when drawn into conflict with the dominant interests in the Western world in the course of the nationalist struggle, they have nursed the ambition of recreating a modified version of the Western society in their own countries. The dominant elites in countries like India have, therefore, seldom put into the forefront the question of a total 'cultural revolution'. The value problem has in this way never been posed as the central problem of Indian renaissance by any school of thought, whether It be liberal, Marxist or Indian-traditionalist.

The elitist dream of creating a modified version of the Western society has, however, resulted only in producing grotesque caricatures in many developing countries. The experience of the last quarter century has shown that in these countries the bourgeois emerges as a lumpen bourgeois, the petty-bourgeois as a lumpen petty-bourgeois and the proletariat as a lumpen proletariat. Transplanted social structures thus turn into the very negation of what they represented in their original milieu. Far from being the carriers of productive values and orientations, these classes turn into bulwarks of social parasitism. Even socialism in this social setting degenerates into vulgar socialism; it turns either into a naked pursuit of power, or a negative, even violent, reaction to deprivation.

A sharp break is therefore necessary from the colonial and neo-colonial tradition of identifying development with mechanical transplantation of institutions and cultures from the Western to non-Western setting. Abandoning the habit of continuously looking outwards, it is necessary now to look inwards and to move towards innovation of patterns and paths suited to one's own total milieu. The basic weakness of this mechanical transplantation is that it does not release the creativity of the most important social force in the developing countries *viz.* the peasantry. In fact, it causes the uprooting of peasants from old ways without integrating them into a new social framework. The peasants in all past models of development have been the object rather than the subject of social change. Peasant interests have generally been sacrificed at the altar of the modernisation process. To repeat these patterns in agrarian countries like India is to invite disaster for millions; it also amounts to reducing modernisation into a destructive rather than a regenerative force for the peasantry, which still constitutes the backbone of ancient countries such as India.

14

Socio-Cultural Influence

Socialisation is a process of social growth through social learning. An individual is born into a society; a society is a group of people who depend upon one another for the satisfaction of their various needs, and who have also developed certain patterns of organization that enable them to live together and survive as a group. These prescribed patterns of behaviour and other socially approved ways are aspects of culture. Culture then may be defined as, the sum total of values, expectations, beliefs, attitudes, customs, and traditions shared by the members of a group or nation.

The first socializing agent of a child is the family followed by his membership in school, religious institution, club, etc. Each cultural group has its own ways of dealing with universal problems like, the care and training of children, feeding and sheltering the group members etc. which are passed on to successive generations as the culture of the that society. To understand how culture influences behaviour we must see how the processes of perception, motivation, thinking, and acting are affected. Thus for example, in a society where fishing is important, individuals of that society are able to discriminate minute changes in the weather and in the conditions of the sea, which would otherwise go unnoticed by most members of different society. The myths, rites, religious ceremonies, literature and paintings of different cultures reveal their beliefs about their world. In short percepts, concepts, beliefs, motives, values, habits, customs and norms are the products of learning and not of inheritance.

People learn to behave in accordance with their culture because there is continuity in the culture. This continuity helps to strengthen the tendency to behave in the approved manner and at the same time to weaken the tendency to behave in an unapproved manner. Much of this training takes place in childhood. Rewards and punishments shape the behaviour of the young child to acquire the habits, which are typical to the culture.

Cultural Changes. Although cultures have developed certain patterns of behaviour, they are not transmitted like hair-looms from generation to generation; instead, they are constantly changing, sometimes slowly and sometimes rapidly. The reasons for cultural changes are many fold and complex; they may be brought about by climatic conditions, by exhaution of natural resources, by technological advances as observed in modem times and even by certain ideologies. Since the behaviour of the individual is shaped by the culture from the time he is born, he is, for most part not aware of the subtle power of cultural influences on him. However, when he becomes aware of these changes he is faced with the problem of conflict. To illustrate, a person brought up in an orthodox and traditional way of life may resent the modern outlook of the present generation and hence is unable to reconcile himself to the cultural changes.

Social Structure

As stated earlier, each culture has its own distinct patterns of behaviour, so also each culture has its own social structure. Every society is interrelated with many types of relations. Social relations may be broadly classified into three headings: (1) Primary social relations, (2) relations of the individual to the group, (3) relations between groups. Taking the first, direct person-to-person relationships constitute the primary interactions of social life. They are primary because person-to-person relations are the earliest social experiences both in the history of the individual and his group. They are also primary in importance because it is the early parent-child relationship, which largely determines the adult personality.

Regarding the second type of relationship the two processes of social facilitation and social inhibition help to determine the relationship of the individual to his group. In every day life social facilitation is observed in such obvious cases as people's eating more and drinking more when in company then when alone. Experiments have shown that workers turn out more work with others busy at the same type of work than in isolation. Similarly, the same experiments have demonstrated the process of social inhibition. Thus while the speed and amount of performance increases in a co-acting group, the quality of performance often goes down. Finally, regarding the relations between groups has been shown to be guided by two processes, namely socio-economic interest groups and social participation groups.

Status and Role. In a society much of the structuring arises from differences among people in the goods and services they produce. One person may be engaged in making garments, another in making shoes and the third in controlling the production of the factory. In such a structure we will find that some people are more important to the society than others. In other words, society assigns certain roles for individuals to perform. In some societies as in India where the society is caste ridden, the social structure is rather rigid, whereas in other societies where class system prevails it is very flexible. In an established society the people are categorized according to differences that are important to meet the needs of society. Thus society assigns to each person what social scientists call a status-age status, sex status, occupational status, social status etc. Each status is a position representing differences among the people in relation to the exchange of goods and services to satisfy the needs of society.

Different people may occupy a particular status at different times and, their statuses may change from time to time. Each status has a role to perform. It is a pattern of behaviour that a person is expected to exhibit according to a particular status. For instance boys and girls at a very early age learn that different behaviours are expected of them. A father as the head of the family has a role becoming to his status. Similarly an employer, a teacher and a mother have different roles to play. The distinction between status and role is as follows:

The former applies to position in the social structure whereas the latter is the behaviour that goes along that position. In a modern society, which has a complex social structure, a person at the same time occupies many statuses and consequently has many roles to perform. Thus for instance a person is the head of the family, teacher, employee, church member, etc. He, therefore, finds himself in multiple statuses and multiple roles. The status and role are important and basic concepts in understanding social structure.

Conflict of Roles. Changes in status put a person in a conflict of roles, and this often happens in a society as complex as ours. He finds that the role he learnt in one status is no longer appropriate in a new status. He becomes uncertain of what role to play and when he is forced to decide he is caught up into a motivational conflict. The consequence of this conflict may be frustration, anxiety, hostility, and failure to adjust. Many of the problems of the adolescents arise because of the difficulty to adjust to the changing behaviour patterns, that is, roles expected of them as they progress from childhood to adulthood.

Conflicts of roles become very important problems in the lives of some individuals. Thus for instance, in our country inspite of equality guaranteed by the constitution, the schedule caste experiences acute problems with conflict of roles. Inequality, iniquities and segregation in housing, education, temples, business, and in other available services precipitate the schedule caste people into conflicts. Their expectations to rise in social esteem, their striving toward upward mobility as a result of education beyond that of their parents, does not seem to be realized in actuality.

Social Classes. In every society, the statuses are arranged on a scale on a scale of prestige. In other words, the people regard some statuses more favourable than others and accordingly wealth, power, respect and honours are given. Research studies have shown that people rank different occupations according to social status. Occupations like physician, banker, or business manager are ranked very high whereas, clerk or salesman has an intermediate rank, and unskilled factory workers are ranked very low. In our society the scale of prestige becomes the basis of caste system. Each person belongs to one of these four and his membership to a particular caste is indicated by his speech, dress, or some other symbol. Further, each caste is restricted to certain occupations and consequently to certain kinds of social behaviour.

In Western society where the prestige scale is the basis of social classes, the formalization of classes is not so rigid. There is greater class mobility in the sense that a person of a lower class has every opportunity to rise in status and thus come up on the prestige scale. The social-class system often maintains cultural, economic and social barriers which prevents social participation and thus a great majority of the children of the lower classes are deprived of the opportunity of learning any culture except that of their own group. Social class system affects individual's experience such as, how he spends his leisure time, what types of things he considers important, what type of job he will try to get, and how he will perceive others as well as he perceived. Although social class system seems to be necessary to maintain the social structure, it is not far from inherent defects, which are real hurdles in the way of progress in the way of lower classes or castes.

The social classes not only differ in status but also in the attitudes of their members. This difference in attitudes is clearly seen in the training and education of a child, and in child rearing practices. Middle class parents tend to be more strict than the upper class parents. The working class parents are more likely to use physical punishment to their children than the middle class parents. The higher class people often aspire to business and occupational profession than the lower class people. Finally, studies have shown that the children from the upper and middle class families tend to have a higher level of achievement motivation than children from the lower class families. It is clear from these differences among different social classes that the attitudes and personalities of the members of different classes differ. They differ in prestige, in attractiveness to others, in freedom to talk, in attitudes and beliefs, in child rearing practices, in educational goals, and even in certain motivations.

Social Groups. Each person grows up in some social group, which he has not chosen; usually he grows up in a family. However, in the course of his development he learns that some of his motives can easily be satisfied if he joins other people. The group membership may be sometimes formal and sometimes informal. The behaviour of joining a group can be analized just like any other behaviour. Group membership becomes a goal for him because he perceives that his joining a group will directly or indirectly satisfy many of his needs. The incentive value of a group sometimes lies in the fact that individual's goals are identical with the goals of the group.

A group may be attractive to a person because be enjoys the activities which group membership allows him to take part in. For example, if a man likes to play cricket, he will be motivated to join the cricket club. A group may also attract an individual because he enjoys being with the other members of the group. In this case he perceives the group as a means for satisfying his affiliation motives. On the other hand, the factors, which lead an individual to join the group, may have little to do with the actual goals and activities of the group. Thus a person may become a member of the group merely because of its prestige in the eyes of others. Or a person may find a group attractive because it provides an opportunity to achieve goals, make use of his club membership to get better business contacts. An individual is attracted towards a group because of satisfaction of his needs. A salesman, for example, may be attracted towards a group because of satisfaction of his needs. The greater the perceived probability that group membership will satisfy his motives the greater the probability that membership will become a goal for him.

Group Cohesiveness. The cohesiveness of a group depends upon the motive of each individual in the group. Some common factors, which influence cohesiveness are: (1) common fate and (2) clarity of goals and means.

One major factor which determine the cohesiveness of a group is the degree to which the members of a group feel they share a common fate with all other members. For example, friendly interaction among workers in a garment factory increased when they were all given a raise by the management. This indication that their fortunes would rise together helped to increase cohesiveness. Similarly, a common threat to a group has shown to increase cohesiveness. Thus, when people are threatened the members organize themselves into cohesive groups. The sharing of common fate convinces the members of a group that they would succeed or fail together.

The better the individuals in the group understand the group goals the means adopted to achieve the goals, and to what extent their personal actions contribute to the goal, the greater the cohesiveness of the group. It has been suggested that greater the interaction among the members of a group, the greater will be the cohesiveness of a group. However, there is one exception to be noted, that unpleasant interaction among the members of a group tries to decrease cohesiveness, rather than increase it.

As it was stated earlier, people join groups for several reasons. Research studies have shown that, in general, groups can be classified into task-oriented groups, whose main purpose is to perform a specific task, and interaction oriented groups, whose main purpose is to provide an opportunity for people to interact with one another. A production unit in a company is an example of a task-oriented group; whereas, a social club is an example of interaction - oriented group. Many groups sometimes have goals, which include both functions. Thus for instance, a humanitarian organization may be setup to do good work in the community as well as to provide an opportunity for better inter-action among the members of a group.

Conformity to Group Norms. The behaviour of members of a group is influenced through group norms. A norm is a standard of behaviour so important in a society that conformity to it is rewarded and deviation from it is punished. Since most of us acquire the need for social approval and do not wish to incur disapproval, we do what is expected of us. We must somehow or the other conform to the expectations of the group or suffer the disapproval of the members of the group. These expectations constitute the group norms. Whenever a group is formed, group norms like statuses and social structure seem to emerge. An important aspect of the behaviour of practically every group is the way in which its members interact and communicate with one another. The longer people interact, and the more they interact, the more they tend to adopt common ways of perceiving and interpreting the world and evolving common standards for the behaviour of each group member. Group norms seem to have a demand quality. Thus an individual not only tends to see and act the way other group members do but he must do so. To enforce the demand, the group members devise different degrees of punishment ranging from capital punishment to a social snub.

People tend to conform to group norms for various reasons. One has already been mentioned. Those who go against the norms incur social disapproval or punishment. The desire for social approval is inherent in every individual so much so that we try to seek social approval from the members of the group but even from complete strangers. Another reason for social conformity is individual's belief is that the opinions of his group are correct, or at least probably correct. If the individual finds the situation somewhat ambiguous and he does not know what exactly is expected of him, he is likely to compare his behaviour with the behaviour of others in the same situation. This type of social comparison need not always lead to conformity, but "going along" with someone else is often chosen as the appropriate behaviour.

Research studies on social interaction and communication in small groups, have shown that the group behaviour of the individuals can be analyzed into 12 categories such as: (1) shows solidarity, (2) shows tension release, (3) shows agreement, (4) gives suggestion, (5) gives opinion, (6) gives information, (7) asks for information, (8) asks for opinion, (9) asks for suggestion, (10) shows disagreement, (11) shows tension, (12) shows antagonism. These categories evoke positive and negative reactions depending upon the type of social interaction in question.

Social Communication

Psychologists have devised methods to study both the direction and the content of group communication.

Communications with a group are guided not only by whom the members of the group wish to talk to but also by whom they are permitted to talk to. Thus for instance a junior executive may talk to his boss, but cannot override the boss's decision. Similarly, the working man seldom gets a chance to talk to the company's president. The channels of communication therefore are restricted and the pattern of closed-communication and open-communication channels is known as the communication structure. Obstacles to communication channels may be either physical or psychological. For example, it is physically impossible for a radio listener to communicate with the announcer. Similarly, a student is afraid to speak to a famous professor because he experiences a psychological block.

The effects of various communication nets on group action can be studied experimentally by opening and closing channels of communication. The channels of communication in three types of class room procedures such as, lecture, teacher-entered question-and answer, and group discussion. An arrow from one person to another indicates that the former communicates with the latter.

The conductivity of a communication net refers to the freeness of interaction. It is usually measured by the proportion of actual communication channels to the potential number of communication channels. In one study Leavitt examined the relationship between conductivity and satisfaction in the group and been found that the greater the conductivity of the communication net the more the members of the group liked the task and were more satisfied with it. Further, he also found that the position of a person in the communication net was related to his satisfaction. The more central an individual's position, that is, the more people he can communicate with directly or through an intermediary, the better he liked the task and the more satisfied he was with the job done.

LEADERSHIP

It is a characteristic of every group whether small or big to have a leader The phenomenon of leadership is evidenced in the play of children, in the games of adults, in trade unions in an industry and in several other situations. The moral is that groups need leaders if they are to pull together as a team. How leadership evolves has been a controversial problem and students of human affairs inspite of their efforts to evaluate the role of leaders in group behaviour, have not come to any final agreement. Leaders are either necessary and history is made by them or leaders are merely the expression of popular needs. The first view is called the "leader principle" or the "great-man theory" of history. It holds that people drift along in aimless confusion until a gifted leader assumes command and tells them what to do. He may accomplish social change for good or bad, but the truth is that he appears to accomplish much more than he actually does. For example, Hitler is haid to have killed millions of people, but literally speaking, he himself did not kill them and yet he is credited with such events as killing and conquering.

The second view is the sociological view. It says that history makes or selects the man, and not vice versa. Social and cultural developments are thought to follow their own laws, and the presence of a particular person as leader is purely coincidental. For example, if a society is at war, a peaceful leader will not be tolerated; in other words, every leader has to follow the needs of the group. In brief, sometimes the leader acquires the leadership influence as a result of his assigned role in an alreaay structured group according to the needs of the group. Sometimes, the group has no pre-determined structure and the leader emerges from the group.

Functions of a Leader. The leader, whether designated or emergent, exerts influence on the members of his group in fulfilling his functions. Krech, Crutchfield and Ballachey, distinguish 13 possible functions of a leader. Table 14.1, gives the different functions which a leader is supposed to perform. It is true that not all leaders perform all these functions in every group, and the relative importance of each function varies according to the nature of each group. All leadership functions are not necessarily carried out by a single person even in a well-structured group with a designated leader. When the designated leader in a well-structured group fails to perform his functions, a second leader may emerge. Bales (1950), found that in unstructured small groups, two leaders often emerged. One person was characterized by the group as doing the most to guide and control the discussion and as having the best ideas. This person was not, however, usually best liked. The function of resolving tensions and preserving group unity fell on another member of the group who was usually chosen as one best liked by his fellow members.

Table 14.1

1. Executive
2. Planner
3. Policy-maker
4. Expert
5. External Group Representative
6. Controller of Internal Relations
7. Purveyor of Punishments and Rewards
8. Arbitrator and Mediator
9. Exemplar or Model
10. Substitute for Individual Responsibility
11. Ideologist
12. Father Figure
13. Scapegoat.

In an unstructured group when the members have interacted for some period, a structure emerges, with a leader and some followers. A number of investigations studying different groups, have been carried out. Mann reviewed the literature in the field of leadership and found some traits that are mentioned consistently as characteristics of leaders. In general, leaders tend to be more intelligent, better adjusted, more dominant, more masculine, less conservative and more socially perceptive than the other members of the group. It is important to note that this is not simply a list of personality characteristics of an individual, but a list of relationships between the individual and the group. This suggests that there is no single leader personality for all types of groups. The kind of person who becomes a leader depends on both, the characteristics of the group members and the nature of the group task. Gibb has shown that leadership ratings for the same person vary when groups are confronted with various tasks.

Types of Leadership. Basically, a leader is a person who influences a group to follow the course of action he advocates. The leader is really the major influencer because he influences the members of the groups to accept his proposals. Leadership can be either formal leadership of informal leadership.

Formal Leadership. The formal leader influences the members of his group primarily because he occupies a formally recognized position. He is the president, chairman or king. His role is to attempt to influence his followers and the role of the followers is to follow him. Frequently, the followers accept the formal leader's ideas because the leader has authority over them and dispenses rewards and punishments. However, any influence based upon the threat of punishment is not likely to be long lasting. The followers, obviously, will obey the orders only so long as they fear getting caught. Such leadership cannot be very effective, though in some situations, such as in war or extreme economic crisis, it may be workable out of sheer necessity. Generally, a leader is most effective when his followers accept his ideas because they truly believe in them.

Informal Leadership. The informal leader does not derive his influence from a formal position and yet, he may be quite a successful influencer in his group. The group members follow his lead because his personal qualities convince them that they can satisfy their own needs by accepting his ideas. Usually, in such a situation the group members not knowing how to attain their goals on their own, they turn to the informal leader for ways and means of achieving their group goals. The group members perceive in their informal leader the quality of proficiency in handling the tasks confronting the group. The group frequently relies on the leader's past performance. Past performance, however, is not the only basis for accepting an informal leader's ideas. A person who is well liked has a much better chance of having his ideas accepted, and thus of influencing people, than one who is less popular. Likes and dislikes, therefore, serve to influence the members of the group in choosing a leader.

Finally, evidence shows that the more assertive the individual is, more likely is that he will be chosen a leader than the less assertive person, at least in first stages of group's existence. The assertive person is the individual who talks a great deal and advances a relatively large number of ideas. If he is not arrogant and aggressive in asserting himself, his active participation makes him stand out in a group. Further, since the assertive person usually advances his ideas with confidence the members of the group come to feel that his ideas are correct.

The social influences on the individual may come from organized groups or unorganized groups. An organized group is an assembly of people physically present like a congregation in a church, or an audience in an auditorium. An unorganized group, on the other hand, is an assembly of people joined together temporarily to solve an issue but with no plans for the future.

The most striking instances of the influences upon the individual are observed in crowd and mob behaviour. A crowd may be said to be an assembly of people attracted to a common focus of the attention sharing similar emotions. It may be a group of curious and fearful spectators of an accident, or sympathetic onlookers at a fire, or even excited fans at sports and games. If the common emotion is very intense, specially if it is anger, and if adequate action is not taken, the crowd turns into a mob.

Some of the factors, which seem to be respectable for mob action and mob behaviour are:

(1) Background Factors. Mob behaviour is most likely to occur where there are long-standing frustrations, which arise sudden general susceptibility because of either accumulated hostility towards particular groups. For example, people in very low socio-economic conditions can be potential mobs towards those of high socio-economic conditions. Similarly, generalized hostility of frustrated men and common antagonisms towards employers can result in mob behaviour.

(2) Precipitating Factors. In such situations some incident occurs, which generates a crowd by focusing the attention on it and initiating common emotions. At once, there is intensification of emotion, which changes a crowd into a mob. The speeches and gestures of people expressing similar emotions serve to increase the feelings of the individual. His increased feelings intensify the feelings of others. For example, when a person of low caste attacks a woman of high caste, this incident is sufficient to break a crowd into a mob fury.

(3) Reinforcing Factors. Since the individuals in a crowd are excited by intense emotions, critical thought is given up thus producing psychological effects which reinforce the participants. The characteristics of mob behaviour are a sense of universality. The individual feels that everyone is with him in what he is doing. Secondly, he experiences a sense of power in the sense that he can do whatever he likes and nothing can stop him. Finally, there is a sense of anonymity because he can get out of the mob and claim no responsibility for the violence and fury.

ATTITUDE AND OPINIONS

An attitude is an organization of concepts, beliefs, motives, habits, and acts associated with a particular object. The concepts and beliefs associated with an attitude are referred to as the cognitive component; the habits, as the action component; and the motives, as the affective component. We say that an attitude is formed when the above components are so interrelated that specific feelings, emotions and reaction tendencies become consistently associated with a particular way of thinking about certain persons or events. In the early stages of attitude formation, its components are not well systematized so that they can be modified by new experiences. However, gradually when they are well organized over a period of time, they tend to become rigid and stereotyped.

For the most part of our lives we are not fully conscious of the extensive influence they have on our social behaviour. But on close self-analysis we find that attitudes function within ourselves and we become sensitive to the attitudes of others. Actually, we try to infer the attitudes of others accordingly to regulate our behaviour. In a social group, from limited samples of another's behaviour we conclude, that he is liberal, understanding, or prejudiced, and then react to him in what we consider to be an appropriate manner. The study of attitudes has become a major problem for social psychologists because it is a complex psychological phenomenon that has great social significance on individual's behaviour.

Components of an Attitude

The Cognitive Component. Attitudes vary from one another in a number of ways other than their specific content. In the cognitive component, we find the specificity of the concept of the object and also the degree of differentiation of an attitude as to how many beliefs and concepts are associated with the object. For example, a person may have an attitude towards Jawaharlal Nehru as a statesman, towards statesmen in general or towards celebrities. Similarly a politician's attitude towards Nehru is more differentiated than that of a person who has little experience in politics. In the former case specificity, and in the latter the degree of differentiation can be noticed.

The Action Component. Attitudes have been observed to differ in their relation to overt behaviour. Some attitudes may have many habits associated with them, others have few. Sometimes the action which goes with an attitude is merely a verbal expression and this is called an opinion. But, the action component of an attitude may include a number of action tendencies. For example, people develop favourable attitudes towards one political party. These may be expressed either by voting on election day, or by long heated discussions with others or by actively participating in political campaign.

The Affective Component. Two of the dimensions, which belong to this component are position and intensity. The former refers to the degree of expectancy of pleasantness or unpleasantness associated with the object whereas, the latter refers to the strength of the affective expectancy. For example, a person's attitude towards a surgeon about to operate on him may include a very strong expectancy about the amount of pain. Here the position of the object is rather negative but the attitude is very intense.

The Function of Attitudes. Attitudes play an important part in determining our behaviour. They influence our perceptions and judgement of others, they determine the speed and efficiency of learning, they help in the choice of groups we associate with, the professions we decide upon, and even the ideologies we cherish. To illustrate how attitudes affect various forms of behaviour, how they give form and structure to personality, we may take the simple example of workers who tend to display an organised pattern of attitudes towards their work, colleagues, superiors, and friends outside their work place. That attitudes are basic features of personality influencing behaviour has been shown in the study of attitudes of minority group members. In our country the attitudes of the majority community may not be very tolerant towards the minority groups. This is clear from the complaints made and concessions sought by the minority groups from the central government.

The Formation of Attitudes

We have already defined an attitude as an organization of concepts, beliefs, habits, and motives associated with an object. The formation of attitudes then consists of learning various concepts, beliefs, habits, and motives. The formation of attitudes follows the basic principles of learning. There are three interrelated principles, which help to explain how attitudes are learned; the principles are of association, transfer, and need satisfaction.

Broadly speaking, we acquire feelings and reaction tendencies, the two essential components of attitudes, through association and need satisfaction. In other words, we learn to fear and avoid people, things or events associated with unpleasant happenings, and to like and approach those people, things and events associated with pleasant happenings. In the first case by avoiding and in the second case by approaching we seem to satisfy the basic need for pleasure or comfort. For example, our most basic attitudes are acquired in infancy through interaction with our parents and other members of our family. An infant develops favourable attitudes towards parents and other members of the family simply because they care for his needs. Their presence becomes associated with his comfort and general well being. In course of time, as parents become associated with punishments as well as pleasures, the child's attitudes towards them become complex and ambivalent.

Although feelings and reaction tendencies towards others are learned through association and need satisfaction, we acquire our thoughts and beliefs, which is the third component of attitudes in a different way. Actually speaking, we learn attitudes through transfer in the same way as we learn meanings of concepts through instructions; for example, a child develops a meaning say for "tiger" when told it is a "catlike" animal having the same features. In this way, social agents like parents and teachers can transfer attitudes by suggesting how best we should reorganize and integrate certain of our basic ideas. Thus for instance, parent or a teacher can transfer completely favourable attitudes towards Schedule castes of tribes by describing them as illtreated, suppressed and yet hard working, friendly and lively; or by transferring a negative attitude by describing them as lazy, undependable and untrustworthy. We also develop attitudes by adopting the attitudes of other important people outside the family circle. As we grow older, we tend to incorporate attitudes that seem appropriate for belonging to groups we consider important. Sometimes we even change attitudes as a means of leaving one group and becoming part of another.

The affective component of an attitude is considered by many psychologists to be at the core of the attitude. It may be associated with several of the human motives. Some psychologists have suggested that the formation and change of attitudes is probably different for attitudes with different motivations. Katz suggests four different motivational basis for attitudes: (1) utilitarian, (2) value-expressive, (3) ego-defensive, and (4) knowledge. An attitude with a utilitarian basis is associated with the survival, safety, and some of the social motives of the, individual. Katz suggests that a person acquires utilitarian attitudes through experience with the object.

A value-expressive attitude is based on a person's motive for self-esteem and self-actualization; for example, a person who values world law will find satisfaction in expressing favourable attitudes towards the United Nations. The formation of value-expressive attitudes seem to depend on a person's perception of the relation between the object, the attitude, and his ideal of himself.

Ego-defensive. These attitudes like the value-expressive attitudes are also related to the motive for self-esteem but in a negative way. These attitudes are formed to defend the ego from his anxieties and hence they can be called defence mechanisms. Thus for instance, many psychologists are of the opinion that prejudice towards minority groups may in some people represent projection or displacement of feelings of hostility and inferiority onto the minority groups. Some studies have shown that people who were dissatisfied with their economic conditions tended to express hostile attitudes towards the minority than those who were satisfied.

Attitudes with a Knowledge. These attitudes are acquired in relation to competence motives, specially the motives to have a clear and consistent view of the world. Such attitudes are formed in one of the three ways: (1) by actively seeking more information, or (2) by adopting towards the object the attitudes of other people, or (3) by adopting attitudes towards the object that are consistent with the rest of his thinking. The best example one could think of the second way of formation of attitudes (adopting the attitudes of others) is that of stereotypes regarding other groups or nationalities.

Some attitudes have very little effect on an individual's thinking and behaviour; others have a great effect on thinking and behaviour in different situations. The greater the effect of an attitude on thinking an benaviour the more central it is. Some psychologists suggest that the centrality of an attitude is partly due to the strength of the motives associated with the object and partly due to persistent presence of the object in the individual's environment. Some attitudes are closely related to one another; that is, they share common or similar concepts, beliefs, motive and habits. Such a cluster of attitudes is called the attitude system.

Attitude Change

Since attitudes are learned, it should be easy to modify their intensity or even replace an undesirable one by learning a desirable one. But it is not an easy task because attitudes are not easily modified or replaced as they are learned. Once attitudes are formed, they become an integral part of individual's personality, affecting his whole style of behaviour. Attempts to modify attitudes succeed only in altering the thought-belief component without affecting the feelings and reaction tendencies so that gradually the attitude may revert to its former state. Those attitudes formed in the home or through early experiences in groups are specially responsible in forming the structure of attitude network, and hence are resistant to modification.

In order to change the cognitive component, the persuaders should construct arguments to change the beliefs of their audiences. Studies have shown that presenting both sides of an issue is more effective in attitude change rather than making a counter-propaganda. Regarding the affective component, the attitude change can be brought about by associating a disliked object with pleasurable feelings and thereby producing changes in beliefs and actions. Some investigators have suggested that the use of fear or punishment associated with an object can succeed in changing the attitudes. However, such a method of negative reward is found not to have the same effect as when a disliked object is associated with pleasurable feelings.

Finally, a person's beliefs and feelings about an object can be changed by changing individual's behaviour towards it (action component). Thus for instance, expressing opinion contrary to one's attitudes can lead to attitude change, specially if the behaviour is unexpectedly rewarded. Similarly, contact with minority groups can lead to the formation of positive attitudes if the contacts are on an equal status basis, or if they are rewarded, or if the goals of the minority group are the same or those of the majority of the people.

Measurement of Attitudes and Opinions. Social psychologists have devised a number of techniques for measuring attitudes; these techniques are called attitude scales. Often a person's attitude is measured by asking him to indicate his agreement or disagreement with a number of statement dealing with the same subject. The major problem in developing an attitude scale is to select a series of statements that will have the following characteristics: (1) an attitude scale should discriminate between people holding different attitudes; (2) the scale should cover the entire range of positions on the attitude; and (3) it should avoid statements that imply positions on several attitude at the same time.

SOCIAL PREJUDICE

The term prejudice as earlier defined referred to an unfavourable attitude towards a person, object or event. However, the term social prejudice refers to a hostile attitude towards some social group. Any attitude of hostility towards Pakistanis, or Schedule caste members, or communists, or any other group is a prejudice. Prejudices are attitudes, and like any other attitudes, they are subject to the principles of attitude formation and maintenance. Prejudices are learned in two possible ways: (1) from contact with the object of the prejudice or (2) from contact with others who have the prejudice. Although they are learned in both ways, studies indicate that they are more commonly acquired by contact with people who have them. For example, it has been shown that there is a high co-relation between the prejudices of parents and those of their children. This is so because parents often train their children to be prejudiced. Parents are not the only teachers of prejudice; prejudices can be acquired through schoolmates, teachers and communication media like newspapers, radio, and television. In a study on regional and communal attitudes of the university students of Bombay, de Souza found that the Maharashtrians had a negative image of the South Indians and Muslims.

Fundamentally prejudices have their basis in preferences, the simple judgements of pleasantness and unpleasantness that everyone makes. Such judgements are not rational. Once learned, prejudices do not die out through forgetting or disuse but they continue to serve the purpose of gratifying an individual's needs. They alter his perception and memory in such a way that his everyday experiences lend support to his prejudices.

There are three big advantages which race prejudice seems to offer. They are (1) economic gain, (2) gain in status and (3) outlet for hostility.

(1) *Economic Gain.* It is a common knowledge that in a competitive society where one person's success depends upon other person's failure, puts a premium upon anything which gives an advantage in the struggle. For example, in Nazi Germany, the affluent Jews were persecuted by the local Germans. In our own country, the emmergence of regionalism is the best example of racial prejudice stemming from economic gain.

(2) ***Gain in Social Status.*** With rapid industrialization and urbanization there has been a gulf between lower status people and higher status people. All of us have a desire for superiority and social recognition; all of us are pleased to look down upon those who are low in social status. Those at the bottom of society struggle to gratify their desire for recognition and superiority; prejudice then is reinforced by the desire to gain in status.

(3) ***Outlet for Hostility.*** Frustration seems to encourage the rise of prejudice. Hostility and aggression usually originate in the frustration of needs. Aggression resulting from frustration either because of economic gain or superior social status is often directed towards others.

Besides the above three mentioned advantages, perception and judgement support prejudice. Prejudice alters perception in such a way that we tend to see what we want to see or even what we believe we are going to see. Such distorted perception and judgement lead to social consequences of prejudice like segregation. For example, people living in slum areas are thought to be dirty, lazy and without any ambition. Consequently, the segregated minority is forced to use inferior facilities under inconvenient or unsanitary conditions simply because segregation allows majority groups living in better social conditions to give vent to their prejudices on to the minority groups.

To eliminate social prejudices, which hinder social progress by producing social conflicts, many suggestions have been made. Firstly, frustration, which involves social, economic and political frustrations should be reduced by promoting the understanding among different groups, by spreading education and by providing facilities for self-advancement.

●●●

Index